Merryn Williams read English at New Hall, Cambridge and obtained a doctorate for her work on Thomas Hardy. Formerly a lecturer at the Open University, she is now editor of *The Interpreter's House*, a national poetry and short story journal. Her published critical works include *Women in the English Novel, 1800–1900* (Macmillan, 1984), *Six Women Novelists* (Macmillan, 1987), *Preface to Hardy* (Longman, 1993) and *Wilfred Owen* (Seren, 1993). She has published three volumes of poetry and was winner of the Second Light Network Poetry Competition 2003, judged by Elaine Feinstein. She also edited an anthology of poetry, *The Georgians 1901–1930* (Shoestring Press 2010). Merryn Williams lives in Oxford.

EFFIE: A VICTORIAN SCANDAL

'A woman, let her be as good as she may, has got to put up with the life her husband makes for her.'

George Eliot, *Middlemarch*, Chapter 25

Merryn Williams

Book Guild Publishing
Sussex, England

First published in Great Britain in 2010
by The Book Guild Ltd
Pavilion View
19 New Road
Brighton, BN1 1UF

Typesetting in Garamond by
Keyboard Services, Luton, Bedfordshire

Printed and bound in Great Britain by
4edge Ltd, Hockley, Essex

A catalogue record for this book is available from
The British Library

ISBN 978 1 84624 916 7

For David Hemp
Richard and Rosalind Evans

Contents

CONTENTS

Introduction

Effie Gray was the wife of two distinguished Victorians, John Ruskin and John Everett Millais, in an age when divorce was almost impossible. The annulment of her first marriage was one of the great scandals of the 1850s and would follow all three of them around until the last of them died. Even then, although families and disciples tried to hush it up, it was not forgotten. The story was told again and again, in a mutilated form, and if one of the three was blamed it was usually her. The letters which they all wrote during the crisis remained unpublished for another century. Millais preferred to express his feelings in paint, and some of his greatest works are images of Effie and Ruskin.

What was unusual was not that the first marriage went sour but that Effie was able to break away legally and reinvent herself as Mrs Millais. Of course, there was a price to pay. Her reputation would always be slightly spotted; Queen Victoria refused to receive her and many people thought – still think – that she behaved badly. There were no tabloid newspapers in those days but, then as now, there was a great deal of malice, fault-finding and unwholesome interest in 'celebrities'. Then, Thomas Carlyle said that no woman had a right to complain about her husband's behaviour; now, critics say that Effie was a commonplace woman who dragged down two great men. The real Effie Gray was a brave, gifted and essentially decent young woman who wanted with all her heart to be respectable. But she was trapped in a situation which did no good to anyone, and in extremity, people sometimes find their way around the rules.

Few other careers were open to her, so she became what is called a Muse. Her face, slightly changed, looks past the crowds in Tate Britain from *The Order of Release*; her influence lurks behind Ruskin's *King of the Golden River* and 'Of Queens' Gardens', which describes his ideal wife. George Eliot, who also had a scandal in her life, brooded over her story and reinterpreted it in *Middlemarch*.

Gladstone believed that 'all three were perfectly blameless'. I do not disguise my sympathy for Effie or my liking for Millais, but this book is not an attack on Ruskin. He was a man of great nobility who found relationships difficult, especially with women, and who was not always sane. The valuable part of his work is still very relevant in the twenty-first century, but, as Effie said, that has nothing to do with domestic life.

PART ONE

EFFIE GRAY

1

The Fair Maid of Perth
1828–47

And how should Dorothea not marry? – a girl so handsome and with such prospects?

Middlemarch, Chapter 1

On a day in late October, 1817, John Thomas Ruskin, the tenant of Old Bowerswell House in Perth, suddenly appeared in front of his niece Margaret with a terrible gash in his throat. She immediately stopped the bleeding with a towel, called a doctor and helped sew up the edges of the wound. Everything possible was done, but a few days later, he died. Very soon afterwards, Margaret married the old man's son, as she had wanted to do for years, and moved to London. For the rest of her long life she hated Perth and Scotland and refused to set foot inside that house.

If his grandfather had not committed suicide, John Ruskin would probably not have been born and the history of Victorian thought would have been different. That tragedy would reverberate down the generations and affect several other lives.

Ten years later, when Mr George Gray, Writer to the Signet, was looking for a place to bring his new wife, his eye fell on the same house, Bowerswell (pronounced Bower's Well). Built in 1800, it stood a short way up the steep lane which runs up Kinnoull Hill, surrounded by tall trees and with an ancient well in the grounds. He thought it needed some improvements, perhaps the whole house ought to be pulled down and rebuilt, but the situation was superb. The garden had enough space for a long yew walk and holly hedges, a bowling green. Behind it, the hill rose 729 feet to give wonderful views of the parks and spires of

Perth, the mighty River Tay and the higher hills to the north. Generations of his family would admire 'the rolling Strath of Tay, the lavishly tinted and ever-changing woods, the distant hills, now purple with heather, now white with ice and snow, the majestic river'.[1] Mr Gray knew what the former tenant had done, but he was not superstitious.

George Gray and Sophia Jameson were married and moved into Bowerswell on 18th June 1827. He was twenty-nine; she was nineteen and the daughter of Andrew Jameson, Sheriff Substitute of Fife. A photograph taken some thirty years later shows a tall balding man and a woman who looks surprisingly good after having given birth to fifteen children. Those who knew them thought that Mrs Gray was 'a sweet, quiet and sensible person, an excellent manager without bustle or conceit'; her grandson remembered her as bright and cheerful. Mr Gray was said to be 'thoroughly good-natured, open and hospitable with excellent temper and warm-heartedness, he has also shown that he possesses no small share of common sense and judgement in the way he has improved his fortune and brought himself and family into the best society his neighbourhood affords'.[2]

A Writer to the Signet is a senior Scottish lawyer. George Gray is described in official documents sometimes as a solicitor, sometimes as a banker. He did not stick to the legal profession but dabbled in commerce, and it would get him into trouble.

On 7th May 1828 the couple's first child, Euphemia Chalmers Gray, was born in the bedroom where old Ruskin had died. Her parents called her Phemy, but after she left home she was usually known as Effie. In the same year Sir Walter Scott published a novel called *The Fair Maid of Perth*, and this name stuck to her too.

The town, which was the ancient capital of Scotland, had a population of about 20,000. Tall ships still sailed upriver to the port of Perth, although in Effie's lifetime it would lose most of its trade to Dundee. Weaving, dyeing, whisky and salmon-farming were the chief industries. The west bank of the Tay was lined with grand Georgian buildings whose gardens ran down to the waterfront (the wynds and vennels where the workers lived were less visible). Seagulls swooped around the cobbled streets and swans nested on the willow-covered islands. Bowerswell is on the quieter east bank, about fifteen minutes' walk downhill and across the wide old bridge to the centre of town.

Perth was, and is, a friendly place; it was also small enough for people to know every detail of their neighbours' lives. The Grays were a cultured, affluent, good-natured family, highly respected in their circle and regular worshippers at Kinnoull parish church. Effie's probable future seemed to be a quiet, small-town life and marriage to a fellow Scot; however, she was less than two weeks old when she got involved with the Ruskins.

The John Ruskin who had killed himself had a daughter, Jessie Richardson, a widow with four children who still lived in the riverside suburb of Bridgend. Her brother, John James Ruskin, was a sherry merchant in London who sometimes visited her, bringing his wife and son. In the same month of May 1828 Jessie died and her very distressed brother was left to wind up her affairs. He took her daughter, Mary, into his home and started the three sons in careers. Mr Gray was an unofficial guardian to these boys and he and John James exchanged regular letters about them. But living so far apart (there was no railway to Perth then), the two families seldom met.

Effie grew into a pretty, fair-haired and highly intelligent little girl. Her brother George was born seventeen months later; he and she would be friends all their lives. Two more boys were born and died young; then three girls, Sophia, Mary and Jane, and another boy, Andrew. Their mother brought them up with the help of a nurse, Jeannie (Janet Gray, perhaps a poor relation), who remained at Bowerswell for decades and was much loved. By the time Effie left home at the age of twelve she was the eldest of six living children.

Her parents had enrolled her in a boarding school, Avonbank in Stratford, which in those days was a quiet market town with no theatre. It seems strange to send a beloved child so far from home, but they rightly thought that she could cope, and probably wanted her to get a good English education so she could mix in 'society'. In fact, her very definite Perth accent would never go away.

Mr and Mrs Gray took her by steamer to London in August 1840 and went on for a tour of Germany, leaving her for a few days with the Ruskin family before the schoolmistress took charge of her. Her first letter home shows that she was thrilled:

After you left me in London I enjoyed myself very much indeed. Mr Ruskin took me to see all the sights. I was very much pleased with the Zoological Gardens and with Westminster Abbey ... I am very fond of school and Avon Bank is a beautiful place. I have a great deal to tell you about school. There is a Mr Walker here a very amusing man he is giving lectures on natural philosophy which are delightful and he tells us a great many things of which I never heard of [sic] before.[3]

5

Avonbank had been known as the Miss Byerleys' School for Young Ladies when it was opened in 1810 by a group of sisters, cultured intelligent women who had inherited legacies from their great-uncle Josiah Wedgwood. They offered girls a basic education in 'English Reading, Spelling, Grammar and Composition, in Geography, and the Use of the Globes, and in Ancient and Modern History ... in the French language, Music, Drawing, Dancing, and Writing and Arithmetic'. And sewing, of course; every nineteenth-century girl learned to sew. 'The school was planned on liberal lines and there was nothing mean even in its appointments ... the very china in daily use was a gift from Josiah Wedgwood'.[4] Their most distinguished former pupil was Elizabeth Stevenson, now known as Mrs Gaskell.

Effie would have shared a bedroom in a spacious and elegant white house, built around 1700, with wide lawns running down to the river. On Sundays they walked the short distance to Holy Trinity Church with its elaborate Clopton chapel and Shakespeare's tomb. Today the house has gone, but the gardens, which belong to the Royal Shakespeare Theatre, are not very different. Her school-days were happy and interesting. She won prizes for general attention, French and history, learned to play the piano to a high standard, and made many friends. When a German girl joined the school, Effie was the only child who tried to talk to her in her own language. The Misses Mary and Harriet Ainsworth, who took over at around the time she arrived, found her a star pupil. She was popular because of 'her artless affectionate disposition and her wish for improvement', and she was a good dancer with a 'very clear and beautiful-toned voice'.[5]

She spent a full year at Stratford without seeing her family, who expected to have her back for the summer holidays of 1841. But at the beginning of July her six-year-old sister, Sophia, died at Bowerswell of scarlet fever, and her parents thought it unsafe for her to come home. Effie wrote to her father in a very wobbly hand:

My dearest Papa,
   You cannot think how sorry I am at hearing the sad news I felt sure that something must be the matter when no one was writing to me Miss Ainsworth told me in the kindest manner possible it is a sad loss to us all she was such a dear child ... You cannot think how kind Miss Ainsworth has been to me I do not know how to repay her I suppose Mama is in great distress Give her my very kindest love and all the children and my hand is shaking so

6

I cannot write any more believe me very dear Papa your most affect. Daughter E. Gray.[6]

She was taken to the Ruskins the following week by her uncle Melville Jameson, who noted that she was an unusually mature thirteen-year-old: 'She has made I think the most gratifying progress, not only in her mere school knowledge but what is of more importance, in her observation of men and things – her remarks are really excellent on many subjects'.[7]

John Ruskin senior, his wife Margaret and their son lived in a semi-detached villa at Herne Hill, which was then almost in the country and had beautiful views. There was a pleasant garden full of lilac and apple trees, where they grew fruit and vegetables, and their table was kept well supplied with fresh food and fine wine. Every weekday Mr Ruskin went to his office, came back for dinner and often, in the evenings, read aloud from the Waverley novels. Effie had seen little or nothing of the Ruskins when she was a child. She knew that the couple had lived in her house before she was born, and had been involved in a tragedy; she may also have known that they had had some hard struggles in their youth. He was a rather formidable-looking man of fifty-six, with 'a full crop of bristly grey hair and very bushy dark eyebrows'.[8] His wife, who was his first cousin and four years older, was tall and had a squint in one eye. She was an excellent housekeeper and a devout evangelical Christian. The other members of the household were their niece Mary Richardson, a meek young woman of about twenty-five, who was very conscious of not being the favourite child, and their adored son John. He was an undergraduate at Christ Church, Oxford, but his studies had been interrupted by bad health and he had been convalescing in Italy.

The young John Ruskin was tall, thin, narrow-shouldered, with reddish hair, a beaky nose and intense blue eyes; his voice had a Scottish/Northumbrian burr. His mouth was slightly disfigured where a dog had bitten him in childhood, but few people noticed, as he had an attractive smile and charming manners. He and Effie were soon great friends; before he left to take another cure at Leamington Spa he promised to write her a fairy story.

But next month, more dreadful news came from Scotland. Sophia had died on 2nd July; on 2nd August, five-year-old Mary died, also of scarlet fever, and six days later three-year-old Jane. Andrew, aged eighteen months, survived.

We may faintly imagine the grief of Effie's parents, and Effie herself, though trying to conceal her feelings for the sake of those around her, would have been deeply shocked. Her letter to her mother, just after she had heard of the third death, shows this child who had not seen her parents for a year trying very hard to console them:

My dearest Mama,

I now make an exertion to write a few lines to you because I think you will like it before the event occurred this morning I had still some hope left and was in some degree happy because every thing I thought was about the recovery – but since the Divine Hand has been pleased to take her to him as well as the other two We must make up our minds as well as we can. How is dear little Andrew what a fine little boy he is. Do not you feel great comfort when you have Miss Thomson with you I think she is a very nice person, she will be a nice companion for you...

Do not be at all uneasy on my account for they are very kind to me here. Try and keep yourself up my dearest Mama for Papa's sake were you not glad to see Grandpapa do not write to me till you feel yourself quite able. Give Papa my kindest love and believe me your most affec. Daughter

E. Gray[9]

It is likely that Effie's adult personality was formed in that first year away from home; her stoicism, her habit of putting the best face on things, her eager interest in new experiences and her natural friendliness and good manners can all be seen in the child's letters. But it had been a long exile. Throughout her life, at times of strain, she would always head back to Bowerswell.

She remained for several weeks at the Ruskins' or with other friends; mean¬while, John in Leamington had not forgotten her. His diary for 15th September 1841 records that he was working on 'Phemy Gray's fairy tale. Poor thing – she wants something to amuse her now'.[10] *The King of the Golden River*, his sole work of fiction, was written 'at the request of a very young lady, and solely for her amusement without any idea of publication'.[11] When it did appear, in 1850, it immediately became a children's classic.

The story reflects Ruskin's idealism and his love of the Alps, which had haunted him like a passion since he was a teenager. Like many fairy tales it starts with three brothers; two bad and one, the youngest, good. The elder brothers have the use of a delightful fertile valley, but ruin it through their selfish and short-sighted behaviour. Then they are told they can turn their river to gold, but only on condition that they carry a flask of holy water to the head of a valley, untouched. They refuse to give any of the water to thirsty people they meet on the way, and are turned into black stones:

> ... the water which has been refused to the cry of the weary and dying is unholy, though it has been blessed by every saint in heaven; and the water which is found in the vessel of mercy is holy, though it had been defiled by corpses.[12]

Only the youngest brother, who cares more about his fellow creatures than money, passes the test. The river does not literally turn to gold but makes the valley fertile once more. It is a straightforward morality tale, but it is also prophetic. If Ruskin were alive now he would certainly say that the human race could not survive if its members did not look after each other and the planet.

The story was finished and posted to Bowerswell around the end of September. By this time Effie was at home, where she would stay for the next two years. Mrs Gray thought she should go back after a while to her school and friends, but her father could not bear to part with her. She spent this time very quietly, helping her mother and working on her music and languages with a governess, Joanna Thomson. Two more children were born; Robert in 1842 and Sophie, named after her dead sister, in 1843. Mr Gray, spending money lavishly, began to have a new house constructed near the old one, which was eventually pulled down. The second Bowerswell, a listed building in the local pinkish-grey stone, is still standing.

Effie returned to school in the new year of 1844 and on her way was again the guest of the Ruskins, who had moved to a fine Georgian house at 163 Denmark Hill. It stood in seven acres of land and had its own small farm. John's diary says that 'Phemy', now fifteen, was 'very graceful but has lost something of her good looks'.[13] He was also much amused because she asked whether ladies could vote in elections. But he was fond of her and probably gave her some advice about reading; Effie would say much later that he had been 'influencing my mind and overlooking my education for years'.[14] He noted that she was 'very good natured; took off her bonnet as soon as she came in from town and sat down, though tired, to play to me'.[15]

She spent six more months at Avonbank, leaving for good in the summer. She had made several friends, and would go on exchanging visits with them and corresponding with her teachers. In November of that year her four-year-old brother, Andrew, died after several days of illness. A long gap, which would get longer, was opening up between Effie and George and the younger group of children.

She was now sixteen, and a particularly charming teenager. Women outnumbered men at the time and a great many middle-class girls never found husbands, but there seems to have been no question of whether Effie would get married, only when and to whom. At five foot six she was rather tall for a Victorian woman; her hair was 'golden auburn', her cheeks pink, and she was always beautifully turned out. She had had an excellent education; only a few exceptional women were better informed. She played the piano seriously (Mendelssohn was a particular favourite), spoke good French and German and could hold an interesting conversation with just about anyone. Today a girl of her type would go to university, get a good job and perhaps combine it after a few years with marriage and children. In those days, she seemed well equipped to be the wife of some distinguished man.

We know that she had a devastating effect on men of all ages, but she also got on well with women. Some of them said she was not beautiful, exactly, but it was less her features than her lively and friendly nature that made her attractive. Even Ruskin, when he was most angry with her, admitted that she was all 'grace and pleasantness'[16] to everyone she met. Since many people would attack Effie, in her lifetime and afterwards, it is worth saying that she was a devoted daughter and sister; there was never any suggestion that she behaved badly to other women and her surviving letters are quite free from spiteful remarks.

'Women and girls of the higher and middle classes lived a pleasant if uneventful life', wrote Charles Dickens' daughter Kate, '... plenty of rather monotonous amusements such as garden parties, croquet, long walks, drives and rides and in the evening, occasional rather dull dinner parties, dances and the always popular opera and theatre parties'.[17] Effie threw herself into what amusements were available. She went dancing – supervised, of course – with various young men in Perth, one of whom, William MacLeod, an officer in a Highland regiment, fell in love with her. He went to India and, as she was still very young, the relationship ended naturally. She stayed at Ewell Castle near Epsom when she was seventeen and briefly met a lanky teenager, 'Jack' Millais, who was very much struck. In the same year, 1846, she visited the Ruskins again and their son showed signs of interest, but his parents rushed him away to the Continent before it could develop.

The young John Ruskin was becoming quite well known. Still only in his twenties, he had published a ground-breaking book, *Modern Painters*, which made such an impression that when he got back to England he found himself 'very celebrated in the literary world'.[18] The phrase is Effie's. She came for a longer visit in April 1847 and at first saw little of him, as he was always being invited out:

> Mrs Ruskin is at present dusting her china which operation she performs daily. We live very quietly; in the morning after breakfast I practice for two hours, then Mrs Ruskin reads 'The Pirate' in John's study. He draws and I knit till lunch, then we drive or walk till dinner-time at five or six after which we have tea and I play all the evening till bedtime.[19]

Mrs Ruskin was fond of Effie, seeing her as a substitute for her niece Mary, who had just left to get married, but she had been careful to tell her on the first evening that John was almost engaged. The young woman they had in mind was Charlotte Lockhart, the granddaughter of the great Sir Walter Scott. Nothing came of this, for the good reason that neither he nor she was interested, but Mr Ruskin very much wanted it to happen as it would have been a grand marriage for his son. He began to fear that Effie would distract him and soon after her arrival, when she was doing little more than play the piano and watch his wife dusting china, he wrote her father an astonishing letter.

'We have been friends for so many years standing', he began ominously, that he was sure he could speak frankly. When his son John was a teenager he had fallen in love with an unsuitable girl – 'the passion however was powerful and almost threatened my son's life'. They were still concerned about his health and now feared he might fall in love with Effie because 'no young man of taste and feeling could long look upon her with indifference'. They had nothing against her, but his mother did not want him to marry a Scottish person – 'she has had so much misery herself in Perth that she has quite a superstitious dread of her son connecting himself in the most remote degree with the place'. Besides, John had met a young lady 'who has engaged his affections and to whom he has made proposals the result of which is not yet known'.[20] Could he, therefore, avoid embarrassment by moving his daughter somewhere else?

Mr Gray, very much surprised, wrote back that, of course, he would immediately arrange for Effie to stay with other friends. He could not help adding:

It strikes me forcibly that Mrs Ruskin could have quietly given Phemy a hint that John was under engagement ... I know well that Phemy has always expressed herself favourably of John as a person for whom she had a high respect as a man of talent and refined manners, but I know also that she has a great deal of good sense and maidenly pride and is the very last person in the world that would either give her affections to one in John's present position or, were he entirely free, accept of him at the expense of wounding his mother's feelings.[21]

That should have ended it, but John found out and was upset at the prospect of losing Effie. Mr Ruskin was forced to write to her father again, saying grudgingly that she could stay:

His Mother and myself see every day that he is too sensibly affected by Miss Gray's presence for his own peace – Still no sudden steps can be taken without too much wounding his feelings and showing a distrust in the Strength of mind which not knowing his own Danger, he would ill brook from any one – I hope with your knowledge of the Circumstances and Miss Gray's great good sense, we may let the visit take its course.[22]

Effie was not fully aware of what was going on and at this point certainly was not in love. Mrs Ruskin urged her to remain for a few more weeks, while reiterating that her son was engaged. She wrote home:

I cannot understand the affair nor I suppose can you but at any rate if I tell you anything about them I trust you will keep it entirely to yourselves as Mr Ruskin never told me he had written to Papa about it. In fact Mrs Ruskin tells me that nobody knows and she only told me in case, as she says, that John and I should *love each other*, wasn't it good, I could not help laughing but thanked her for her caution which however I *did* not *require* as I consider him the same as married and should never think of such a thing. However I think this little gossip will amuse you but be sure it goes no further as I should dislike it exceedingly.[23]

She remained with the Ruskins, on and off, for a total of two months. They went to the French Theatre and heard Jenny Lind sing. John spent more and more time with Effie, repeatedly drawing her and then tearing up the paper. On her nineteenth birthday he presented her with a poem, 'For a Birthday in May', which begins:

> Thorn, and meadow grass – sweet sister,
> Twine them as I may,
> Deemest thou a darksome garland
> For thy natal day?
> Thou thyself art fairer, sister,
> Than all the flowers in May.[24]

It was not very good poetry but it was flattering. Ruskin had not yet made up his mind, but he was extremely interested in her and it showed. Effie soon realised that he was not committed to Charlotte Lockhart, and as the month of May went on she began to think she was falling in love. She had known him for a long time; he was by far the most attractive and distinguished man in her circle. Every evening he waited outside her room to take her down to dinner, and afterwards she played the piano. The old people quickly went to sleep, leaving the young ones virtually alone.

But after all that, John did not propose. Effie now sensed that his father was uneasy and certainly knew that neither parent wished her to join the family. She left them in mid-June; the plan was that she should go on another visit but as soon as she was out of the Ruskins' house she wrote to her father begging to be allowed to come home. She was baffled and upset by their behaviour, and the friendship between the two families had already come under strain.

2

The Graduate of Oxford
1819–48

It had occurred to him that he must not any longer defer his intention of matrimony, and he had reflected that in taking a wife, a man of good position should expect and carefully choose a blooming young lady – the younger the better, because more educable and submissive – of a rank equal to his own, of religious principles, virtuous disposition, and good understanding.

Middlemarch, Chapter 29

So far, the story has been told from Effie's point of view. But the Ruskin family had a long history of which she was not fully aware, and for them, the lights and shadows fell with a certain difference.

John Thomas Ruskin, the grandfather of the great critic, was an Englishman who had moved to Scotland, where he worked as a grocer and commercial traveller, and married a minister's daughter, Catherine Tweddale. They had two children, Jessie and John James, who was born in 1785 and educated at Edinburgh High School. As a teenager, he studied art and would always love paintings and literature. He was so intelligent and hard-working that he could easily have become a professional man, but this was not allowed. The girl was married off to a tanner in Perth and the sixteen-year-old boy was taken from school and sent to London to be a clerk in a wine importing firm.

Around this time Catherine sent for her husband's niece, Margaret Cock, whose mother had been the landlady of the King's Head in Croydon, and who changed her name to the more genteel Cox. She lived with the couple for the next thirteen years, during which time old Ruskin's behaviour got steadily worse. In 1808 he almost went bankrupt, but his son promised to pay his debts, and eventually did. On his visits home he had grown close to his cousin, who was perhaps more in love than he was, but the old man did his best to thwart their marriage.

They were engaged for fully nine years, Margaret putting up with her uncle's dreadful temper and improving her mind by reading the best books she could get.

Although he had never wanted to go into 'trade' (which was considered vulgar), John James worked hard and conscientiously and did very well. He met a Spaniard, Pedro Domecq, who gave his name to a range of sherries, and they established the City firm of Ruskin, Telford and Domecq. But he still could not afford to marry because he was supporting his father (now insane and unable to work) and slowly clearing his debts. By the autumn of 1817 the older Ruskins and Margaret were living in Perth as the tenants of Bowerswell Villa. In October Catherine collapsed and died and, a fortnight later, John Thomas Ruskin cut his throat. Some relief must have mingled with the horror. Three months later, the 'now not very young people'[1] were quietly married and moved south.

This was the reason for Mrs Ruskin's 'insuperable dislike' of Perth. She came back a few times in the next ten years while her husband's sister was alive, but nothing would persuade her to go inside Bowerswell.

John Ruskin was born in London on 8th February 1819, in the same year as Queen Victoria and George Eliot. His mother was thirty-seven and would have no more children. She felt he was the reward for the long dark years she had endured in her uncle's house, and dedicated him to God before he was born.

From the age of three he lived at 28 Herne Hill, where Effie first met him, and some of his earliest memories were of following his mother around the garden. She was a strict disciplinarian, and he was 'always summarily whipped if I cried, did not do as I was bid, or tumbled on the stairs',[2] so he became a quiet and obedient child. He was educated at home, by tutors and his parents, although at fourteen he briefly attended a day school where the other pupils treated him like a girl. He read the entire Bible and learned Latin with his mother, while his father introduced him to Byron, Shakespeare and Scott. He was 'withdrawn from the sherry trade as an unclean thing',[3] and never wished to take it up. Indeed he decided, when he overheard his father talking business with colleagues, that he had absolutely no sympathy with the 'commercial mind'.[4]

Every summer Mr Ruskin went travelling on business and took his family, sometimes touring for months by carriage. John was shown around various stately homes and saw some of the finest landscapes in England and Wales. He wrote a great many indifferent poems; 'between 14 and

15' he had 'indited thousands of lines'.[5] Some of these were published while he was still a teenager. He also learned to draw and, after visiting Derbyshire, became fascinated by rocks and minerals.

A thirteenth birthday present was a de luxe edition of the long poem *Italy*, by the elderly and then very well-known Samuel Rogers. It was illustrated with pictures of Venice, Florence, Rome and the Alps, some by Turner, and after a while Mrs Ruskin suggested that they should visit these wonderful places themselves. From then on they spent several summers in Europe, where the young boy was overwhelmed by the nature and architecture. Turner and the Alps would become two of the great passions of his life.

When he was an old man, John Ruskin looked back on his extraordinary childhood and said that he was deeply grateful to his parents. They had given him absolute devotion, comfort, leisure, an ample income and every opportunity to develop his mind. His father, as anyone who reads his letters can see, was a remarkable man; later John and he discussed religion more freely than they could have done in his mother's presence. She too was highly intelligent, but she had an authoritarian temperament and a narrow, literal-minded faith. He would always be very close to them, but he knew they had been too protective and isolated him from his generation, so that he found it difficult to form friendships. 'When affection did come', he wrote, 'it came with violence utterly rampant and unmanageable'.[6]

Pedro Domecq had four daughters who visited Herne Hill when Ruskin was seventeen, and he fell desperately in love with the sophisticated fifteen-year-old Adèle. She laughed at him (and anyway was unsuitable, being a Roman Catholic), but he remained obsessed by her for years. After she left he tried to fill his mind with other things, going to lectures at King's College and visiting Dulwich art gallery and the Royal Academy. The three pictures which Turner, an eccentric and reclusive man in his sixties, exhibited in 1836 struck him as works of genius. He was furious when *Blackwood's Magazine* abused them and wrote a long response, which his father decided to send not to *Blackwood's* but to Turner himself. A short, dry note came back from the great painter:

My dear Sir,
  I beg to thank you for your zeal, kindness, and the trouble you have taken in my behalf, in regard of the criticism of *Blackwood's Magazine* for October, respecting my works; but I never move in these matters, they are of no import...[7]

Turner was not a man who easily made friends, and they would never be close, but from this time on he would faintly approve of the young critic and Ruskin would tell everyone that he was a sublime artist, Shakespeare's equal. At his son's request, Ruskin senior bought several Turner watercolours and, most magnificent of all, *The Slave Ship*, a surprise birthday present in 1844.

At the age of not quite eighteen he entered Christ Church, Oxford, the first member of his family to go to university. Henry Liddell, the Dean, noted that he was 'a very strange fellow ... living quite in his own way among the odd set of hunting and sporting men that gentlemen-commoners usually are'.[8] Most of these young men had no interest in the life of the mind and shocked him by flaunting pictures of naked women, but they did not bully him, if only because he was able to give them very good wine. He made one lifelong friend, Henry Acland (1815–1900), who became the Regius Professor of Medicine. But the bonds with his parents did not slacken; his mother moved into lodgings in the High Street and he had tea with her daily, his father joining them at weekends.

Adèle spent a Christmas break with the family and Ruskin noted that 'though extremely lovely at fifteen, Adèle was not prettier than French girls in general at eighteen'.[9] But he was still infatuated. In April 1840, when he had been overworking and had just heard that she was married, he started coughing blood in his rooms at Oxford and his parents immediately took him away. It looked like tuberculosis. The family went for a long stay in Italy and he recovered, but he did not take his degree for another two years, and then it was a Fourth.

Yet already his achievements were considerable. He had won the Newdigate Prize for poetry, had published verses and essays, met Turner and Wordsworth and become a fellow of the Geological Society. In Italy he had toured the great buildings and galleries, contemplating the book which would make his name. He came home in the summer of 1841, which is when he wrote *The King of the Golden River* for Effie. In 1842 the family moved to the much grander house in Denmark Hill, where several Turners were hung in the breakfast-room. This was partly so that John could have a suitable setting to entertain friends.

Ever since childhood the young man had been a compulsive writer (his collected works, not counting letters and diaries, would eventually fill thirty-nine volumes). However, he gave up writing poetry in his twenties; his real medium was magnificent, sonorous prose. He also practised drawing every day, but had no ambition to be an artist. Instead he saw himself as a teacher, perhaps a preacher on a new theme, man's relationship with art. In May 1843, when he was twenty-four, he published the book which would make him famous:

Modern Painters:
Their Superiority in the Art of Landscape Painting
To all
The Ancient Masters
proved by examples of
The True, the Beautiful and the Intellectual,
From the
Works of Modern Artists,
especially
From those of J.M.W. Turner, Esq. R.A.
By a Graduate of Oxford.

This volume (the first of five) attacked admired painters like Canaletto, Claude and the Dutch masters, whose work he thought tame. By contrast, Turner – especially the late, Impressionistic Turner – was 'the greatest landscape painter who has ever lived'.[10] At this time Ruskin was still an orthodox Christian and believed that nature was God's handiwork. No picture of a sunset could equal the sunset itself, but Turner had come closer than anyone to painting 'the exhaustless living energy with which the universe is filled'.[11] He urged readers to look not at old masters but at the sea, clouds, cataracts, storms, sunlight, 'the pure and holy hills, treated as a link between heaven and earth'.[12] Not everyone could visit galleries, but anyone who had eyes could look at the sky, which was constantly changing, and almost impossible to paint well. Young artists were advised to go to nature in a spirit of reverence and paint what they actually saw.

His splendid language and high ideals made a deep impression on his readers. They included Wordsworth, Tennyson, George Eliot, Charlotte Brontë, Elizabeth Gaskell and the young William Holman Hunt. A second volume, discussing the idea of beauty, appeared in 1846. The Graduate's identity soon leaked out and it became obvious that he had one of the finest minds of his generation. His parents, and many other people, had no doubt that he was destined for greatness.

This was the situation in late June 1847, when the nineteen-year-old Effie headed unhappily back to Scotland. Ruskin was twenty-eight and still living at home, with a growing reputation but no independent income. His parents still worried about his health, which in fact was good, and still involved themselves far too much in his life. They had not given up hope that he would marry Charlotte Lockhart, and feared that he might become dangerously ill if he was thwarted in love.

Effie was bewildered by a family so different from her own. She spent two days on the steamer, which made her seasick, and was glad to get home to Bowerswell. Her brother George was now working in his father's office in South Street and there were four more children, all under six: Robert, Sophie, Alice and John. Effie soon became re-absorbed in the life of Perth, and no doubt her mother pointed out that there were plenty of other young men. She had written to her from London that 'John Ruskin will certainly be in Scotland ... but you need not expect to see him at Bowerswell. He cannot come for various reasons and as you know Mrs Ruskin would be miserable every moment he was in Perth or under our roof which would be much worse. It is extraordinary to me how a woman of her powers of mind and extreme clearness of understanding can be so superstitious'.[13]

Ruskin did pass through Perth on 25th August, on his way to the Highlands, and looked in at Mr Gray's office but did not meet his family. All expectation from him, as Jane Austen might have said, was now absolutely over. From everything we know about Effie, she would have behaved with dignity. In any case, she now had much more to worry about than a failed romance.

Mr Gray had been spending money lavishly on English schools, continental holidays and the rebuilding of Bowerswell, and had bought shares in – among other things – the Scottish Central Railway Company. It seemed safe, when railways were so obviously the transport of the future and Perth was just about to be connected with the rest of the island. But there was a huge slump and by August, like thousands of other speculators, he was in serious trouble. As well, Mrs Gray was expecting her thirteenth baby.

What they did not yet know was that Ruskin had been miserable when he avoided Effie, 'thinking that my own pain was perhaps much less than hers'.[14] He told his parents about it in letters from the Highlands and they, remembering how ill he had been after the trouble with Adèle, were alarmed. Mr Ruskin still thought Effie was an artful girl, and knew about the Grays' difficulties, but he was prepared to give way if his son's health and happiness depended on it. Mrs Ruskin, who had lived with Effie for weeks, was more positive:

She is very lovely, with the least vanity I have ever seen in any one, she has much social kindly feeling, this in a wife would be invaluable to you for you cannot go out of the world altogether and in your intercourse with it she would be indeed a helpmate for you. I think her also very prudent in her expenses without the slightest meanness, her taste in dress really good, her appearance such as we may all be proud of, her family and connections equal if not superior to our own – her temper I think must be excellent or she would not have borne so easily your fault finding and her natural abilities are much above the common ... I do think Effie so open, so frank and upright, that she will not deceive you, and you may tell her if she takes you and makes you happy that we shall receive her with joy and that I will study her happiness and cherish her with my whole heart ... Effie is fitted to make an excellent wife and you happy and if she loves you as I think she does and has done from childhood she will be most happy with you.[15]

None of them were in any doubt that Effie would agree. Ruskin invited himself to Bowerswell and hung around for a week at the beginning of October, but still did not propose. Effie had been hurt by his behaviour and was careful not to give him much encouragement. The family was trying to keep up appearances; other young men called at the house and he soon found that several of them admired her:

She is surrounded by people who pay her attentions, and though I believe most of them inferior in some points to myself, far more calculated to catch a girl's fancy. Still – Miss Gray and I are old friends, I have every reason to think that if I were to try – I could make her more than a friend – and if – after I leave here this time – she holds out for six months more I believe I shall ask her to come to Switzerland with me next year – and if she will not – or if she takes anybody else in the mean time – I am really afraid I shall enjoy my tour much less than usual – though no disappointment of this kind would affect me as the first did.[16]

This sounds bad. He certainly was not passionately in love with Effie yet. But seeing her courted by other men increased his interest, and he found himself very depressed when he went away. Soon afterwards he wrote to her proposing marriage, and was accepted.

21

A legend sprang up afterwards that she had been engaged to someone else and jilted him, supposedly for the Ruskin money. Mrs Gaskell wrote years later, 'Effie Grey [*sic*] *was engaged at the very time she accepted Mr Ruskin* he did not know of it till after their marriage',[17] but Mrs Gaskell never knew her well. Effie could not have been engaged when she was in London that spring as no such thing is mentioned in her letters. Nor was she officially linked to anyone in Perth, though she did have an admirer called Mr Tasker, whom Ruskin met, and who he thought was 'feeling his way', but she 'saved him the mortification of direct refusal'.[18] She also wrote to William MacLeod and told him she was going to be married; Ruskin knew about him too. No doubt she saw and danced with other young men after she came home, but all her letters and actions show that at this time she was in love with Ruskin.

No one seems to have worried about the fact that she was very young. Her mother had married at nineteen and been happy; it did not seem unusual. Effie's flirtations had all been fairly innocent. She did not yet know much about men and was basically a good Presbyterian girl who wanted to spread her wings a little way, have an interesting time, and then settle down for life with a husband and children.

Having written back to Ruskin agreeing to marry him, she did not see him again for five months. Of course he lived a long way off, but there was nothing to stop him getting on a train and coming north. Instead, he wrote her several letters saying how much he loved her and revealing that he was particularly excited by her effect on other men: 'How proud of you I shall be ... Fancy us – at the Opera again, together ... And I shall see everyone gazing at you – and think – "Yes – you may look as much as you please, but she is *mine*, now, *mine*, all mine"'.[19]

Even Mrs Ruskin thought his behaviour a little strange – 'as you say you love her more the oftener you write to her may you not be in some degree surrounding her with imaginary charms?'[20] There was talk of Effie going to London for a visit, but she would not have left home until her mother was safe. The baby, Melville, was born on 30th November, then the whole family went down with flu and Effie ran the house for several weeks. She herself seems to have found Ruskin's letters satisfactory, writing to him four months after she had last seen him:

I do not know how I can sufficiently thank you for your inestimable letter this morning so full of tenderness and affection almost too kind and good, you will quite spoil me, my love, it almost made me weep with joy to think myself so beloved, not but that I was fully impressed with that before, but this morning's letter almost made me rejoice too much in thinking that so much happiness was permitted to me who am so unworthy of it.[21]

They did not meet as an engaged couple until March, when she went to Edinburgh for a friend's wedding and they fixed their own wedding date for April 10th.

All this time Mr Gray's finances were giving enormous concern and Effie's coming marriage to the son of old friends seemed the only bright spot. Ruskin's parents had written welcoming her into the family, but when the marriage contract was drawn up Mr Ruskin was dismayed to find that her father had nothing to give her. He wrote to him three weeks before the wedding, saying bluntly that presumably he would have to go bankrupt. And it was no use, he warned Mr Gray, to expect anything from his son:

John knows my Severity in money matters – that though I give where I can – were he to be Security for a Single hundred for the best friend he has – he should never see a shilling more of my money.[22]

John himself was told, around this time, that his prospective father-in-law might be ruined, but assured him sincerely that he did not mind. 'It grieves me much that I can be of so little service to you', he wrote, 'there are however modes in which hereafter I may be able to relieve you from some anxiety'.[23] His ability to help was limited because he had no income of his own, but he would look after Effie, and perhaps in future they could take care of her little sisters, Sophie and Alice.

Away from these unpleasant matters, the Ruskin family looked forward to their summer tour of Europe. Ruskin had been telling Effie how much he wanted to show her the Alps. He had gone abroad once without his parents, in 1845, but this time it was planned that all four should go together. He confided, 'there are little things that often sadden me now, in my father and mother – Still – I am always happiest when I am most dutiful – and although you may be sure, Effie love, that I will not sacrifice my wife's comfort in any degree to an exaggerated idea of filial duty – still, I think you will find you can give so much pleasure on this journey by very little self-denial, that you will not in the end have reason to wish it had been otherwise planned ... And remember, love, we owe them *a little* – all our present happiness and our future'.[24]

Somewhere at the back of his mind was the consciousness that they could climb mountains together only if she did not get pregnant.

Meanwhile, tremendous events in Europe were affecting thousands of other lives. In the last week of February 1848 the citizens of Paris revolted and Louis-Philippe, King of the French, was expelled. This added to Mr Gray's troubles, as he had bought shares in a French railway company which were now worthless, but he hung on and did not go bankrupt. In March there were rebellions against the Austrian emperor in Vienna, Hungary, Poland and Italy. Suddenly it seemed unsafe to make a wedding journey to the Continent. Instead the young couple would tour the Highlands and the Lake District, by themselves.

Ruskin came to Bowerswell, with his valet George Hobbs,[25] twelve days before the wedding. He was distressed by the Grays' circumstances, bitterly disappointed that he could not go to Europe, and his stay was quite long enough to convince him that he did not like small children. There were five of them, who naturally made a great deal of noise, and Melville, now aged four months, would have cried. His parents stayed away. Mr Ruskin explained in an awkward letter that his wife could not get over her horror of Perth; he also felt he should not go far from home because the Chartists were planning a mammoth demonstration in London. But he generously settled £10,000 on Effie; the income would be drawn by her husband and would be their main means of support.

Monday 10th April 1848 was a fine day in Scotland. Four hundred miles to the south, 20,000 people marched to Kennington Common calling for Parliament to accept the six demands of the Charter: universal manhood suffrage, secret ballots, equal electoral districts, no property qualifications, annual parliaments, payment of MPs. Two art students, John Everett Millais and William Holman Hunt, walked beside the crowd, fascinated. The respectable classes, terrified of a French-style revolution, had barricaded their windows and armed a number of special constables, just in case. William Rossetti, an eighteen-year-old clerk in the Excise Office, had been given a thick stick but probably would not have used it as his sympathies were with the Chartists. In the end it rained heavily and the great crowd dispersed without violence, and without getting what it wanted. Hunt had promised Millais' parents to keep the younger boy out of trouble and dragged him away before the end.

Effie Gray and John Ruskin were married quietly by a Scottish minister in the drawing room at Bowerswell that same afternoon. Afterwards they left their friends celebrating and drove (with his manservant) to Blair Atholl, where they were to spend the first stage of their honeymoon.

The wedding night would go down in history.

PART TWO

EFFIE RUSKIN

3

The Virgin Wife 1848–9

Hence he determined to abandon himself to the stream of feeling, and
perhaps was surprised to find what an exceedingly shallow rill it was.

Middlemarch, Chapter 7

The new Mr and Mrs Ruskin arrived at their inn very late, after an
exhausting build-up to the wedding and a drive of over thirty miles.
What happened, or rather did not happen next was described by both
of them six years later. Effie would say that at the time she knew nothing
about sex. Ruskin would say that they agreed not to consummate the
marriage, because he did not want children, or not yet:

> It may be thought strange that I *could* abstain from a woman
> who to most people was so attractive. But though her face was
> beautiful, her person was not formed to excite passion. On the
> contrary, there were certain circumstances in her person which
> completely checked it.[1]

Later he told Effie 'that he had imagined women were quite different
to what he saw I was, and that the reason he did not make me his
Wife was because he was disgusted with my person the first evening'.[2]
    Ruskin's knowledge of the female body was academic. He may have
looked at the pictures of naked women which had been passed around
his Oxford college, but these pictures may not have been realistic. Or
Effie may have been losing blood on the first night; later he would
accuse her of having an internal disease. It seems likely that he lowered
the dress from her 'snowy shoulders' (his phrase) and then found that
he could not go through with it. There are no more details.
    The sad and unmentionable truth was that Ruskin could feel real
passion only for very young girls. Adèle had been fifteen when he first

29

saw her; Effie had been twelve. As each grew older, he gradually became less and less attracted. His sex drive, though it did exist, was much weaker than most men's, and it is almost certain that he never had a full sexual relationship in his entire life.

Naturally, he did not tell his new wife that her 'person' left him cold. Instead he talked about his dislike of children and his wish to take her to Europe and the Alps, without burdens. Effie did not know how unusual his behaviour was, but she did know that it was a wife's duty to obey her husband. Possibly she was afraid of the unknown and agreed that it made sense to postpone pregnancy. The state of their marriage would remain a secret between them for several years to come.

For the next two weeks they travelled, quite happily, through the Highlands and Lake District. Ruskin, who went nowhere without George Hobbs, was impressed that Effie got on 'capitally well without any maid', and amused by her general friendliness:

> Effie talks to everybody she can make stand still, everywhere and anywhere ... I found her inside the Turnpike engaged in confidential conversation with the Turnpike woman ... then at Killin, she got over an old man ... and before I knew what she was about – she was sitting at the fire drinking the old gentleman's health in whisky – and paying him compliments on his clean butter tubs. We met some people on the road today, as we were walking – whom she addressed as if she had known them thirty years – and if I hadn't remonstrated, a little farther on, she would have been quite thick with a party of Tinkers.[3]

Judging from her early letters home, she worried only about her parents' problems. She begged them not to fret and pointed out that they would never have to spend money on her again. They came back to Denmark Hill at the end of April and moved in temporarily with the older Ruskins. 'Mrs R overwhelms me with presents', Effie wrote, '... Mr and Mrs R. are as kind as can be ... I never saw anything like John, he is just perfect!!!!'[4] She was taken to a Royal Academy private view, to a literary breakfast with Samuel Rogers, to the Henry Aclands at Oxford, and was one of the few women ever to be allowed inside Turner's house:

> He was so kind and took us into his room without a fire and bare and miserly but he ran and brought out his wine and biscuits and

we all drank each other's health, and then he took us up to his gallery where we saw *such* pictures. I would pawn all I had for the *Old Temeraire* but he has been offered £1000 and we won't have it.[5]

'I am glad to see Phemy gets John to go out a little', Mr Ruskin wrote. 'He has met with most of the first men for some years back but he is very indifferent to general Society ... Phemy is much better calculated for society than he is – He is best in *print*'.[6]

It was too good to last.

The first tensions had to do with her brother George, a pleasant and inoffensive boy of eighteen. He had been expensively educated, at Charterhouse and in Germany, but now the Grays' affairs seemed so desperate that they thought of sending him to London as a clerk. They had hoped that Mr Ruskin could help him find a job; it did not seem much to ask of an old friend. But he was reluctant, and the situation was deeply embarrassing for Effie:

John and I often talk about him but we can make no plan and John thinks and so do I that there is no chance of his father taking him, and it is a delicate point for us because John you see has no separate business of his own to enable him to speak independently ... I cannot help being distressed about you all and I often cry at night when I think what a load hangs over you and that I cannot help you in the least degree, but it would be much worse if you did not tell me for then I would fancy things were worse than they are.[7]

Then there was the postponed continental holiday. The Ruskins were vehemently opposed to the revolutions which were shaking Europe at the time John and Effie got married, and annoyed by the ruin of their plans. Instead, in July, all four of them went to Salisbury. Ruskin's ever-active mind had been preoccupied for some time with the glories of medieval buildings and he was working hard on *The Seven Lamps of Architecture*. After he had sketched the cathedral for a few days, he became unwell. His father assumed he had worn himself out by exertions in the marital bed, which amused him. Mrs Ruskin feared that he was seriously ill; Effie knew he was not. There was a trivial argument about a blue pill. Ruskin thought that Effie had been rude to his mother and took the old lady's side.

But by August it seemed safe for the younger couple to go to France. There had been a short-lived radical government which believed in universal manhood suffrage, but it had been ousted, and in late June the workers in Paris rioted and 1500 were killed. Effie was shocked by the 'awful loss of life'[8] but Ruskin wrote coldly:

> The sound of mortars and howitzers in the streets of Paris is the sweetest music I have heard this many a day not excepting even dear Effies – I regret as everyone must the fearful balance of slaughter on the wrong side – Still – it will be the severest warning: it has shown to the mob that they are not omnipotent.[9]

This may surprise those who think of Ruskin as the working man's friend, but he hated revolution, not only because of his Tory background but also because he feared any threat to ancient buildings. The sight of workmen 'actually before our eyes knocking down the time worn black with age pinnacles and sticking up in their place new stone ones'[10] almost drove him mad.

The couple toured Normandy, where he made drawings of the finest cathedrals and churches, and took notes. It was Effie's job to copy them out neatly, otherwise there was little for her to do. Ruskin told his father that she would quietly sit down, sometimes for three hours at a stretch, while he drew and wrote. 'She chats away with the people and is getting on fast with her French'.[11]

But unfortunately they were pursued by letters from both families going over the arguments about George. Mr Ruskin thought, correctly, that the boy was unlikely ever to be a successful businessman, and feared his son might be embarrassed by a relation in 'trade'. He wrote to Effie's father:

> On the subject of disposing of George I would not presume to influence or interfere but as I am ever frank with all persons I would wish to guard you against expectations from me – I will do all I can for Phemy but for twenty reasons I promise nothing for George ... I only hope that in this change of destination you are not looking at all to me and that he is not looking to London as a place of pleasure – I name this because I have always thought (though it may be erroneously) that George's Education has been one rather of pleasure and Excitement than of work ... Before taking the irretrievable step George should fully understand what

he probably comes here to – To a solitary Lodging or some family in the City to whom his Board is an object – His Sister and Brother in Law if family matters admit of it, will not be in London 4 months a year these 7 years and when here they will be absorbed by Society to which though they have the will they have not the power to give him admission – as a professional man, as a Lawyer occasionally visiting London, they might, as a Brokers Clerk in the City they cannot.[12]

Effie was aware of the tensions between the two families, which stayed only just within the bounds of good manners. Her father was shocked by Mr Ruskin's aggressive tone and wrote, 'He overlooks my reasons entirely and thinks only of George becoming a burden upon him or you, which we never dream't of'.[13] Meanwhile, unknown to her, John was writing to his father:

... as for G.G., I shall take care that he shall give you no trouble nor interfere with my society – I am very sorry he is coming and of course must be prepared for some things that I shall not like – but I shall make him understand his position – and, although I cannot exclude him from seeing his sister – yet I shall keep my study inviolable – Effie will have to choose between *him* and *me*.[14]

He had already told Effie that he did not want her old friends to disturb him. Later on he thought it over and decided it was his Christian duty to put up with his wife's family to some extent.

Meanwhile the Grays were struggling on, still expecting to lose their home. Effie tried to write cheerfully and sent them all the money she could spare. Her hair began to come out in handfuls when she brushed it, and she was often in tears. John wrote that 'even when poor Effie was crying last night I felt it by no means as a husband should – but rather a bore – however I comforted her in a very dutiful way'.[15] She was terribly distressed when she heard that her favourite aunt, Jessie Jameson, had died, a month after giving birth to a baby who died too. (Another aunt would also die in childbirth later that year.) The good news, which reached them in October, was that George had found a place in a legal firm in Edinburgh. She wrote home:

I hope this will be the last said upon an unpleasant subject which corresponding upon has done no good, but it ought to end in each party thinking no wrong is intended on either side, and I think you ought to excuse Mr R's suspicious character when you consider the claims he has upon him ... but be sure no ill was intended so there let the subject drop.[16]

They returned to England in the autumn and moved into the fashionable Park Street, but Ruskin often spent his days at his parents' house, without his wife. By Christmas Mr Gray's affairs had improved, and Effie urged her mother to visit them. Before that she had to get through Christmas at Denmark Hill, and it went badly. She was very unwell, but Mrs Ruskin would not allow her to stay upstairs while she entertained Turner and other guests. Now that Effie was a member of the family, her mother-in-law felt free to bully her. 'I am aware that Mrs Ruskin gives Lectures', her own husband admitted, 'and being above 60 will speak to a very young person in a way that is not pleasant before others'.[17] Ruskin described the incident rather callously – 'finding her one day in tears when she ought to have been dressing for dinner, she gave her a scold – which if she had not been ill she would have deserved'.[18]

When Mrs Gray reached London in January 1849, she was shocked by the change in her daughter. The girl who had set off so hopefully on her honeymoon only nine months ago was very weak, coughing badly and unable to sleep. Mrs Ruskin, as we know from her private letters, had no sympathy.

The plan was for all four of them to set off that spring for the delayed tour of Switzerland, but in February Effie returned to Bowerswell with her mother, intending to stay only a few weeks. But all the children were suffering from whooping cough, and on 1st March Robert, a bright six-year-old, died. 'You seem to be afflicted beyond the ordinary Lot of Man', Mr Ruskin wrote to the Grays, 'in the Loss of so many sweet Children'.[19] With her family in so much grief, and herself so pulled down, it seemed impossible to go on holiday. She decided to stay where she was, and did not see John Ruskin again for nine months.

Effie spent her first wedding anniversary and her twenty-first birthday in Perth, where she was the object of much gossip. Why was she staying for so long with her parents while her husband and *his* parents were touring Europe? Perhaps she had come home to have a baby? But the months went by, and no baby appeared. Some people, it seems, already suspected the truth, and described her as 'the virgin wife'. The Grays were aware of what was being said and feared that the young couple might become permanently estranged.

To be fair, the elder Ruskins also thought it an odd arrangement. 'I should disapprove entirely of this', Mr Ruskin wrote, 'were my Son going abroad for his pleasure – but it seems as much a matter of business as my travelling to Liverpool ... They must however arrange their comings and goings with each other'.[20]

Ruskin crossed the channel in April, just after finishing the *Seven Lamps*, with his parents and Hobbs. In May, Mr Gray came to a settlement with the bank. But Effie did not get better, and in the same month consulted James Simpson, the pioneer of chloroform, who was then Professor of Midwifery at Edinburgh University. If he gave her a full physical examination he would have found that she was still a virgin and may have told her the facts of life. He certainly advised her, then or later, to have a child.

Ruskin, who was having a delightful time, hinted in his letters that this might soon happen. He wrote to her quite frequently and, at first, affectionately:

Do you know, pet, it seems almost a dream to me that we have been married: I look forward to meeting you: and to your *next* bridal night: and to the time when I shall again draw your dress from your snowy shoulders: and lean my cheek upon them, as if you were still my betrothed only: and I had never held you in my arms.[21]

'I think it will be much nicer next time, we shall neither of us be frightened',[22] he told her, and agreed when she mentioned her affection for her little sister Alice that he would like 'a little Alice of our own'.[23] 'Indeed I long for you my pet', he wrote cheerfully from the Jura, 'but I have much here to occupy me and keep me interested – and so I am able to bear the longing better perhaps than you, who have only the routine of home'.[24] And, by the way, could she make some notes on the history of Venice for his new book?

But although her in-laws were enjoying their holiday, it nagged at them that something had gone wrong between them and Effie. They had hoped she could fit into the family like their niece Mary (who died that summer while they were abroad) and, unfortunately, they could not keep their worries to themselves. Ruskin complained, in the last letter quoted, that she should have 'thrown herself openly upon' his parents, although presumably he would not have been pleased had she told them all. He was even more annoyed when he heard that Effie was suffering from 'nerves', which he and his mother tended to think were her own fault.

Then Mr Ruskin decided to write frankly to Effie's father. He and his wife had been hurt by her coldness, he said, and surprised that she had stayed behind in Scotland. She ought to realise that her husband had gone abroad for work, not pleasure, and should not try to bring him home prematurely:

> About your Daughter both Mrs Ruskin and myself must continue to be anxious and as I use no reserve I will confess to you that the feeling is mingled with sorrow and disappointment ... You may tell her that Mrs Ruskin and I, although the change was unexpected, can entirely forgive her rejection of our kindness or good offices but we do expect from the Love which we hope and believe, she bears my Son that she will try to make his pleasures hers, to like what he likes, for his sake, and to hear of the places which he loves with pleasure, and if I might take the liberty of prescribing for her own comfort and amendment, I should urge an effort to be made to sacrifice every feeling to duty, to become interested and delighted in what her Husband may be accomplishing by a short absence, and to find a satisfaction in causing him no unnecessary anxiety.[25]

Effie's parents had already noticed that she did not get letters from Mr and Mrs Ruskin. Her father walked round the garden with her and begged her to tell him what was wrong, but how could she tell him? All he understood, and said when he wrote back, was that young people were better left alone:

> Phemy has the greatest affection for John – Her earnest wish is to have the same for you and Mrs Ruskin ... You do not make allowance for her state of health ... neither do you consider that her natural manners are thoroughly scotch by which I mean that she makes no display of feeling even to those to whom she is much attached ... If I may be permitted to hint a word by way of advice it would be simply that Mrs Ruskin and you should leave John and Phemy as much as possible to themselves – married people are rather restive under the control and supervision of Parents tho' proceeding from the kindest and most affectionate motives. Do not take amiss what I say for I have but one desire and that is to see you all happy.

He added that of course Effie understood the importance of John's work and 'no selfish desire on her part would induce her to wish him to return till he has accomplished the objects for which he went abroad'.[26]

Effie's own letters are lost, but she certainly tried to improve matters, and wrote 'a very sweet letter'[27] to Mrs Ruskin in June. But the discussion dragged on and grew harsher. In July Ruskin himself joined in, with a letter to Effie's father which argued passionately that his parents had always been extremely kind to her and that she was mentally ill:

> If she had not been seriously ill, I *should* have had fault to find with her: but the state of her feelings I ascribe now, simply to bodily weakness: that is to say – and this is a serious and distressing admission – to a nervous disease affecting the brain ... If Effie had *in sound mind* been annoyed by the contemptible trifles which *have* annoyed her; if she had cast back from her the kindness and the affection with which my parents received her, and refused to do her duty to them, under any circumstances whatever but those of an illness bordering in many of its features on incipient insanity, I should not now have written you this letter respecting her ... I hope to see her outgrow with her girls frocks – that contemptible dread of interference and petulant resistance of authority which begins in pride – and is nourished in folly – and ends in pain – 'Restiveness' I am accustomed to regard as unpromising character even in horses and asses – I look for meekness and gentleness in woman.[28]

Effie would have been much more shocked by this letter than by those of his father, who for all his bossiness and tactlessness really did want to make peace. Her parents probably did not show it to her, but they preserved it, and some years later her mother wrote on the envelope, 'Remarkable Letter of J. Ruskin's in which he artfully puts down his then so-called *wife*'s unhappiness to any thing but the real cause which he himself only knew'.

In the late summer of 1849 the Ruskins started for home. They suggested that Effie should join them in London, but so many neighbours had been commenting on Ruskin's long absence that the Grays thought he should first come to Perth and be seen in public with his wife. This provoked another angry letter, this time to Effie:

> As for your wish that I should come to Scotland – that is also perfectly natural – nor have I the slightest objection to come for

you: only do not mistake womanly pride for womanly affection: You say that 'you should have thought the first thing I should have done after eight months absence, would have been to come for you'. Why, you foolish little puss, do not you see that part of my reason for wishing you to come to London was that I might get you a couple of days sooner; and do not you see also, that if love, instead of pride, had prompted your reply, you would never have thought of what I *ought* to do, or your *right* to ask, you would only have thought of being with me as soon as you could ... I do not intend to allow you to dictate to me what is right, nor even to take upon you the office of my mistress in knowledge of the world – If you knew a little more of it, you would be more cautious how you wrote impertinent letters to your Husband.

The whole affair however is too trivial to occupy me longer – and I am not going to treat you like a child, and refuse you your cake because you don't kiss your hand for it properly: I shall come to Perth for you as soon as I get home: only have your calls and ceremonies over, as I shall not stay there.[29]

At this point, a modern young woman might have decided she had had enough. For Effie, that was not an option. She may have reflected that it was nearly two years since they had got engaged, and that for more than half that time they had been living apart. The long quiet months at home had done her good. Perhaps after talking things over with her mother, she had an idea.

4

The Stones of Venice 1849–51

But this stupendous fragmentariness heightened the dream-like strangeness of her bridal life ... Ruins and basilicas, palaces and colossi, set in the midst of a sordid present.

Middlemarch, Chapter 20

'When I came home I found my wife much better', Ruskin wrote, 'and very desirous of some change of scene. She asked me to take her to Venice, and as I had need of some notes ... I was glad to take her there'.[1]

They had both been following the news. Venice had declared itself a republic in March 1848 and held out bravely for over a year against the Austrian army. Throughout the summer of 1849 the city had been bombed and blockaded; Ruskin had written to Effie that he would 'give up all architectural studies'[2] if they knocked it down. It surrendered only on August 22nd, when people were dying in great numbers from cholera and almost starving.

Ruskin arrived in Perth in September, as promised, and Effie suggested that, now the siege had ended, he should go with her to Venice and work on his new book. She must have been thrilled by his description of the city in *Modern Painters*:

Thank heaven, we are in sunshine again, and what sunshine! ... Do we dream, or does the white forked sail drift nearer, and nearer yet, diminishing the blue sea between us with the fulness of its wings? It pauses now, but the quivering of its bright reflection troubles the shadows of the sea, those azure, fathomless depths of crystal mystery, on which the swiftness of the poised gondola floats double, its black beak lifted like the crest of a dark ocean bird, its scarlet draperies flashed back from the kindling surface, and its bent oar breaking the radiant water into a dart of gold. Dream-like and dim, but glorious, the unnumbered palaces lift their shafts out of the hollow sea – pale ranks of motionless flame – their mighty towers sent up to heaven like tongues of more eager fire – their grey domes looming vast and dark, like eclipsed worlds – their sculptured arabesques and purple marble fading farther and fainter, league beyond league lost in the light of distance ... Yes, Mr Turner, we are in Venice now![3]

Ruskin had not been there for four years and was delighted with her plan. He and Effie would come out into the sunshine again. They would make a new start.

Effie invited a friend, Charlotte Ker, to go with them. It is unusual to take a third person on a second honeymoon, but she knew she could expect to spend a good deal of time without her husband, who would also be taking his valet George Hobbs. So, less than a month after returning from Europe, Ruskin was on his travels again, and with his parents' approval. He took Effie to London, where she tried hard to get back on good terms with her in-laws:

I had some private conversation with Mr Ruskin; what an extraordinary man he is; he was quite delighted that I spoke to him, evidently, and said he had nothing to blame me for and thought I had behaved beautifully. I begged him to tell me what he was not pleased with. He said there was nothing but he thought sometimes John could not make me happy which was a new light certainly on the subject. However we settled it all in the best possible manner, but who can know what such a man thinks!! ... By the way, a capital joke Mr Ruskin heard when he came home that the report was that I was so unhappy with John that proceedings were instituted for a separation. He was fearfully angry.[4]

People were still talking about this odd couple and it would not stop. Effie and John left England, with Hobbs and Charlotte, on 3rd October, and drove by carriage to northern Italy. For the first time she saw the Alps, Romeo and Juliet's Verona, Leonardo's *Last Supper*. Austrian soldiers were everywhere and she wrote from Milan, 'I am a thorough Italian here and hate oppression, therefore wish them far enough'.[5] But Ruskin corrected her; at this time he believed that the Austrians were 'the only protection of Italy from utter dissolution'.[6] In Venice they would meet several Austrian officers and the Italians who supported them, the *austriacanti*. The patriots, or *italianissimi*, kept away.

When they got there they found that the railway had been blown up but the monuments, to Ruskin's huge relief, were still standing. Effie found it 'the most exquisite place I have ever seen'. They moved into the Hotel Danieli, a marble palace whose windows overlooked the water. She wrote home that 'it is most delicious, always mild, never damp, the skies and sunsets of the most heavenly colours, and the sea and canals so fresh and calm and green with the streets of Palaces, and no marks of the year-and-a-half blockade they are just recovering from'.[7]

There were very few English people in the city, but they did make friends with Rawdon Brown, a bachelor scholar of forty-three who had lived there for the last fifteen years. 'I never wake in the morning, but I thank God that he has let me pass my days in Venice',[8] he wrote. Effie called him 'a most agreeable, clever literary person',[9] and he opened doors for them both.

Ruskin, as he had made clear before they started, was here to work. He went out daily with an Italian servant to study architecture:

> John excites the liveliest astonishment to all and sundry in Venice and I do not think they have made up their minds yet whether he is very mad or very wise. Nothing interrupts him and whether the Square is crowded or empty he is either seen with a black cloth over his head taking Daguerrotypes or climbing about the capitals covered with dust, or else with cobwebs exactly as if he had just arrived from taking a voyage with the old woman on her broomstick. Then when he comes down he stands very meekly to be brushed down by Domenico quite regardless of the scores of idlers who cannot understand him at all.[10]

It does not look as if they discussed his book, except in the most general terms. Effie said that she thought *The Stones of Venice* 'will be worth something but it is not easy to find out for he finds that he has so many things to write about that have never been written about before that he requires to bring out one before another is able to be understood'.[11]

For four months in Venice they were quite content, each doing what he or she preferred. We hear of them playing chess and throwing a ball around the huge cold rooms to keep warm. Ruskin's hints that they might begin a sexual relationship were not followed up. He was charming to her, because she was making no demands on him, but he was still sure that he did not want children and in some part of his mind he still thought (as no one else ever did) that she was unhinged. It was probably discussed, and perhaps it was around this time that he said they would make love when she was twenty-five. He would certainly have picked a date well in the future, and she was not yet twenty-two.

Effie dismissed the subject for the time being – 'we follow our different occupations and never interfere with one another and are always happy'.[12] She and Charlotte worked hard at their Italian and German. They explored the islands by gondola and bought some sparkling Venetian glass. They went to the opera, sometimes with Ruskin, and admired the Titians, Veroneses and Tintorettos. Sundays were spent quietly reading the Bible or going to the German Protestant church.

But she was conscious that there was a great deal of 'misery and wickedness'[13] in the city. Her family had always been involved with charities in Perth, and she was eager to help where she could. She bought some lace from an old woman who was almost starving, tried to get a young man excused from conscription, and made friends with the Dominican friars – Fate Bene Fratelli – who looked after the sick, and had behaved heroically during the siege. Later she would send them a tube of chloroform from London. She was shown the island of San Giuliano, from which Venice had been bombed, and wrote sombrely, 'I never in reading realized what War could do till we saw this place'.[14]

It was unusual for two young foreign women to go about on their own. They were not seriously molested, but Italians, probably attracted by her fair hair, followed them around and sometimes threw bouquets at them. One admirer said to Ruskin, 'Ah! Monsieur, comme votre femme est belle!'[15] They got to know more people and she grew quite popular. An Austrian officer called Paulizza, who had overseen the balloon-bombing, became friendly with them and may have fallen in love with Effie. Rumours were getting back to Perth, and she had to explain to her mother: 'I never could love anybody else in the world but John and the way these Italian women go on is so perfectly disgusting to me that it even removes from me any desire to coquetry which John declares I possess very highly, but he thinks it charming, so do not I ... I am one of the odd of the earth and have no talent whatever for intrigue as every thing with me must be as open as the day'.[16] This had happened before and would happen again. Ruskin was well aware that other men found his wife very attractive and, knowing she would behave herself, felt proud and pleased to be her legal owner.

For Effie, the great advantage of Venice was that she had total freedom and was exploring a foreign culture – 'we ladies like to see and know every thing and I find I am much happier following my own plans and pursuits and never troubling John, or he me'.[17] So when they headed home, in March 1850, she was disappointed. Ruskin promised they would soon return so that he could continue his book.

They reached London in April and were reunited with the old Ruskins, to whom Effie had written regularly while they were abroad. It went quite well. Then they moved back into Park Street, but most days Ruskin had himself driven to his parents' house after breakfast. Effie suggested he should work at home so that she could sometimes see him, but he said he liked to be surrounded by his Turners, and that she could easily amuse herself.

She went riding, practised the piano, made several new friends. One of them was Elizabeth Eastlake, formerly Rigby, whose husband Charles was the keeper of the National Gallery. Later that year he was elected President of the Royal Academy and knighted. His wife had been a successful writer before marrying at the age of nearly forty; in 1849 she had published a brutal anonymous review of *Jane Eyre*. She was almost six feet tall and her husband much shorter. Later she would play an important part in Effie's story.

In June, along with several other ladies, Effie was presented at a reception in Buckingham Palace and found it 'broiling but amusing ... The Queen looked immensely stout and red but was very calm', she reported. 'I kissed her hand which was fat and red too'.[18]

Much of the talk that spring and summer would have been about art. The Ruskins had come home just before the 1850 Summer Exhibition, and this year a group of young men who called themselves the Pre-Raphaelite Brotherhood were in the news. One of them had done a shocking picture called *Christ in the House of his Parents*, or *The Carpenter's Shop*. Ruskin was asked to take a careful look at it, but thought little of it.

As Mrs Gray was pregnant again, Effie went to Bowerswell and stayed there from August to October, when Albert was born. It was ironic that her mother, at forty-two, was having a baby when she was unsure that she, in her early twenties, ever would. Both sets of parents were probably surprised that she had not become pregnant, but asked no questions, so far as we know. Still feeling unwell (perhaps it was psychomatic), she consulted Mr Simpson again, and wrote to Rawdon Brown:

I quite think with you that if I had children my health might be quite restored. Simpson and several of the best medical men have said so to me ... but you would require to win over John too, for he hates children and does not wish any children to interfere with his plans of studies. I often think I would be a much happier, better, person if I was more like the rest of my sex in this respect.[19]

In those days there was only one way to avoid having children. Certainly Ruskin's lack of interest in his wife had been noticed, and some men thought there might be a chance for them. A Russian aristocrat whom she had met in Venice called on her; she turned him away. Another idle young man who hung around her was Clare Ford, the brother of some friends. Effie urged him to reform his way of life but made it clear that she did not have affairs.

That spring she sat for two portraits, commissioned by old Mr Ruskin. One, by Thomas Richmond, shows a glamorous young woman in a blue cloak, standing on a terrace. Effie thought it made her look prettier than she really was. The other, by G.F. Watts, is in chalks and has more character.

In March 1851 the first volume of *The Stones of Venice* was published, and Effie and John began making plans to go back. In May, the Great Exhibition opened its doors (Effie went, without her husband), as did the Summer Exhibition at the Royal Academy. There were more attacks on the absurd Pre-Raphaelites. 'We cannot censure at present as amply or as strongly as we desire to do', wrote the *Times*, 'that strange disorder of the mind or the eyes which continues to rage with unabated absurdity among a class of artists who style themselves P.R.B.'[20] Ruskin had walked past their pictures, as people do, without really looking at them, but soon afterwards the poet Coventry Patmore urged him to look again. He and his wife Emily (the original Angel in the House) were family friends, and he knew the young artists, one of whom, J E Millais, had submitted a painting called *The Woodman's Daughter*, suggested by Patmore's poem of that name. He told Ruskin that these young men were very talented and needed a defender.

So Ruskin, perhaps accompanied by Effie, went again to the National Gallery and studied the new Pre-Raphaelite submissions with care. He looked at William Holman Hunt's *Valentine Rescuing Sylvia from Proteus*, and was struck by its 'perfect truth, power and finish'.[21] Then there was *Convent Thoughts* by Charles Collins, brother of Wilkie, which shows a nun contemplating a flower. Ruskin had no Catholic sympathies but was impressed by the careful drawing of water lilies. There too was Millais' *Woodman's Daughter*, which was not completely successful.

But the same artist had two other entries that year. *Mariana* was based on a Tennyson poem, derived from *Measure for Measure*. A youngish woman in a deep blue dress is standing in a luxuriously-furnished room, looking out of her window for a lover who is never going to come. Dead leaves blow on to the floor where a mouse is scratching. Her pose, head thrown back and a loose girdle slipping from her waist, suggests extreme boredom and frustration. This picture was surrounded by crowds of women.

The third painting was *The Return of the Dove to the Ark*. Two girls, the wives of Noah's sons, are cradling a dove which has flown back from the flood area with an olive branch. Their robes are green, white and purple, and they are standing on a layer of straw, so brilliantly pictured that almost every stalk is distinct. The left-hand girl has strong serious features, 'far above affected prettiness',[22] which reminded one snobbish critic of a laundry maid. Ruskin also thought she looked plebeian, but he was struck by 'the tender and beautiful expression of the stooping figure, and the intense harmony of colour in the exquisitely finished draperies'.[23] He wanted his father to buy it, but it was already sold. Today these pictures hang in Tate Britain and the Ashmolean Museum.

He went home and wrote a letter to the Times, signed 'The Author of *Modern Painters*'. He was careful to say that he had not met the Pre-Raphaelites, and indeed could see several small blemishes in their work. But he protested against the attacks:

> I believe these young artists to be at a most critical point of their career – at a turning-point, from which they may either sink into nothingness or rise to very real greatness ... They know very little of ancient paintings who suppose the work of these young artists to resemble them ... They intend to return to early days in this one point only – that, as far as in them lies, they will draw either what they see, or what they suppose might have been the actual facts of the scene they desire to represent, irrespective of any conventional rules of picture-making; and they have chosen their unfortunate though not inaccurate name because all artists did this before Raphael's time, and after Raphael's time did *not* this, but sought to paint fair pictures rather than represent stern facts.[24]

This was published on 13th May. A second letter appeared on the 30th, which wished them well, and hoped that these young men 'may, as they gain experience, lay in our England the foundations of a school of art nobler than the world has seen for three hundred years'.[25]

Of course the Pre-Raphaelites were thrilled. In June, after a decent interval, Ruskin received a letter of thanks, signed J E Millais and W Holman Hunt. The address was that of a modest terraced house in Gower Street, where Millais lived with his parents and brother and painted in a converted greenhouse. Ruskin and Effie promptly drove there to call on him.

He was anxious to meet the new generation of artists and establish himself as their friend and patron. Turner was now over seventy and failing; besides, Turner had not really needed him. He had been a Royal Academician before Ruskin was born and they had never been close. But Ruskin thought he could make a real difference to the reputation of these young men and, moreover, improve their work by educating them in the principles of *Modern Painters*.

Mr and Mrs Millais, who had been distressed by the attacks, were delighted to meet him and introduced their son, a very tall young man with a bush of curly fair hair. He had pleasant easy manners and they both found him charming. Almost at once they 'carried him off to their house at Camberwell and induced him to stay with them for a week'[26] before they went abroad. Ruskin asked him to come as far as Switzerland, to study the Alps and cataracts, but he declined, as he was going to paint out of doors that summer with his friend Holman Hunt. So Effie and Ruskin returned to Venice at the beginning of August, without him.

5

The Marvellous Boy
1829–53

'No, not a gardener', said Celia; 'a gentleman with a sketch-book. He had light-brown curls. I only saw his back. But he was quite young.'
Middlemarch, Chapter 9

John Everett Millais was a child prodigy. No other British artist has ever been admitted to the Royal Academy schools at such a tender age or painted such extraordinary pictures before he was old enough to vote.

When the Ruskins entered his life he was just twenty-two, having been born on 8th June 1829, one year after her and ten years after him. His father, John William Millais, was 'a native of Jersey, a musician, professional or semi-professional ... a rather fine-looking, easy-going, hearty, and very good-natured man. The mother was a much more energetic and active character'.[1] Mary Millais, born Evamy, was eleven years older than her husband and had been married before, to a draper. Johnny, or Jack, as he was known, was their youngest child. He had two half-brothers, Clement and Henry Hodgkinson, a sister, Emily, who married an American, and a brother, William, one year older, who also became an artist but was nothing like so talented or hard-working.

His name was French, and for a while the family lived in Brittany, but he probably never spoke any language but English. Most of his early childhood was spent in St Helier in Jersey, playing on the sand with William much like any other active little boy. But from an early age he was extremely good at sketching, and several adults who saw his pencil drawings could hardly believe they had been done by a child. His mother, who educated him at home, moved the entire family to London in 1838 so that the nine-year-old could get the best possible training. Armed with an introduction, she took him to the elderly President of the Royal Academy, Martin Archer Shee (1769–1850), who was surprised and impressed.

The Academy, founded in 1768 with Joshua Reynolds as its first president, would overarch John Millais' entire working life. In those days it was based in the National Gallery in Trafalgar Square. Every year it selected the most talented boys (not girls) who offered themselves and trained them without charge. Every spring, then as now, hopeful artists submitted their work for the Summer Exhibition, the highlight of the London season. A man who did well might be elected an Associate Royal Academician and eventually get the coveted title of RA. All that lay in the future.

He went first to Henry Sass's school in Bloomsbury (where Gabriel Rossetti was a pupil a few years later), and then was accepted by the Academy at the record-breaking age of eleven years and six months. The other students were teenagers or young men, and some of them were bullies. On one occasion Jack was hung upside down from a window until he lost consciousness, and might have died if some passers-by had not banged on the door. Later he shot up to six feet, although still weighing only nine stone. An early picture shows him with floating curls and in a fancy costume, but when he was older he had his hair cut and dressed conventionally. He won one medal after another and sold small pictures to help the family budget. His father did not have a full-time job, and the boy was the main wage-earner while still in his teens.

At this time he appeared to have everything – a devoted family, an astonishing talent, a charming personality and striking good looks. According to William Rossetti, 'Millais was a very handsome, or more strictly, a beautiful youth: his face came nearer to the type which we term angelic than perhaps any other male visage that I have seen'.[2] But, unlike some charming people, he was kind-hearted and responsible. Anthony Trollope would write, 'To see him has always been a pleasure. His voice has been a sweet sound in my ears ... These words, should he ever see them, will come to him from the grave, and will tell him of my regard – as one living man never tells another'.[3]

William Holman Hunt first met the Academy's star pupil when Millais bounced up to him as he was at work in the British Museum:

'I say, are not you the fellow who was doing that good drawing in Room XIII?'

'Yes, that was me.'

'That's a good drawing. You ought to be at the Academy.'

'That is exactly my opinion. Unfortunately, the Council have twice decided the other way.'

'You just send the drawing you are doing now, and you'll be in like a shot. You take my word for it; I ought to know. I got the first medal last year in the Antique, and it wasn't the first one I have received, I can tell you. Now, remember, your drawing will get you into the Academy.'[4]

Millais was fifteen at the time and an obvious high flyer. Hunt, who was two years older, had had a far tougher life. His family was not well off and wanted him to get a proper job; only his dogged determination kept him drawing. The boys became close friends, sometimes even painting bits of each other's pictures. Hunt never forgot how he was always made welcome in the Millais family and how they forced him to accept some money when he was in difficulties. He was amused by the way the youthful genius handled his parents, deciding that 'the time has come when I cannot have my studio made into a general sitting room',[5] and barring the door. Afterwards they all had tea together, quite amiably.

The young Jack Millais sometimes visited friends in Ewell, where he had first glimpsed the young Effie Gray. He was interested in a girl called Fanny, who upset him by marrying an older man. At other times he stayed in Oxford with his half-brother Henry Hodgkinson and his wife Mary, and there made contact with the art dealer James Wyatt and with Thomas Combe, printer to the University. Combe and his wife were a childless couple, devout Anglo-Catholics, who bought some of his earliest works. The boy saw the wonderful group of medieval paintings which became the core of the Ashmolean Museum's western art collection. Outstanding was Uccello's *The Hunt* (1470), which shows a dark forest with a group of small figures in bright red disappearing into the trees. This may have suggested the background of *The Woodman's Daughter*, which was painted near Oxford; it certainly gave him a respect for Italian artists before Raphael.

There were other influences. As a teenager 'he was sent for by people unknown to him, but who knew him to be a young artist, to draw a portrait of a girl in her coffin before her burial'.[6] He was deeply affected, and later drew a picture of himself standing by the coffin. *The Death of Romeo and Juliet* is another teenage sketch. Death had not yet come really close to Millais but it haunted his imagination, and he was dreaming about girls, rather than actually seeking them out. He was programmed, as a young man, to fall chivalrously in love with an unattainable woman. Isabella, Mariana, Ophelia, the lovers in the *Huguenot* – none will get what they desire.

His first ambitious oil painting, *Pizarro Seizing the Inca of Peru*, was exhibited at the Academy in 1846, when he was not quite seventeen. He seemed unstoppable, but in 1848 (around the time he went on the Chartist demonstration and Effie got married), the hanging committee rejected his *Cymon and Iphigenia*. That was an unpleasant shock and made him receptive to Hunt when he said the Academicians were hopelessly out of touch. The older youth had read Ruskin's *Modern Painters* and been overwhelmed. Millais did not read it.

The Pre-Raphaelite Brotherhood was founded that year by a group of young men who were determined 'ever to do battle against the frivolous art of the day'.[7] Hunt and Millais were joined by 'the mysterious and un-English'[8] Gabriel Rossetti, a poet from a brilliant Anglo-Italian family, who suggested they should confine themselves to the magic number seven and use a password. The other members were Fred Stephens and James Collinson, painters; Thomas Woolner, a sculptor, and Rossetti's brother William, who wrote art criticism in his spare time and was a very fine character, which Gabriel was not. They were all aged between nineteen and twenty-two. Other painters who did not join the secret seven (Ford Madox Brown, Charles Collins, Walter Deverell, Arthur Hughes) were also loosely called Pre-Raphaelites.

The group would last only for a short time and its members had quite different styles. The strongest bonds were between the two Rossettis, as was natural, and between Millais and Hunt. What they had in common was impatience with the old men who ran the Academy, and the fact that they all 'belonged to the middle or lower-middle class of society ... Of any access to "the upper classes" through family ties there was not a trace'.[9]

'The P.R.B.s were all high-thinking young men', wrote William Rossetti, 'assuredly not exempt from several of the infirmities of human nature, but bent upon working up to a true ideal in art, and marked by habits generally abstemious rather than otherwise. To deny themselves the good things of this life when forthcoming was not their nature, but, having next to no money to spend, they stuck to necessities and eschewed superficialities'.[10] They met in each others' homes over cups of tea, sat up late having intense conversations, went for moonlit walks or night¬time boating on the Thames. For a very short time they published a house magazine, unfortunately named *The Germ*. Their heroes included Christ, Shakespeare, Keats and Tennyson. Many of their pictures were inspired by dead poets and told a story.

Millais, whose work had been conventional up to then, abruptly changed his style. His first Pre-Raphaelite painting was *Isabella*, based on the Boccaccio story and the Keats poem. It shows two lovers sitting at a crowded table, absorbed in each other. The girl's brother, who is determined to part them, viciously kicks a dog. The picture's impact depends on its subtext; we know that Isabella's lover will be murdered and that she will die of grief. Already the very young artist was brilliant at painting faces. The man who bullied him is the brother of Isabella, who was posed by his sister-in-law Mary Hodgkinson; William Rossetti is Lorenzo; Gabriel is in the background draining a glass.

This picture, which made an immediate impact, was signed J E Millais 1849 PRB. Soon the meaning of the initials leaked out and the PRBs found themselves being laughed at. An impression got around that they were all Roman Catholics, although only one, Collinson, actually converted. Millais' close friend Charles Collins was devout, and Hunt also aspired to be a Christian painter and was nicknamed Holy Hunt in his old age. Millais himself was not particularly religious, although he had been exposed to High Church images in Oxford and they got into some of his paintings. *The Carpenter's Shop*, exhibited in 1850, was inspired by a sermon of Pusey's in the University church.

This picture shows the child Jesus with a bleeding hand, surrounded by concerned members of his family while sheep gaze through the workshop door. He is not seriously hurt, but the wounding foreshadows his crucifixion. Millais painted it in a real carpenter's shop and the tools, planks and wood shavings are entirely convincing; he had also asked a working man to pose for the figure of Joseph so he could copy his arm muscles. The head is his father's; the mother of Jesus, who kneels beside him with an agonised look, was again posed by Mary Hodgkinson.

No one is likely to be shocked by this picture today. It is a sad, serious work, painted with 'sacred earnestness' and 'high aspiration',[11] but at the time it seemed blasphemous. Instead of idealised figures with haloes, the Holy Family were depicted as hard-pressed working people; there is dirt on the floor; the child carrying the water bowl appears to have rickets. Several critics abused it, including Dickens:

In the foreground of that carpenter's shop is a hideous, wry-necked, blubbering, red-haired boy in a nightgown, who appears to have received a poke playing in an adjacent gutter, and to be holding it up for the contemplation of a kneeling woman so horrible in her ugliness that (supposing it were possible for any human creature to exist for a moment with that dislocated throat) she would stand out from the rest of the company as a monster in the vilest cabaret in France or in the lowest gin-shop in England.[12]

The attacks on Millais and his friends, but particularly him, were renewed after the next Academy exhibition. Some critics disliked the Catholic symbols in *Mariana*, and feared that *The Return of the Dove* really meant that Protestants would in due course return to Rome. It was at this point, the summer of 1851, that Ruskin wrote his two letters to the *Times* and artist and writer eventually met. While Ruskin and Effie headed again for Venice, Millais and Hunt went to Ewell near Kingston-on-Thames. One was planning *The Hireling Shepherd*; the other was about to paint *Ophelia*.

They stayed in the country, sometimes visited by other artists, from July till November. Millais chose a spot by the river Hogsmill and did the entire background – water weeds, a willow tree, dog-roses, meadowsweet – planning to add the figure of the drowning girl when he returned to London. Afterwards he had time to start a second picture, which he thought would be less important. He had discovered an interesting red-brick wall, covered with moss and ivy, and painted it through several weeks that autumn. In front of this wall he intended to place two ordinary lovers, but Hunt argued that that would be uninteresting. Instead, he suggested two lovers being tugged apart by historical forces. A scene from the Wars of the Roses, perhaps? A Roundhead girl and a Cavalier? Millais thought it over and remembered a scene from Meyerbeer's opera *Les Huguenots*. The place is France, the time the St Bartholomew's Day massacre of 1572. A brave young man, a member of the Protestant minority, is being urged to put on the white ribbon which will protect him from murder. His fiancée is a Catholic but is only interested in saving his life. Their faces and intertwined hands show their deep love for each other, the young woman's terror and the man's determination to die rather than renounce his beliefs. There are blood-red petals near the ground.

That same autumn, Hunt had the idea for *The Light of the World*, and started work on it by the cold light of a full moon. Millais discussed it with him and agreed not to paint the same subject. At twenty-two and twenty-four they had already conceived their most celebrated, perhaps their best works. Hunt hoped they would co-operate many more times, but as he noted sadly in his old age, 'never did we live again together in such daily spirit-stirring emulation'.[13]

Millais did not paint Ophelia herself until he got back to his studio, where she was posed by Rossetti's girlfriend Elizabeth Siddal, who made herself ill by lying for hours in a bath, in an expensive dirty silver dress. He also painted the matchless figures in the second picture: *A Huguenot, on St Bartholomew's Day, refusing to shield himself from danger by wearing the Roman Catholic badge.* They were exhibited together at the Royal Academy in 1852, and caused a sensation. Ruskin's father, who wrote to him regularly, told him all about the reviews.

The young Ruskins' second stay in Venice was longer than the first, and they were out of England for almost a year. They got on perfectly well; they always did when his parents were not around. Effie went to several parties, including a magnificent water pageant to welcome the Emperor of Austria. Ruskin still believed the occupation was necessary, but found himself annoyed by the sight of guns in St Mark's Square and soldiers all over the historic city. He was also beginning, for the first time in his sheltered life, to brood about the dreadful contrasts between the rich and the poor.

'Mrs Ruskin is a very pretty woman and is a good deal neglected by her husband, not for other women but for what he calls literature',[14] wrote an acquaintance. She read or played the piano to him when he wanted but most of the time had to make her own entertainment. She fitted happily into Venetian high society, 'not being stiff or shy like most English'.[15] In the week before Christmas, Turner died. He did not leave Ruskin any pictures, as might have been hoped, but made him an executor of his will, which bequeathed virtually everything to the nation. Ruskin corresponded anxiously with his father, who had opened Turner's neglected house in Queen Anne Street to find masses of drawings and sketches, but decided not to return yet, as he had not quite finished taking notes.

He told him that once he and Effie were back, they would stay in England for the foreseeable future. He wanted to be near his parents in their declining years (his mother was now seventy) and suggested that they might all four live under the same roof, if the old people could put up with his wife. Otherwise, he would live about half a mile away, but this must be in some quiet place where he would not be disturbed. They decided on a villa in Herne Hill, the other half of Ruskin's childhood home:

I do not speak of Effie in this arrangement – as it is a necessary one – and therefore I can give her no choice. She will be unhappy

– that is her fault – not mine – the only real regret I have, however is on her account – as I have pride in seeing her shining as she does in society – and pain in seeing her deprived, in her youth and beauty, of that which 10 years hence she cannot have – the Alps will not wrinkle – so *my* pleasure is always in store – but her cheeks will: and the loss of life from 24 to 27 in a cottage at Norwood is not a pleasant thing for a woman of her temper – But this cannot be helped.[16]

Effie's comparative happiness in Venice was clouded by the thought of going back. She said in a letter home that it might have been better if she had never got married, 'for then the Ruskins would not have had me to grumble at and I would always have been with my mother and you and amongst the places I shall always love best. But then poor John would not have been so happy as he is with me and it is always something that he thinks me perfect'.[17] She was mistaken; Ruskin did not think so. Whatever pleasant things he may have said, at around the same time he was cold-bloodedly discussing her character:

Therefore I am always either kind or indifferent to Effie – I never scold – simply take *my own way* and let her have hers – love her, as it is easy to do – and never vex myself – If she did anything definitely wrong – gambled – or spent money – or lost her character – it would be another affair – but as she is very good and prudent in her general conduct – the only way is to let her do as she likes – so long as she does not interfere with *me*: and that, she has long ago learned – won't do.[18]

Meanwhile Mr Ruskin sent more letters to the Grays, who must have dreaded the sight of his handwriting, complaining that she was pleasure-loving and extravagant. This was unjust; it was John who was spending vast amounts on engravings and books. Effie always managed to look good by updating her dresses, but she gave up her 'modelling master' to save money and did not overspend her allowance. Nor was she materialistic; when some not very valuable jewellery was stolen near the end of their visit she wrote, 'I assure you I would have thrown my Jewels ten times over into the sea than that any person should suffer for me'.[19] (Her husband took the view that 'every person who wears cut jewels merely for the sake of their value is … a slave-driver'[20]). The complaints went on.

By February 1852 she was resigned to the idea of settling near the old people, but not happy. 'They arrange and manage everything ... and when I ventured to say that I ought at least to have been consulted, John said he *never intended as long as they lived to consult me* on any subject of importance as he owed it to them to follow their commands implicitly. Neither they or he think that he has any duty to me in these things at all'.[21]

Reluctantly, she turned her back on Venice in June. There was an absurd episode in Verona, when Ruskin was challenged to a duel by an Austrian officer and sensibly declined. By mid-July they were back in smoky London, and settling into the little house which had been chosen for them at 30 Herne Hill, next door to Ruskin's old home. Effie wrote home tactfully that she liked the garden. John was infuriated by the vulgar furniture.

The real problem was that they were now living south of the river, three or four miles from central London. After all the hectic socialising of the last two years, it was impossible for her to call on friends or go to parties unless she could get hold of a horse-drawn vehicle. In 1852 there were no tube trains, motor buses, cars or bicycles. If a lady walked any distance she would be hampered by her skirts, possibly accosted, and could be in danger after dark. Mrs Ruskin, who believed that Effie should settle down and be a good housewife, allowed her to borrow her carriage, but only once a week. She loved babies, and must have been bitterly disappointed that no grandchild had appeared after four years. Probably she blamed Effie.

Mr Ruskin was more sympathetic. 'They never appeared to me to have more than a decent affection for each other', he wrote, 'John being divided betwixt his wife and his pictures and Phemy betwixt her Husband and her Dress – So that to hope to make them happy and comfortable in a Life which suits Mrs Ruskin and me, seems quite chemerical'.[22] This was slightly unfair to Effie, but the old man was right about the shallowness of their feelings. The 'decent affection' which they still felt for each other would last less than twelve months.

The pattern of their life together was soon fixed. Every morning after breakfast, Ruskin walked over to his parents' house to work in his old study; Effie usually did not see him again till the evening. She looked after the garden, was polite to her in-laws, and kept up a cheerful front, though she was not happy. In September she went to Perth and brought back her little sisters, Sophie and Alice, for a long visit. She also decided that, to avoid gossip, she would not go to public places by herself.

The bright lights of Venice were a long way away. She still very much wanted a baby and, after fitting in for five years with Ruskin's way of life, sensed that something was not right with her marriage. A letter of February 1853, when she had been at home half a year, shows that relations with her in-laws had not improved:

> The Ruskins are bothering me now because I won't visit at all without John or go to Balls alone. How is one to please them? I have never asked John to go to a single place nor told them of many of the kind invitations I have had, yet they know from John I get them. What should I do? If I do go – I must be fatigued, spend money in carriage hires and go alone. If I don't they say that it is my own fault if I have not society and that I may go wherever I like or do what I choose provided I don't *degrade* John by taking him into society ... I think of sending all my invitations to D H to be decided upon, for which ever way I do is sure to be wrong ... They will be kind to me but then I must be their Slave in return. I must praise them as three perfect people and be treated as a fool or a child, whichever suits me best, but then I must never complain or else get a torrent of insults in return.[23]

'D H' is 163 Denmark Hill, a house she had grown to hate.

The children returned to Scotland at the beginning of March. Very soon afterwards, Millais made an unusual request. Ruskin's mind had been full of Turner and Venice since he got home, and Millais had been working hard, giving himself headaches, on two big pictures. However, they must have met occasionally. Now the young man asked Ruskin if he might be allowed to paint his wife.

6

Portrait of John Ruskin
March–December 1853

'It was as I thought: he cared much less for her portrait than his own'.
'He's a cursed white-blooded pedantic coxcomb', said Will.

Middlemarch, Chapter 22

In March 1853, Effie began to pose for the heroic Highland woman in John Everett Millais' *The Order of Release*. This was mildly unconventional. It was one thing to sit for a 'Portrait of Mrs John Ruskin' commissioned by her family, quite another to sit for a 'story painting' which anyone could buy. Everybody knew, after all, that artists' female models were not respectable.

Ruskin was happy to give his permission. He thought Millais was potentially a great painter, Turner's heir, and he hardly cared what Effie did, provided he was left alone. For most of each day he was at Denmark Hill writing *The Stones of Venice*. The young artist moved his painting materials into their attic, occasionally staying overnight.

The Royal Academy Summer Exhibition was a few weeks away. Millais explained that he was submitting two pictures, whose backgrounds were already finished. In each of them a woman was the central figure and he wanted to paint Effie's head – he was not sure for which. One was *The Proscribed Royalist, 1651*, where a Puritan girl visits her lover who is hiding in an oak tree. The other, and much greater, was *The Order of Release, 1746*.

Fortunately Millais decided the Scottish painting needed a Scottish model. Effie certainly told him something about the history and traditions of her homeland, which he had never seen. He worked intensely, painting her from immediately after breakfast until lunch and then through the afternoon until dark. Effie wrote to her mother afterwards that she had a stiff neck and had not had a moment to herself, 'but I was anxious

57

to be as much help to him as possible as the whole importance of this picture is in the success of this head ... He found my head like every one who has tried it immensely difficult and he was greatly delighted last night when he said he had quite got it. The features are at once so curious and the Expression so difficult to catch that he wanted – half a smile.'[1]

Millais worked very 'slowly and finely', to quote Effie again, sometimes doing no more than a square inch a day, and did not show her the picture until it was finished. Nothing went on behind those closed doors which her husband and the rest of the world could not have seen. She was twenty-four; he was twenty-three. They liked each other very much but had no plans to let it go any further. He was an idealistic young man, probably not much more experienced than she was, and in his eyes she was not only a married woman but the wife of a friend. And in any case, he was thinking mainly about his picture.

In late March Effie visited the studio in Gower Street for a final sitting. His parents would have been there; all remained perfectly proper and she was at last allowed to see his two Academy entries. 'I really do not know which I like best', she wrote again to her mother, 'they are both so wonderful, the first as a grand study of nature, trees, moss, foxglove, fircones, birdsnest and old wood contrasting with the splendid Orange Satin and black dress of the Woman – the second as a painting of expression and of human sympathy and incident'.[2] She would have told Millais, too, that she was deeply impressed.

The Order of Release, one of the greatest Victorian paintings, shows a Highlander who has been wounded at Culloden being let out of prison. His head is buried on his wife's shoulder; she grasps his hand and supports their sleeping child on her left arm while with the other she passes the 'freedom paper' to the jailer. It is obvious that she has walked for miles, bare-footed, and probably knocked on several doors to get her husband released. A strong woman, therefore, well used to doing many jobs at once. She does not even look at the jailer; every ounce of energy goes into supporting the man and child while she stares past their exhausted figures into space. There is no joy or relief in her expression; perhaps she is determined not to show emotion in front of the enemy. Her face is the only one we see clearly (the others are half-hidden) and it was that face which struck everyone who saw it a few weeks later when it was unveiled.

'My head you would know anywhere' (Effie added). 'In fact it is exactly like, but as Millais truly says, and I felt, he has not refined the face in this picture as he wished me to look the character. It looks a little stronger than I do but it looks very well indeed and is precisely what he wanted ... any body who has ever seen me once would remember it was somebody they know. The man who has fallen on my shoulder with his head buried is very grand. His arm is wounded and over it hangs the undress Highland jacket of Gray – a Kilt of Gordon Tartan and purple stockings with shoes. I have a purple woolen gown tucked up showing my bare feet and a sort of upper petticot of blue thrown over my head and enveloping the child, a little golden haired thing in Drummond Tartan, who has fallen asleep from fatigue after walking so far, primroses and bluebells it had picked by the way tumbling out of its hand. A splendid Highland Dog, black and Tan, is jumping up on his master. I am holding out the note of release to the Jailor who is in the Doorway. So you see the picture is quite Jacobite and after my own heart.' The only differences between this woman and Effie were that her fair hair had been painted black, to contrast with the child's hair, and that her grim, drained expression was not the one people usually saw. *Blackwood's* reviewer hinted that it was a caricature of the beautiful Mrs Ruskin. 'Her face is plain to a degree ... instead of tenderness she is the hardest looking creature you can imagine ... A friend of ours said aloud, "I would rather remain in prison all my life, or even be hanged, than go out of prison to live with that woman".'[3]

Millais had, of course, got precisely the look he wanted, and perhaps he had seen it move across Effie's face during the long hours she posed. She was not thinking about getting emotionally involved with this brilliant young man; she was thinking about making a last attempt to save her marriage.

On 2nd May 1853 the Summer Exhibition opened; on 7th May Effie turned twenty-five. That was the date on which Ruskin had said, years before, that they would finally make love. He probably hoped she had forgotten. Several things were happening around this time; her brother George came to stay and they moved temporarily into a flat in Mayfair to be near the Academy; Ruskin had finished working and wanted to go out and about. Some time on or around her birthday Effie forced him to have a discussion, or more likely several discussions. These were naturally held in private but it is clear that, during the month of May, unforgivable things were said.

The Order of Release was a tremendous success. The crowds were so thick that it was hardly possible to get near it; Effie was showered with compliments. But she was aware that there was a great difference between her and the woman in the picture; that little family was not in a happy situation but at least its members were bound together by affection. The Highlander (he was modelled by a man called Westall, whom she probably never met) was devoted to his wife and dependent on her; her own husband had made it clear that he did not need her, and it seemed she would never be allowed to have a child. As Ruskin still showed no enthusiasm, she forced herself to ask him on what terms they were to live.

At first Ruskin came back to the old arguments. He disliked children; their way of life would be disrupted if she had a baby; many saints had lived together in chaste marriages. Effie was not convinced. In the end he blurted out the true reason – 'that he had imagined women were quite different to what he saw I was, and that the reason he did not make me his Wife was because he was disgusted with my person the first evening'.[4] He added that she was not fit to bring up children because she was insane. The arguments may have dragged on for weeks but it is clear that, some time during the early summer of 1853, the marriage died. Before that time, the references to Ruskin in her letters are quite affectionate; afterwards they are as brief as possible. Probably she had been hoping that, after five years and one month, there would be some sort of miracle and he would begin to love her. She would never entirely get over his cruel words.

Another woman, having been told by her husband that she was personally repulsive and mad, might have wanted to crawl under her bed and never come out again. Effie's reaction was to go out and meet her friends. On 8th May she told her mother that she had enjoyed her birthday and that Mrs Harriet Beecher Stowe, the author of *Uncle Tom's Cabin*, was in London. At any other time she would have tried to get an introduction, but just now she was too distressed and preoccupied. During the next few days she felt exhausted and had violent headaches. She went alone to a party on the 20th and bumped into Millais. The two very attractive young people were seen talking quietly to one another, looking like a couple.

By June, the London season was breaking up. Ruskin had once before invited Millais to join him for a summer holiday; now he suggested that they and Hunt should go to Scotland, to some wild and lonely place where he could teach them how to paint like Turner. And his wife? Well, she would have to come too, and indeed might be able to make herself useful. It is likely that they were furious with each other but told no one about their deep division. Ruskin looked forward to discussing art and nature with the two Pre-Raphaelites; Effie was glad to be getting away from her in-laws and nearer to Perth. She grew quite excited by the prospect of looking after a group of artists and wrote, 'for the next two months I fancy John and the two Millais and Holman Hunt will be very busy sketching and walking over the Mountains and I shall occupy myself in trying to make them all as comfortable as I can, for we shall not have a very extensive establishment and there seems no certainty of any thing to eat but Trout out of the Tummel or the Garry, but it would amuse you to hear the Pre-Raphaelites and John talk. They seem to think that they will have everything just for the asking and laugh at me for preparing a great hamper of sherry and tea and sugar which I expect they will be extremely glad to partake of in case of returning home any day wet through with Scotch mist.'[5]

In the end, Holman Hunt did not come. He was 'going to Syria to paint sacred subjects',[6] and expected to leave England very soon. So the party which left London on 21st June consisted of the Ruskins, their manservant Frederick Crawley, and Millais. Effie hoped they would not return until Christmas, because her husband had been asked to lecture in Edinburgh in November, and of course she planned to visit her family at some stage.

They stayed for the first week in Northumberland, with the naturalist Sir Walter Trevelyan and his wife Pauline. With hindsight, their hosts described the situation to William Bell Scott:

Already apparently before they reached Northumberland, the handsome hero had won the heart of the unhappy Mrs Ruskin, whose attentions from her husband had it seems consisted in his keeping a notebook of the defects in her carriage or speech. More than that the lovers had evidently come to an understanding with each other, founded apparently on loathing of the owner of the notebook. Mrs Ruskin used to escape after breakfast, and joined by Millais was not heard of until the late hour of dinner. Lady Trevelyan hinted remonstrance, took alarm in fact, but not caring to speak confidentially to the lady who acted so strangely in her house, got Sir Walter to rouse the apparently oblivious husband. Her quick eye had of course discerned something of a telegraphic nature between the lovers, and she was mystified by Ruskin's inexplicable sillyness as she inadvertently called it to me. Sir Walter was also mystified, having pretty good eyes of his own, but was less given to forming conclusions or speaking of what was passing, he agreed however to take Ruskin into his confidence. But that innocent creature poo-poohed him. Really he didn't *believe* there was any harm in their *pleasing* themselves. He did not see what harm they could do: they were only children! He had often *tried* to keep her in order. Years after when I could venture to talk over the affair with Sir Walter, I asked him how he explained this mode of taking the warning. He confessed to having thought over the matter, and was inclined to conclude that John Ruskin wanted to get rid of his wife; had it been any other man he would have so concluded, but then the individual in question did not know much about love-making.[7]

The notebook certainly did exist, but as yet there was no understanding. This is proved by a letter Millais wrote from Northumberland, 'Today I have been drawing Mrs Ruskin who is the sweetest creature that ever lived; she is the most pleasant companion one could wish. Ruskin is benign and kind.'[8] Effie was probably sick of hearing her husband hold forth to an admiring audience and longed to be out of doors. Her spirits rose as they got further away from London. 'I was so happy', she wrote, 'running into the woods and down the Trout streams without a Bonnet or walking the Poney over the bleak Border Moors to a Mountain Tarn they have where hundreds of young sea-gulls were just beginning to fly'.[9] Millais, dazzled, went after her.

They were joined by William Millais, who was also a painter, in watercolours, and had a fine tenor voice. He was an affable young man, not at all jealous of his brilliant younger brother. The party moved on to Edinburgh and then through Callander. On 2nd July they reached the tiny village of Brig o' Turk (Bridge of the Wild Boar), and moved into the New Trossachs Inn. Later they decided it was too expensive and worked out other sleeping arrangements.

The inn was on the edge of Loch Achray, with magnificent views of the mountains Ben Venue and Ben Ledi (2400 and 2900 feet high), and within easy walking distance of two more lochs, Venachar to the east and Katrine to the west. A stream, Finglas Water, rushed down from the hills in a succession of deep pools and cascades. Today Glen Finglas reservoir lies above it, and the lower part of the stream is more shallow than in Effie's day.

Millais, on his first sight of Scotland, was overwhelmed by the brilliant purples of the mountains, clouds and heather. He wrote again to Hunt saying 'you would go mad if you saw some of this scenery it is so fine'. They had decided to stay for a while 'as I am going to paint Ruskin's portrait by one of these rocky streams ... The Ruskins *are most perfect people*', he went on, 'always anxious and ready to sacrifice their interest in our behalf. She is the most delightful unselfish kind-hearted creature I ever knew, it is impossible to help liking her – he is gentle and forbearing.'[10] For some reason, though, he was feeling thoroughly depressed.

Ruskin's father had commissioned Millais to paint his son and he wanted a background of rocks and flowing water in the style of Turner, who had passed through the village twenty years before. 'Millais has fixed on his place', Ruskin wrote home on 6th July, '– a lovely piece of worn rock, with foaming water, and weeds, and moss, and a noble overhanging bank of dark crag – and I am to be standing looking quietly down the stream – just the sort of thing I used to do for hours together – he is very happy at the idea of doing it and I think you will be proud of the picture – and we shall have the two most wonderful torrents in the world, Turner's St Gothard – and Millais' Glenfinlas. He is going to take the utmost possible pains with it – and says he can paint rocks and water better than anything else – I am sure the foam of the torrent will be something quite new in art'.[11]

But the picture could not be begun at once, for two reasons; it rained most of the time and a canvas had to be ordered from Edinburgh. This was twenty-eight inches high and twenty-four wide, distinctly smaller than *The Order of Release*. To pass the time they played battledore and shuttlecock, and Millais did a small portrait of Effie in a green top, with a wreath of foxgloves in her hair. She is sewing, and her wedding ring is not visible. Another tiny picture shows her, sewing again, on the rocks beside the stream.

A week after they had arrived, most of the party left the inn. William stayed where he was while Ruskin, Effie and Millais moved into the schoolmaster's house. Effie wrote cheerfully to her mother, 'John Millais and I have each two little dens where we have room to sleep and turn in but no place whatever to put anything in, there being no drawers, but I have established a file of nails from which my clothes hang and John sleeps on the Sofa in the Parlour'. She had made herself a rough linsey wolsey dress and was 'quite independent of weather and [would] sit out all day on the rocks'.[12] There was plenty of porridge, cream and eggs, the Millais brothers caught trout, and all three gentlemen splashed about in the stream, building dams like children.

Effie was enjoying herself in the friendly company of two handsome and unattached young men and perhaps did not think too hard about where it was heading. Millais, however, was restless. The two little cupboards where they slept were on either side of the parlour where Ruskin made his bed, and it struck him as very strange that the man did not want to be alone with his wife. He taught her to draw and found that she made remarkable progress. They gave each other jokey names; he called her the Countess rather than Effie (which was too intimate) or Mrs Ruskin. He injured his thumb; she tied it up and trimmed his hair. His letters frequently say what a delightful person she is; however – 'Her husband is a good fellow but not of our kind, his soul is always with the clouds and out of reach of ordinary mortals – I mean that he theorises about the vastness of space and looks at a lovely little stream in practical contempt'.[13]

All this was going on in the first six weeks before his brother went home. When William was an old man and two of the other three were dead he wrote for the record (using Effie's birth initials, ECG):

> I may say that I think that Ruskin did not act wisely in putting JEM and ECG continually together – Every afternoon by way of exercise Ruskin and I spent our time with pickaxe and barrow and spade to try to cut a canal across a bend in the river – whilst he preferred that ECG should roam the hills with JEM & presently they did not return until quite late – Ruskin's remark to me was, 'how well your brother and my wife gets on together'! – a very dangerous experiment & had it not been *for their integrity* evil consequences must have ensued.[14]

At the end of July Millais finally started *John Ruskin*. He would do many other portraits of famous men but none with such an impressive background. In the finished work, a correctly dressed Victorian gentleman stands on a rock, holding his hat and stick, while the torrents gush around him. We get the impression of enormous intellectual power and pent-up emotion. The likeness is perfect.

The actual place, a mile above the bridge, was identified in the 1990s, and is almost unchanged.[15] To get there you scramble down a steep bank to reach a sunless spot at the bottom of a ravine – 'all dark rocks with plants hanging down over them and the foaming water below'.[16] Millais began with the background. He worked very slowly, as his habit was, and the midges gave him a terrible time. The weather had improved, and after he had painted for several hours, usually in the afternoon, they all wanted to go walking. The early autumn colours were extraordinary, and it did not get dark until very late.

By this time Millais was amazed by Ruskin's attitude to the lovely young woman he had married. There is a story that one day, when Effie could not cross a stream in her long skirt (the men having jumped over easily) her husband coldly told her that she knew the way home. He had also started noting down various remarks of hers for future reference. When William left in mid-August, Effie accompanied him as far as Perth with a female neighbour, then spent a few days with her family. Ruskin suggested that Millais should go too and that they should travel back together (which would have caused comment). Millais refused. He now suspected that Ruskin actually wanted them to have an affair.

Effie returned and they resumed their long walks in the hills, sometimes staying out until after dark. Neither of them had meant it to happen, but at some point they admitted they were helplessly in love. The only things we know for certain are that Effie told him she was still a virgin, and that they did not sleep together. No doubt there were passionate kisses and some bitter tears.

Meanwhile the three of them kept up the charade of being an ordinary married couple on holiday with the husband's young friend. Ruskin sat indoors, finishing the index to *The Stones of Venice* and preparing his lectures on Architecture, Decoration, Turner and Pre-Raphaelitism. Millais returned to the inn (the nights, with Effie only a few feet away, were beginning to torture him), and then moved back to the cottage again. In the mornings they all talked through the curtains as they got dressed. The portrait made very slow progress and Ruskin's father grew impatient, but Ruskin himself was delighted with the scenery which framed his figure, the ash bough, the creepers, the tiny plants, the silver lichen on the dark rocks.

Is it possible that he did not know what was going on? Plenty of people, then and now, were sure that he wanted Effie to compromise herself so that he could get a legal separation, perhaps even a divorce. But he was an unusual man. More likely he was simply absorbed in his work, relieved that Effie was no longer making emotional demands on him and not very interested in how the two young people felt.

They were desperately unhappy. So far as they could see, they had three choices: renunciation, a sly affair or an open elopement – and the second and third seemed impossible. They were both Christians, in a mild way, and accepted the sexual morality of their time. If they had

had an affair Ruskin might not have noticed immediately, but if Effie had become pregnant (as she surely would have), he would have known the child could not be his. He would then probably have repudiated her and perhaps used old Mr Ruskin's money to obtain a divorce. He certainly could have divorced her for adultery, if she had committed it, when the law was changed four years later. The Divorce Act of 1857 would permit men to free themselves from a faithless wife, but not the other way round. It did not allow people to end a marriage merely because they were miserable.

Running away together seemed an even wilder notion. Had they done so, Effie would have become a social outcast; no respectable woman could have been seen with her. Any children would have been illegitimate. Her family in Perth would be appalled and ashamed. George Eliot, who was contemplating the same step at about the same time, took it only after long thought and knowing she would lose some of her friends. Her parents were dead and she was happy to work in solitude; she was not a natural extrovert as Effie was. Besides, Millais was just starting his career and Effie feared that any scandal would harm it. This may not have been true (Turner, who never married, had had more than one mistress and two natural children) but it preyed on her mind, and Millais was well aware that an affair or elopement would have far worse consequences for her than for him.

This was what tormented him as the Trossachs summer reddened into autumn. He knew there was no hope, he knew that for her own sake he had to leave her, but he could not bear to do so yet, and he was committed to finishing Ruskin's portrait. It was obvious that this would not happen for some time. He wrote to Hunt that he was utterly miserable but could not tell him why in a letter. 'Here I am at 24 years of age sick of everything, after having won the artistic battle and certain to realise a respectable competence as long as I can use my eyes, and yet I don't believe there is a more wretched being alive than the much envied J E Millais'.[17]

Early in October a painter friend, Mike Halliday, visited Brig o' Turk and saw that something serious was going on. Around the same time Effie told her husband 'that if she ever were to suffer the pains of eternal torment, they could not be worse to her than going home to live at Herne Hill with me'.[18] On the 16th Ruskin wrote to his mother:

I wish that the country agreed with Millais as well as it does with me, but I don't know how to manage him and he does not know how to manage himself. He paints till his limbs are numb, and his back has as many aches as joints in it. He won't take exercise in the regular way, but sometimes starts and takes races of seven or eight miles if he is in the humour: sometimes won't, or can't, eat any breakfast or dinner, sometimes eats enormously without seeming to enjoy anything. Sometimes he is all excitement, sometimes depressed, sick and faint as a woman, always restless and unhappy. I think I never saw such a miserable person on the whole. He is really very ill tonight, has gone early to bed and complains of a feeling of complete faintness and lethargy, with headache. I don't know what to do with him. The faintness seems so excessive, sometimes appearing almost hysterical.[19]

Millais' misery was deepened by the news that another young painter, his friend Walter Deverell, who was responsible for a family of little brothers and sisters, was dying of Bright's disease. He was a good-looking, talented young man, who is shown in profile in *Isabella*. 'Let me know by return of post his circumstances', he wrote to Hunt, 'whether they require *money, or anything*, as I *would gladly* give all I have in *such a good* cause'.[20] He continued to paint in the bitter cold; only three-quarters of the portrait was done. Ruskin wrote to Hunt too, saying 'here is Everett lying crying upon his bed like a child – or rather with that bitterness which is only in a man's grief – and I don't know what will become of him when you are gone'.[21] He seems to have thought the young man was wretched only because his friend was going to the Middle East, and advised him that it would not be good for his own genius to go there yet.

Neither of the two Pre-Raphaelites took much notice of him. Millais pulled himself together, and assured everyone that he was quite well. But when Ruskin and Effie packed up and left, on 26th October, he sent his unfinished canvas home and followed them in pouring rain to Edinburgh. There for the first time he met Effie's parents, who had come to hear their son-in-law lecture. In a very short time he struck up a warm friendship with her mother, Mrs Sophia Gray.

Ruskin gave his first two lectures on 1st and 4th November at the Philosophical Institution in Queen Street, each attended by more than a thousand people. The following week Millais said an agonised goodbye to Effie; they had agreed they would not meet again. Back in London, he was elected an Associate of the Royal Academy, one of the youngest men ever to be so honoured.

Meanwhile Ruskin was meditating on 'the utter *unchangeableness* of people ... When we married', he wrote to his father of Effie, 'I expected to change *her* – she expected to change *me*. Neither have succeeded, and both are displeased. When I came down to Scotland with Millais, I expected to do great things for him ... I might as well have tried to make a Highland stream read Euclid, or be methodical. He, on the other hand, thought he could make me like Pre-Raphaelitism and Mendelssohn better than Turner or Bellini. But he has given it up, now'.[22]

By this time any mild liking he had felt for his wife at the beginning of 1853 had changed into active resentment. Effie had a comfortable home; he and his parents had shown her every kindness; he did not interfere with her lifestyle any more than was necessary. How could he concentrate on his work if she continued to make scenes? On 11th November he wrote that 'it might be better that I should declare at once I wanted to be a Protestant monk: separate from my wife'.[23] Both sets of parents now knew that the marriage was in deep trouble.

In London, Millais dined with the old Ruskins at Denmark Hill and discussed the portrait. It was embarrassing, but he did not know how to get out of it. Mr Ruskin wrote to his son that he was an extremely good-looking young man but very thin. In Edinburgh, Effie nursed her mother, who had become unwell. On 21st November she went to Bowerswell with her family, leaving Ruskin to enjoy the single life that suited him best.

Over the next few weeks it was agreed that Effie's little sister, Sophie, should return with the unhappy couple to London; Effie could teach her and have a companion while Ruskin was out of the house. There were also plans for him and his parents to tour Switzerland in the summer of 1854. They did not want Effie and decided that she should be dropped off in Germany to stay with friends.

Effie and Millais were still writing to each other, letters which do not survive. Just before Christmas and once she felt better (for all we know it was anxiety about her daughter that had made her ill), Mrs Gray wrote to Millais and begged that this should stop. She liked the young man, she wished her family had never got mixed up with the Ruskins, but Effie was going back to London, where he was, and she was afraid of a horrible scandal. Millais wrote back:

Believe me *I will do everything you can desire of me*, so keep your mind perfectly at rest – I should never have written to your daughter had not Ruskin been cognisant to the correspondence, and approving of it, or at least not admitting a care in the matter – If he is such a plotting and scheming fellow, as to take notes secretly to bring against his wife, such a quiet scoundrel ought to be ducked in a mill pond. His conduct is so provokingly gentle that it is folly to kick against such a man. From this time, I will never write again to his wife, as it will *be better,* and will exclude the possibility of his further complaining, although sufficient has past to enable him to do so, at any time he may think fit. One is never safe against such a brooding selfish lot as those Ruskins. His absence in the Highlands seemed purposely to give me an opportunity of being in his wife's society – His wickedness must be without parallel if he kept himself away to the end that has come about, as I am sometimes inclined to think. Altogether his conduct is incomprehensible – he is either crazed, or anything but a desirable acquaintance.

The *worst of all is the wretchedness* of her position. Whenever they go to visit she will be left to herself in the company of any stranger present, for Ruskin appears to delight in selfish solitude. Why he ever had the audacity of marrying with no better intentions is a mystery to me. I must confess that it appears to me that he cares for nothing beyond his Mother and Father, which makes the insolence of his finding fault with his wife (to whom he has acted from the beginning most disgustingly) more apparent. I shall never dine at Denmark Hill again, and will not call at Herne Hill to see either, but will leave a card which will suffice. I shall be out of England next year so that there can be no more interference from me. If I have meddled more than my place would justify it was from the flagrant nature of the affair – I am only anxious to do the best for your daughter. I consider Ruskin's treatment of her so sickening that for quietness' sake she should as much as possible prevent his travelling, or staying a summer in company with a friend, *who cannot but observe* his hopeless apathy in *everything regarding her happiness.* I cannot conceal the truth from you, that she has more to put up with than any living woman. Again I must promise you that I will never more give occasion for the Ruskins to further aggravate her on my account. *Everything on my part will be as you wish* – I have scarcely time to sign to save post

Ever yours sincerely

J E Millais

69

I will write tomorrow more intelligibly
I think the Ruskins must not perceive too great a desire on your part to keep quiet, and submit to anything, as they will imagine it to be fear. She has all the right on her side and believe me the Father would see that also if he knew all.[24]

Neither Effie's nor Ruskin's parents 'knew all' yet. The next day, December 20th, Millais wrote again to Mrs Gray:

I am afraid my answer to your kind and judicious letter was dreadfully incoherent, but now I will endeavour to reply more satisfactorily.

Although you know John Ruskin's odd propensity for roaming away by himself from all human creatures and their habitations, yet you cannot be aware of the abstracted way in which he neglects his wife. It is utterly impossible for a friend to sojourn with them for any length of time without absolutely being compelled in common courtesy to attend to her. I assure you that Ruskin only expressed approval and delight at perceiving that your daughter and myself agreed so well together, and when *I spoke to him about his extraordinary indifference to her attractions* (which could not be but excessively unpleasing, and conducive to her unhappiness) he only apathetically laughed and said he thought all women ought to depend upon themselves for engrossing employment, and such like cold inhuman absurdities. There was something so revolting to me about this sickly treatment of her just cause of complaint and discontent, that I never again ventured to speak on the subject, as I could not depend upon keeping my temper. When she and my brother visited Bowerswell, he was all for my accompanying them, and returning with her; which I refused to do, although I knew he would have been quite as happy without my society. In fact he appeared *purposely to connive at the result* – seemingly callous, and methodically writing all that he himself brought about, to his parents, like a boy of ten years of age. He is an undeniable giant as an author, but a poor weak creature in everything else, bland, and heartless, and unworthy – with his great talents – of *any* woman possessing affection, and sensibility.

Do not imagine that I am induced through circumstances to speak thus depreciatingly of him, or that this is a hasty conclusion of his character. An open enemy is preferable to a cool friend, and

Ruskin is one of the latter order and therefore odious in my sight – I think his Inquisitorial practice of noting down everything which could forward an excuse for complaining against his own wife, is the *most unmanly, and debased proceeding I ever heard of,* but even that is nothing in comparison with his aggravating unsociability which she has to put up with. You were kind enough to be plain spoken with me in your letter, and I will be the same with you – it is of no use conventionally disguising my opinion from you, however biased it may be, and however painful I cannot resist unreservedly avowing it: you will avert many disagreeable casualties, and greatly increase your daughter's comfort by *permitting always one, or other, of her sisters to be with her.* It is a sufficient inducement (not to speak of her appearance) that these cunning London men detect neglect, and unconcern, on Ruskin's part, and her unhappiness, to make them impudent and importunate. With a companion this evil can be greatly frustrated, as she would not be left by herself to receive strangers, and gallant rakes, who can always find an excuse for calling, and who look upon Ruskin as a kind of milksop. I have met many of these fellows even before I knew Ruskin, and have heard them circulating over dinner tables the most unwarrantable insinuations, and now I find myself continually questioned regarding my experience of their married life.

I believe you will have every reason to be satisfied with me, as your desire is not more earnest than mine to hasten the interests of the Countess. My intention is simply to call and leave a card at Herne Hill and the same at Denmark Hill after which I will carefully avoid (if they should invite me) dining there, by managing to get engaged elsewhere. When the summer comes I shall, I trust, be away on the Continent, after completing Glenfinlas, which I would leave as it is, had not Ruskin spoken about it since, to the effect, that he should consider it an insult to his Father, besides himself, if I did not finish it. Of course I cannot obviate or foresee the chances of meeting the Countess in society, but as she rarely goes out, and myself as seldom, I don't think such a meeting likely. I have written a letter, (the last I will write) telling her I will *not call and see her,* as proposed, to escape the suspicion of the Father, and Mother, who will naturally enquire whether I have been there or not, and will think it strange after our intimacy. *Should she, and yourself,* consider it more prudent for me to call as though nothing had happened I will do so. I regret very much, (in spite of the wonderful advance my pupil has made in her drawing) that I had not taught her more, as I am convinced she will find it one of her greatest, and most absorbing recreations. I will take care to send her sketches and engravings to copy, which she can return by Crawley – by this means a kind of friendship will be continued which will satisfy the curiosity of most people who will imagine I go there as before. Sometimes I uselessly wish that I never had accompanied Ruskin to the Highlands. It may be beneficial in the end to their position, in regard to each other, as it has disturbed the settled dullness of their existence, *and any change was preferable* to the life they have been living (I should rather say the life that *she has been enduring)*, for I believe he is complacent, and happy enough. I have seen nothing but the most placid and patient submission on her part to his will, and yet there is a *stealthy*, bad, dissatisfaction in his nature which is very trying, and disgusting. I sincerely hope that all this is not so new to you, but that you will (from previous knowledge) be prepared to hear what is so distressing for me to recount, and that this unfortunate business may blow over, like all the other calamities and grievances that have gone before us. If I have not answered as you desired pray let me know, as I am only anxious to accede to your wishes...

With many thanks for your kindness, and best remembrances to Mr Gray and your family believe me

John Everett Millais[25]

Around this time Effie travelled south with the ten-year-old Sophie, and was with Ruskin in Durham on Christmas Day. Millais spent it wretchedly, walking about London between church services. By the end of the old year all three were back in the same city. Effie had neuralgia in her face and a twitching eye, which would torment her for the next few months. 'She passes her days in sullen melancholy', Ruskin wrote in a note to Mrs Gray, 'and nothing can help her but an entire change of heart'.[26]

So far as she could see, there was absolutely no hope of a happy outcome. Ruskin would continue to live exactly as he liked and Millais would go abroad and probably be snapped up by some other woman in the next few years. She was twenty-five and believed she had nothing to look forward to. She would never have a child and would be tied to the Ruskin family, who detested her, for as long as they all four lived.

The only obvious alternative was to go back home and be gossiped about in Perth for the rest of her days.

It might have come to that. However, Effie had a secret weapon, of which she was not yet aware.

7

The Eve of St Agnes
January–April 1854

He was going away into the distance of unknown years, and if ever he came back he would be another man ... Their young delight in speaking to each other, and saying what no one else would care to hear, was for ever ended, and become a treasure of the past. For this very reason she dwelt on it without inward check.

Middlemarch, Chapter 55

In the early months of 1854 Millais and Effie were back in London, separated by only a few miles and the Thames but expecting never to meet again, believing it would be wrong if they tried to do so. Both were utterly depressed.

Effie, who had not seen her in-laws for half a year, found herself back in the same routine, with her husband regularly leaving after breakfast to spend his waking hours at Denmark Hill. They still slept in the same bed, though, and she tried to make a new start with the new year. She told him that as 'one of his objections to my conduct was not helping him in his work ... I was quite ready to do anything he might desire'. But Ruskin was too angry for any sort of reconciliation. 'John proceeded to say that his marriage with me was the greatest crime he had ever committed in acting in opposition to his parents ... John's pity and polite behaviour ... is simply put on, he says, because he considers it his duty to be kind to anybody so unhappily diseased'.[1]

She got on in the best way she could. Like many other women, she found solace in work, teaching Sophie each morning and preparing Rawdon Brown's book on Venetian history for an English publisher. She drove into London whenever she was allowed a cab, to see her friends and work at the British Museum. But the twitching of her eye still tormented her, as did the sight of destitute people in the streets. She knew what she had lost; she knew that she could have had a much happier marriage. 'Hope seemed impossible, interest in Life gone'.[2]

Millais was also wretched. His best friend, Holman Hunt, left England on 13th January: 'I had not had time to dine, and Millais rushed to the buffet and seized any likely food he could, tossing it after me into the moving carriage'.[3] He spent a great deal of time with the dying Walter Deverell; the family was very hard up and Millais and Hunt had bought one of his pictures, anonymously. Old Mr Ruskin also visited Deverell at his son's request and described him as a 'gentlemanly young man in the poorest Dwelling's worst Room – a handful of fire on a Black cold day, painting to pass time without purpose or energy'.[4] In the new year he grew weaker and Millais often sat by his bed and read to him, walking home after midnight through the snow. On 2nd February Deverell died, aged twenty-six. For the first time in years Millais had nothing fit to send to the Summer Exhibition. He knew it would be wise to get away and join Hunt, but he was obliged to stay where he was until he had finished two pictures.

He had promised Mr and Mrs Gray to do a watercolour of Sophie. The little girl was driven several times to Gower Street and on one occasion he threw himself on the sofa and begged William to let her in – he could not risk coming face to face with Effie. Sophie was most anxious to co-operate, 'never relaxing until her poor little head wavered about',[5] and he became very fond of her. There was also the great portrait of Ruskin.

Neither the background nor the central figure had yet been finished. Ruskin visited him regularly through the winter as if nothing had happened. 'Surely such a quiet scoundrel as this man never existed', Millais wrote in a fury, 'he comes here sitting as blandly as ever, talking the whole time in apparently a most interested way'.[6] Ruskin now knew perfectly well that his wife and Millais were in love, but was not annoyed with him. Instead, he blamed Effie for distracting the brilliant young artist from his work. 'He is very bland and affable towards me, at times absolutely tender',[7] Millais told Mrs Gray in bewilderment. He found completing the portrait his most hateful task ever; only professionalism and good manners made him push on.

Meanwhile the old Ruskins, who were paying for the picture and waiting impatiently for it to be finished, hardly bothered to conceal their abhorrence of Effie. They were polite when they came face to face, but she was well aware of how they felt. They did their best to turn Sophie against her family – 'Mrs R kissing her and saying she wished she could have the charge of her – for her mother was a weak ignorant woman, and I, a poor, silly creature simply raised into respectability by my husband's talents – that I thought myself very clever and that people made much of me but it was all John's great abilities and that I was merely a Scotch girl with bad manners'.[8] All of which Sophie immediately passed on to her sister.

This comes to us at third hand, of course. Sophie may have exaggerated, Effie may have exaggerated, but we know that Mrs Ruskin grew more cantankerous as she grew older and did not usually hesitate to say what she thought. John Ruskin took the ten-year-old girl for walks and did all he could to get her on his side. 'He says', reported Sophie, 'he is going to begin his harsh treatment whenever you come back from Germany, that there is not time for it to have effect before you go away, but that when you return, as you won't go to Perth and remain there, he is to try what harshness will do to break your spirit. He is hardly ever going to speak to you and is going to spend nearly all his time at D.H. He says, you are so wicked that he was warned by all his friends not to have anything to do with you, but that you were so bold and impudent and made such advances to him that you just threw your snares over him in the same way that you had done over Millais, and that you were all the cause of Millais' present unhappiness'.[9] He added that he would write a book about Effie's behaviour and would bring her sister Alice, then aged eight, for a long visit 'to see how they agree'. Knowing of Ruskin's interest in very young girls, this sounds plausible.

Effie was shocked by the Ruskins' attempts to influence the child (and determined they should not get hold of Alice). 'I cannot think such goings on at all fit for so young a girl. It will teach her, I fear, both to exaggerate a little and to act a part'.[10] It would be unfair to blame the Ruskins for the problems Sophie developed in later life, but they certainly forced her to live for weeks in an unhealthy atmosphere.

Both husband and wife wanted to break away but could not see how. They gave dinner parties and attempted to behave normally, but everyone who was in the house for any length of time knew that they loathed each other. The manservant Crawley knew it; so did a friend, Jane Boswell, who stayed with them for a while and came to the conclusion that Ruskin was mad. Effie was convinced that his parents wanted 'to get rid of me, to have John altogether with them again. At any price they are resolved to do this, but they seem to wish if possible to disgust me to such a degree as to force me – or else get me – into some scrape'.[11] There was an argument over a drawing, *St Agnes' Eve*, inspired by the Keats poem about separated lovers, which Millais had given them. A nun in winter is standing at her window, speechless, celibate, trapped in the snow. Effie thought she could trace a resemblance to Millais himself in the nun's features and looked at it constantly. 'I think I see Millais reading the poem to me and talking about it with me. I wish he was gone – I cannot bear to think of what he must endure painting John'. To her mother, who was almost as distressed as she was, she wrote:

> I would rather do anything than that his name should be dragged before the public, and I agree with you that towards winter, after he has gone and no intercourse between us, that if they do not behave better I must then do something without any disadvantage to either of us. For however much he wishes from his regard for me to help me it would be an irreparable misery to himself ... his character stands so deservedly high that as the founder of a new school, and in a great position in this Country, it would be a lasting sorrow to have that reputation tarnished in the slightest degree. It is a very very important thing for him to keep clear of us altogether and you may tell him not to think it selfish but imperatively necessary and his first duty to go as soon as possible.[12]

Ruskin's behaviour over this picture – he taunted her about why she was not writing to Millais – confirmed the belief she already held that he was trying to push them into one another's arms. It still seems unlikely that he really wanted this, though his father may have. He felt strongly that Millais was the great coming painter and wanted to remain friends – 'as long as he does fine things John will never let him alone but will attach him to himself'.[13] If she refused to have an affair with him, perhaps she might have one with Clare Ford, who resurfaced at this time, or perhaps the confirmed bachelor Rawdon Brown could be persuaded to stay in the house and be left alone with her while he, Ruskin, spent his days at Denmark Hill? Effie firmly declined to do anything which might get her into a 'scrape'. They were all waiting for the Ruskins' Alpine tour, which would start in May, and hoping they would see their way more clearly after several months apart.

Millais was hearing some of these things from Sophie and was also corresponding with their mother. It was agonising to feel that he could do nothing for the woman he helplessly loved. '*It is my opinion that some steps should be speedily taken* to protect her from this incessant harassing behaviour of the Rs. If they are bent upon obtaining a separation you will be obliged (in pity for her sake) to consent, for human nature can never stand such treatment', he wrote. 'I am not sufficiently acquainted with Law to know whether something more than a separation could be obtained, but I think you should enquire into the matter'.[14]

And then, some time in late February or early March, everything changed.

Effie had grown close to Lady Eastlake since their return to London. The older woman felt something like a mother to her (her only child had been stillborn) and could see that the young woman was in a dreadful state of nerves. She loathed Ruskin, who had attacked her husband for his management of the National Gallery, and, as the daughter and sister of gynaecologists, she knew that some marriages were not consummated. Now she told Effie what she had never suspected, that a church court, if informed, might find her marriage null and void. She had spoken to an elderly retired judge, Lord Glenelg, who also thought that it was possible.

Effie took a few days to think over this extraordinary news. It looked as if a small crack, through which she just might squeeze, had finally appeared in the wall of her prison, but if she took advantage of it she would have to tell her parents, and Ruskin's, submit to a physical examination by strangers and invite gossip from all those who knew her and many who did not. She was a modest and reserved person whose instinct was always to put a good face on things. If she exposed her private life in public as no woman, to her knowledge, had done before, might she not only cause more sorrow to her family and achieve nothing in the end? Yet she knew she could not go on living like this for ever, and could lose Millais if she allowed the marriage to drag on for years. In the end she wrote not to her mother, as might have been expected, but to her father, the Writer to the Signet, who would know if there really was a legal way out:

> You are aware that since 1848 to this last year I have never made any formal complaint to you. There were many reasons for my silence, the principal being of course my great love for you and my dear Mother – fearing to trouble you when you were in great difficulties yourselves, when I tried to look on my unfortunate position as one where, whatever I internally suffered, at least removed me from being a burthen on you – and I resolved that no annoyance which I suffered should give you any. I pass over all other discussions

and reasons at present till I see you as I could fill Volumes. To come to the present moment, when even now I was unwilling to tell you all, fearing your anger against John Ruskin who has so illtreated and abused me, and his Parents who have so seconded him, although so far they are innocent, not knowing the gravity of the offence with which I charge him and from which proceeds all the rest. But they have been most guilty in the education they have given him and ought not to have treated me as they have done. I wish neither to be uncharitable nor to take advantage of any of them but I am so ruined and nervous in both mind and body that as they are so anxious to get rid of me, and I have not the satisfaction of feeling that any one is the least the better for my forbearance and suffering, I have duly considered the step I am about to take in telling you all. Feeling very ill last week and in the greatest perplexity about my duty to you – I went and consulted Lady Eastlake and also partly Lord Glenelg, the two persons in London for whom I have most respect. I did not open my mind to the latter as I did to the former but as I could perfectly rely on their prudence and wisdom I took the advice of Lady E to permit her to make the necessary enquiries of How English Law would treat such a case as mine. You may perhaps at first wonder that I should apply to anyone in preference to yourself – but I was still unwilling to ask you to act for me until I saw I could not avoid giving you trouble and that of a most serious nature. I enclose Lady E's most kind and noble letter, it will best show you what she is, as well as perhaps help you, although cases of this description may have come under your own knowledge in the course of your Life. I have therefor simply to tell you that I do not think I am John Ruskin's Wife at all – and I entreat you to assist me to get released from the unnatural position in which I stand to Him. To go back to the day of my marriage the 10th of April 1848. I went as you know away to the Highlands. I had never been told the duties of married persons to each other and knew little or nothing about their relations in the closest union on earth. For days John talked about this relation to me but avowed no intention of making me his Wife. He alleged various reasons, Hatred to children, religious motives, a desire to preserve my beauty, and finally this last year told me his true reason (and this to me is as villainous as all the rest), that he had imagined women were quite different to what he saw I was, and that the reason he did not make me his Wife was because he was disgusted with my person the first evening 10th April. After I began to see things better I argued with him and took the Bible but he soon silenced me and I was not sufficiently awake to what position I was in. Then he said after 6 years he would marry me, when I was 25. This last year we spoke about it. I did say what I thought in May. He then said, as I professed quite a dislike to him, that it would be *sinful* to enter into such a connexion, as if I was not very *wicked* I was at least insane and the responsibility that I might have children was too great, as I was quite unfit to bring them up. These are some of the facts. You may imagine what I have gone through – and besides all this the temptations his neglect threw me in the way of. If he had only been kind, I might have lived and died in my maiden state, but in addition to this brutality his leaving me on every occasion – his threats for the future of a wish to break my spirit – and only last night when he wished to put his arm round me (for I believe he was cold) I bade him leave me, he said he had a good mind to beat me and that he had never admired Romanism so much, as if he had a Confessor for me he would soon bring me to my senses. I don't think, poor creature, he knows anything about human creatures – but he is so gifted otherwise and so cold at the same time that he never thinks of people's feelings and yet with his eloquence will always command admiration. I cannot bear his presence and something you will feel is imperative. Once this year I did threaten him with Law, but I really did not know myself about it, as it was in Edinburgh and he said, 'Well, and if I was to take all the blame?' I think he might not oppose my protest – In point of fact, could He?

I should not think of entering your House excepting as free as I was before I left it. All this you must consider over and find out what you can do. Thank God for all his goodness to me which has enabled me to Live up to this time in his fear and in I trust a virtuous Life – the glory is all his and under him I have been kept from sin by the remembrance of the example you and my dear Mother have ever shown me. If I have not written you clearly enough you must put it down to illness and agitation, for you will hardly wonder this keeping up of appearances makes me often sick.

Your affectionate daughter,
Effie Gray[15]

When this letter (which explained so much, including the absence of grandchildren) reached Bowerswell, Effie's parents could not at first agree what to do. Mr Gray, who had not come across such a case before, advised caution; his idea was to speak privately to Ruskin's father before anything was decided. Mrs Gray, seeing the prospect of a second happier marriage for her daughter, wanted to get things moving. In the same week she passed the news to Millais, who replied:

> I confess in spite of the distress it must occasion that I am glad that you know all. You will better understand now how all the Highland affair came about, and how little right Ruskin has to complain of her conduct. I think the most generous way of looking upon his behaviour is to believe him partially out of his mind. It is needless for me to say how deeply I sympathise with you in this miserable affair and how I pity her in her present position which I trust will be changed.[16]

It was agreed that Mr Gray would travel to London and consult the experts. Meanwhile, Ruskin's behaviour deteriorated; he told Effie that 'my insolence was unpardonable and that the only thing for me was a good beating with a *common* stick'.[17] A letter of 30th March says, 'These two or three mornings I have come down quite exhausted for John has found out a new method ...' A new method of tormenting her, presumably, but the rest of the page has been torn off. This letter continues, 'he will perhaps do some unheard of thing since he seems to think himself quite perfect and really to believe ... me quite mad'.[18]

She urged her father to see a jurist who understood the marriage laws before having any kind of showdown. 'These are matters quite beyond the common run of Life and must be treated by people accustomed to extreme cases'.[19] On 10th April, her wedding anniversary, she wrote begging her mother to come too:

> You really must come here. I think when Jane goes and things begin to be arranged it would be most improper for me to be here alone as I am quite afraid of John and you do not know what he might not do. Brown thinks him quite mad, although he says he may have a method in his madness and suggests that the Grandfather's suicide has still its effects in John's conduct. I am very ill and so nervous that I cannot meet these coming events without your advice and presence as well as Papa's ... This day six years ago we anticipated

very different results. God will defend the right. I am quite decided that to live on any terms with this man is to continue in sin.[20]

It was fortunate that Effie's parents, still vigorous middle-aged people, were able and eager to help. They arrived by steamboat on 14th April, not informing the Ruskins that they were in London, although they did meet Lady Eastlake and Rawdon Brown, who was visiting England and knew what was going on. Mr Gray had discovered that it was indeed possible to annul a marriage on the grounds of non-consummation and that it had happened before. Once they were sure of this, they decided that Effie should come home, letting her husband think that it was only for a few months' holiday while he was abroad. There were good reasons for keeping their real plans a secret; Ruskin had the legal right to force his wife to live with him. Or he might offer to consummate the marriage, which by now was the last thing she wanted. Even marital rape may have been in their minds.

Millais knew what was going on and wrote to Mrs Gray:

I can perfectly understand the dreadful state of mind of the poor Countess, but you *must impress* upon her the weakness of overmuch distress in the matter. She can have *nothing to blame herself for,* and *with that knowledge should go bravely through it.*

It is only the wretchedness of Society that makes us attach so much importance to disclosures of the kind, making thousands endure a slow inward martyrdom for years rather than suffer a temporary exposure of facts. She must also remember that under the circumstances there was no chance of her condition improving with time – I believe he would grow every day more selfish and intolerant, but she knows best what she would have had to contend with, and cannot but feel that an entire change is both now her duty, and the only way of insuring a chance of some enjoyable quiet in her life.[21]

Effie spent much of the next week putting her affairs in order and packing her luggage, including the drawing *St Agnes Eve.* Since Ruskin was never at home in the day he did not suspect what she was doing, and in any case was totally preoccupied elsewhere. As his marriage fell apart, he noted in his diary, 'My head has been so taken up with my glorious new Psalter and I have been so much at Denmark Hill that I could not write here'.[22] The Grays used the time to consult an eminent gynaecologist,

Robert Lee: 'He was perfectly thunderstruck with the case and had read John's Books and thought him a Jesuit – but now he thinks him mad – and shudders at what she must have gone through and said to her to take her course by the Law – that it was the most proper for her to do and the only one a father and mother could approve of'.[23]

On Tuesday, 25th April 1854, Effie got up early and prepared Sophie and herself for the long journey to Scotland. At the last moment she slipped off her wedding ring; the morning was bitterly cold and she would have worn gloves. Ruskin escorted them to King's Cross, where he walked up and down, not saying a word to her, until their train pulled out at half past nine. Frederick Crawley, who was very sympathetic and probably knew that she was not coming back, travelled with them. As soon as they were off, she told the little girl what was happening. Forty minutes down the line, at Hitchin, their parents were waiting. Sophie jumped out; Mrs Gray took her place and Effie passed her father a small parcel. The train moved on.

Mr Gray, with Sophie, returned to London, where he made certain arrangements. They would catch the steamer home next day.

At six o' clock that evening, two messengers knocked on the door of 163 Denmark Hill. The Ruskins all felt much more comfortable now that they were back together and were probably discussing their forthcoming tour of Switzerland. The two men were called out and John was handed a citation, informing him that his wife was seeking to have their marriage annulled. Mr Ruskin got a parcel containing Effie's account book, keys, wedding ring, and a letter for her mother-in-law:

Dear Mrs Ruskin,

You have doubtless been wondering why I did not, as was usual with me, pay you a visit at Denmark Hill to bid you goodbye before going to Scotland, but I felt that owing to the circumstances which induce my addressing you this letter that rendered it not only impossible for me to see you now or indeed ever again – but also required that I should state to you the reasons of my sending you my Keys, House Book wherein will be found a statement of this year's account – together with an explanation of the money received and spent by me, and also you will find enclosed my marriage ring which I return by this means to your son, with whom I can never hold farther intercourse or communication.

You are aware that I was married by the Scottish form in my father's house on the 10th of April 1848.

From that day to this, your son has never made me his wife, or wished to do so, as he at first overcame my judgment, which was ignorant on such points, by a variety of arguments which even showing him the words of Scripture did not refute or cause him to change his opinions in the least about. Whilst we were at Salisbury, when you caused me to be put in another room on account of an illness which he told me his Father supposed to arise from his recent connexion with me, he used to laugh and say his Father was imagining things very different to what they were. His conduct and manner went from bad to worse until I felt I could no longer submit to his threats of personal cruelty and desires to get rid of me in any manner consistent with *his own* safety and comparative freedom. I always resisted the idea of a *separation* and would take no steps in such a matter, and threatened him with the course I have now pursued if he did not treat me in a becoming manner. He said, 'Well what if I do take all the blame you would make a great piece of work for your Father and go home and lose your position'.

I have gone through this winter and thought at last that I must either die or consult my parents to take proper steps to ascertain what relief could be got, since your son almost daily heaps one insult upon another, more especially accusing me of *Insanity*. My Father and Mother came instantly they knew what I suffered to Town and are only sorry I have lived in such an unnatural position so long. I believe you have been all along in total ignorance of this behaviour of your son's. The Law will let you know what I have demanded, and I put it to you and Mr Ruskin to consider what a very great temporal loss, in every point of view, your Son's conduct has entailed upon me for these best six years of my life. Your son first said he would marry me when *I* was 25 – then on arriving at that age last year – I enquired on what terms we were to live, he said I was quite *mad*, quite unfit to bring up children, and beside did not love or respect him sufficiently. I said *that* was quite *impossible* after his perpetual *neglect* – but that I never would refuse to gratify his wishes. He then put it off again and said he should try and break my spirit to enduce me to leave him and return to Perth as I bored him. I think *he* will be glad I have taken this step. I hear that our affairs are perfectly known in London society; and nothing more will be said, since the fact of our marriage not having been consummated was known to *many* and your son's personal neglect of me *notoriously condemned* – this has likewise been the case in Perth. My parents have entirely approved of the steps I have taken and my Mother accompanies me to Scotland. All accounts besides the House Books will be found filed in the store-room and any things at Herne Hill amongst the glass, furniture &c that your son considers my property you will, I feel assured, be good enough [to] send after me.

I remain yours truly

Euphemia C. Gray[24]

Nothing was said about Mrs Ruskin's own behaviour. Perhaps the letter had to be read aloud to her, as her sight by now was very poor.

They were taken completely by surprise. Mr Ruskin, a passionate man himself, would have been amazed to find that his son had no sexual interest in his young wife; John may have been embarrassed but presumably said what he would put in writing two days later. They talked about it far into the night, but of one thing they were quite sure; it was all Effie's fault. Indeed, after the first shock, there was a certain relief. As her train moved slowly north, they agreed they would consult a lawyer and try to minimise the scandal, but would not oppose Effie's wish to end the marriage. They also decided to behave just as usual and to go on holiday, as planned.

Effie and her mother changed trains at Edinburgh and arrived after midnight at Perth, where George was waiting with a cab. It was two in the morning before they reached home. She was very glad to see Bowerswell again, to fall into her own bed and to know that the Ruskins were four hundred miles away.

PART THREE

EFFIE GRAY FALSELY
CALLED RUSKIN

8

The Order of Release
April 1854–July 1855

It was a question whether gratitude which refers to what is done for one's
self ought not to give way to indignation at what is done against another.
And Casaubon had done a wrong to Dorothea in marrying her.

Middlemarch, Chapter 37

When Effie left Herne Hill for the last time, it was a Tuesday. On
Wednesday Mr Ruskin called on his solicitor, and on Thursday John
Ruskin sat down and wrote a statement giving his side of the story:

General Facts

I was married – in her father's house – to Euphemia Chalmers
Gray, on the 10th April 1848. She entered her 21st year on the
7th May in that year. Immediately after our marriage, we agreed
that we would not consummate it, at all events for some little time;
in order that my wife's state of health might not interfere with a
proposed journey on the Continent.

Soon afterwards we agreed that the marriage should not be
consummated until my wife was five and twenty.

Before that period had arrived, I had become aware of points in
her character which caused me to regard with excessive pain the
idea of having children by her, and therefore, neither before nor
after that period, either pressed or forced consummation, but I
offered it again and again, and whenever I offered it, it was refused
by her.

Her feelings of affection towards me appeared gradually to become
extinguished; and were at last replaced by a hatred so great that
she told me, about the end of September or beginning of October,

1853, we being then in Scotland, that if she ever were to suffer the pains of eternal torment, they could not be worse to her than going home to live at Herne Hill with me.

I took her home, nevertheless. We arrived in London on the day after Christmas Day 1853. From that time to this she has remained in resolute anger – venting itself in unexplained insults; and rejecting every attempt of mine to caress her as if I had been a wild beast.

She informed me some days ago – about the 14th or 15th of April, that she intended to go down to Scotland on Tuesday the 25th, to which proposal I assented; understanding that she was to stay with her parents for three months, while I went to Switzerland with my father and mother. I saw her depart by the railway at half past 9 on Tuesday morning, and was surprised to receive the citation to court the same afternoon.

Details relating to the above statement

1st Reasons for our agreement not to consummate marriage

I offered marriage by letter, to Miss Gray, in the autumn of 1847, and was accepted. Letters passed between us almost daily from that time until I went to Scotland in March 1848, to marry her. I met her at her uncle, Mr Sheriff Jameson's at Edinburgh; there some fortnight before our proposed marriage Miss Gray informed me that her father 'had lost immense sums by railroads', and Mr Gray, coming over himself, told me he was entirely ruined, and must leave his house immediately. His distress appeared very great; and the fortnight or ten days preceding our marriage were passed in great suffering both by Miss Gray and myself – in consequence of revelations of ruin – concealed till that time, at least from *me*.

The whole family rested on me for support and encouragement – Mr Gray declaring I was their 'sheet anchor' – But no effort whatever was made to involve me in their embarrassments – nor did I give the slightest hope of my being able to assist Mr Gray, who I believed, must assuredly have become bankrupt. But I expressed no surprise or indignation at the concealment of his affairs from me, although it had entirely destroyed the immediate happiness of my marriage.

Miss Gray appeared in a most weak and nervous state in

consequence of this distress – and I was at first afraid of subjecting her system to any new trials – My own passion was also much subdued by anxiety; and I had no difficulty in refraining from consummation on the first night. On speaking to her on the subject the second night we agreed that it would be better to defer consummation for a little time. For my own part I married in order to have a companion – not for passions sake; and I was particularly anxious that my wife should be well and strong in order that she might be able to climb Swiss hills with me that year. I had seen much grief arise from the double excitement of possession and marriage travelling and was delighted to find that my wife seemed quite relieved at the suggestion. We tried thus living separate for some little time, and then agreed that we would continue to do so till my wife should be five and twenty, as we wished to travel a great deal – and thought that in five years we should be settled for good. The letters written to Miss Gray before our marriage are all in my possession and will show that I had no intention of this kind previously. My wife asked me to give her these letters some days ago – I fortunately refused, thinking she would mislay them, as she did not now care about them, but she doubtless intended to destroy them.

2 Reasons for the aversion felt by my wife towards me.

This aversion had nothing to do with our mode of living together. It arose first from my steady resistance to the endeavours of my wife to withdraw me from the influence of my parents, and to get me into close alliance with her own family. She tried to get me to persuade my Father to put her brother into his countinghouse: and was much offended at my refusal to do so: she then lost no opportunity of speaking against both of my parents; and, every day, was more bitterly mortified at her failure in influencing me. On one occasion, she having been rude to my mother, I rebuked her firmly, and she never forgave either my mother or me.

I married her, thinking her so young and affectionate that I might influence her as I chose, and make of her just such a wife as I wanted. It appeared that *she* married *me* thinking she could make of me just the *husband she* wanted. I was grieved and disappointed at finding I could not change her; and she was humiliated and irritated at finding she could not change me.

I have no doubt she felt at first considerable regard for me, but never a devoted or unselfish one. She had been indulged in all her wishes from her youth; and now felt all restraint an insult. She sometimes expressed doubts of its being *right* to live as we were living; but always continuing to express her wish to live so. I gravely charged her to tell me, if she thought she would be happier in consummating marriage: or healthier, I being willing at any time to consummate it: but I answered to her doubts of its being right, that many of the best characters in church history had preserved virginity in marriage, and that it could not be wrong to do for a time what they had done through life.

It may be thought strange that I *could* abstain from a woman who to most people was so attractive. But though her face was beautiful, her person was not formed to excite passion. On the contrary, there were certain circumstances in her person which completely checked it. I did not think either, that there could be anything in my own person particularly attractive to *her:* but believed that she loved me, as I loved her, with little mingling of desire.

Had she treated me as a kind and devoted wife would have done, I should soon have longed to possess her, body and heart. But every day that we lived together, there was less sympathy between us, and I soon began to observe characteristics which gave me so much grief and anxiety that I wrote to her father saying they could be accounted for in no other way than by supposing that there was slight nervous affection of the brain. It is of no use to trace the progress of alienation. Perhaps the principal cause of it – next to her resolute effort to detach me from my parents, was her always thinking that I ought to attend *her,* instead of *herself* attending me. When I had drawing or writing to do – instead of sitting with me as I drew or wrote, she went about on her own quests: and then complained that 'I left her alone'.

For the last half year, she seems to have had no other end in life than the expression of her anger against me or my parents: and having destroyed her own happiness, she has sought wildly for some method of recovering it, without humbling her pride. This it seems, she thinks she can effect by a separation from me, grounded on an accusation of impotence. Probably she now supposes this accusation a just one – and thinks I deceived her in offering consummation. This can of course be ascertained by medical examination, but after what has now passed, I cannot take her to be my wife or to bear me children. This is the point of difficulty with me. I can prove my virility at once, but I do not wish to receive back into my house this woman who has made such a charge against me.[1]

He signed and dated this paper and passed it on to his father's solicitors. It was not used, and would remain in an office drawer, unread, for the next seventy years.

On Friday, the Royal Academy hosted a private view of the 1854 Summer Exhibition. Lady Eastlake had been telling the story 'whenever and wherever I think the *truth* can do good' as soon as Effie was out of London and, as people crowded in, the delicious scandal circulated 'busily through the rooms'. Millais came in (he wanted to see how Hunt's new pictures were received) and she accosted him: 'We found ourselves suddenly in the *subject*, – my cheek white, his *crimson* ... He had known nothing of the *truth* and asked me with painful blushes if I had'.[2]

Millais had of course known the truth for some time and had confided only in his closest friends, but suddenly all the chattering classes seemed aware that he was involved in the collapse of the marriage. Someone must have talked, and anyway it was well known that his picture of Mrs Ruskin had hung in the last exhibition and that he had spent the summer with her and her husband in Scotland. It was soon being said that they had eloped, and that he was not showing anything this year because the Academy was shocked by his behaviour.

On Saturday Ruskin and his father turned up at the Old Water Colour Exhibition. The painter David Roberts, who was separated from his own wife, 'could not pretend to be ignorant of what all the world was speaking of ... and asked them if it were true'. Ruskin was noncommittal, but the old man was angry. His son had been 'entrapped' by the Grays, he said – 'and as the place was not the best in the world for discussing such a matter he took his precious son by the arm, and said "Come along John – we shall have to *pay* for it – but never mind we have you to ourselves now".'[3] Ruskin was then a man of thirty-five.

As in all break-ups, especially celebrity break-ups, people took sides. It was soon clear that most of them were against Ruskin; the excitable Lady Eastlake said he had been 'struck ... out of the respect of all good people'.[4] He met 'with general condemnation', although there were some who made 'allowances for his peculiar mind, believing him to be partly mad'.[5] Ruskin himself said that only three of his friends remained loyal. In a conversation between the Bishop of Edinburgh, J G Lockhart and some other gentlemen, 'all agreed as to their long detestation of the writings ... and then Mr Hay said, "It is all very well to agree about the writings – but what do you intend to do with the *man* – surely when women are banished from society for their faults, you will never admit such a villain as that", and then Sir Charles and all said that *they* should never receive him, and Mr L growled out his indignation'.[6] Lockhart perhaps was thinking that his own daughter, Charlotte, had had a narrow escape.

Many more things must have been said which were unfit to print, whenever two or three men were gathered together. We get the flavour from a letter of Ford Madox Brown's – 'the vilain [*sic*] has lived with her seven years long and never yet shown any performance, the stones of venice [*sic*] being the only ones as yet of which poor Mrs R has had the advantage'.[7] He did not bother to hide his contempt.

But why was Ruskin supposed to be wicked, rather than unfortunate? Many people believed, as did Effie herself, that he had tried to push his wife into the arms of other men. Or perhaps they thought he was a homosexual who had cynically married an unsuspecting young woman as a 'beard'. And why did Effie say that their situation was well known in London and Perth? There had certainly been talk since the first year about the long separations, the absence of children, the hints that he was unwilling to have them. Or perhaps the average sensual man in the club or pub simply knew by instinct that Ruskin was different.

Lady Eastlake's motives were not completely pure, but she did honestly care about Effie's future. It was so unusual for a wife to run away that she could have ended up as a social outcast, if people had not been convinced that he was exceptionally depraved. She did get quite a lot of sympathy; Ruskin had made many enemies by his habit of saying just what he thought, whereas Effie and Millais were very well liked. But not everybody felt she had done the right thing. The kindly Dr Acland, a deeply religious man, had noticed Ruskin's 'dreadful indifference to his wife'[8] but feared that the Bible did not sanction divorce. Thomas Carlyle went round saying '*that no woman has any right to complain of any treatment whatsoever, and should patiently undergo all misery*'.[9] Carlyle's own marriage was unconsummated, according to his biographer. His wife, Jane, took a more nuanced view:

I know nothing about it, except that I have always pitied Mrs Ruskin, while people generally blame her, – for love of dress and company and flirtation. She was too young and too pretty to be left on her own devices as she was by her Husband, who seemed to wish nothing more of her but the credit of having a pretty, well-dressed Wife.[10]

A few years later, though, she told Hunt that 'if because husband and wife are not in accord they should separate, many marriages would be annulled'.[11]

Pauline Trevelyan, with whom the Ruskins and Millais had stayed in Northumberland, was another staunch friend of Ruskin. Effie is said to have written her several letters, 'beseeching sympathy with the painful position of a wife, who, for the first time in her life knew what love was, confessing that John was loathsome to her, and that at any pains and penalties of exposure and shame she must from him be separated'.[12] She refused to reply.

The story spread far and wide as people wrote to their acquaintances outside London. Gabriel Rossetti heard it in Hastings, where he was staying with Lizzie Siddal. 'Everybody seems to know all about it from the letters I get',[13] he noted, and, 'I suppose it is more the right time to be in favour with her than with him'.[14] However, Ruskin had given him lunch and commissioned a picture the day before Effie's flight, and it made no sense to quarrel with a rich and generous patron. He and Lizzie would extract a good deal of money from him over the next few years.

Mrs Gaskell in Manchester heard the news with horror. She could 'not bear to think of the dreadful hypocrisy if the man who wrote those books is a bad man', and although she also said that everyone knew about Ruskin's bad temper she decided Effie was the guilty party:

> Don't think me hard upon her if I tell you what I have *known* of her. She is very pretty, very clever – and very vain. As a girl when she was staying in Manchester her delight was to add to the list of her offers (27 I think she was *at* then) but she never cared for any one of them. It was her boast to add to this list in every town she visited just like somebody in the Arabian Nights who was making up her list of 1000 lovers. *Effie Grey* [sic] *was engaged at the very time she accepted Mr Ruskin* he did not know of it till after their marriage. I don't think she has any more serious faults than vanity and cold-heartedness \ not to her own people, nor her father's house/ but you know how much suffering they may cause. She really is very close to a charming character; if she had had the small pox she would have been so.[15]

Mrs Gaskell had the novelist's instinct for a good story regardless of the facts, and would get into serious trouble in a few years for her rash statements in the *Life of Charlotte Brontë*. The claim that Effie was engaged at the time she accepted Ruskin has been discussed (in Chapter 2). But the important point is that Mrs Gaskell scarcely knew her; when they met before her marriage she was presumably staying with school friends and could not have been more than eighteen. Perhaps the girls did joke about 'offers' and perhaps Effie claimed to have had twenty-seven (which no one would have taken seriously). It would have been silly adolescent talk if it happened but it went down in black and white, harming her reputation for all time.

Imagine this sort of thing repeated over and over again, in letters which have not survived and conversations which have not been recorded. That summer, the papers were filled with bad news from the Crimean War. There was a cholera epidemic in which thousands died. In July came an interesting new scandal when Miss Marian Evans went abroad with G H Lewes, who was separated from his wife, but people did not stop talking about the Ruskins. Millais had hoped it would be 'but a nine days' wonder and it will be all over'.[16] But it would never be over.

Some of these remarks got back to Effie at Bowerswell in the next fortnight. At first she had felt overwhelming relief: 'I am already better, the quiet of this lovely place and seeing all the children so happy and gay, and feeling that I am really away from those wicked people fills me with such thankfulness that already a quiet happiness has settled on my spirits'.[17] But in the middle of May she collapsed with a violent headache and spent ten days in bed or a chair, unable to move or speak. She knew that her acquaintances, and many who had never met her, were discussing her avidly, and this was hard for a young woman who had always sought to be on friendly terms with those around her and who valued her good name. She was worried, too, because she would soon have to be examined by two male doctors. She was haunted – would be haunted fifteen years later – by Ruskin's claim that she had an 'internal disease'. Perhaps they would find that there really was something abnormal about her; perhaps any man who shared her bed would be repelled.

Millais had taken no part in the vilification of Ruskin. He was not a good hater, and now that everything had changed was inclined to judge him kindly. When people discussed the scandal in front of him, he tried to get away. But to his intense frustration he could not get the portrait finished; Ruskin had written to say that he was going abroad and had no time to sit. Instead he headed back to Brig o' Turk, with his friend Charles Collins, to put the final touches to the background. He made it clear to all those interested that he was not going anywhere near Perth: 'I should indeed be sorry to hear that any friend of mine imagined that I had the *bad taste* to see Mrs R whilst the matter is in lawyers' hands'.[18]

Around the same time, on 24th May, Effie went to London with her father, letting only her closest friends know she was there. All applications for divorce or separation, of which there were very few in those days, had to be handled by the Ecclesiastical Courts in Doctors' Commons. Her husband's family did not appear; they had been out of the country for two weeks. She went first to St Saviour's church, Southwark, where she made a sworn statement about her life with Ruskin, the places they had lived in and the fact that he had refused consummation. Mr Gray had to swear that the couple had shared a home until the previous month. On the 30th, she was interviewed privately by a lawyer and examined in her lodgings by two doctors, Robert Lee and Charles Locock, the Queen's obstetrician, who were paid ten pounds each. They reported:

We found that the usual signs of virginity are perfect and that she is naturally and properly formed and there are no impediments on her part to a proper consummation of the marriage.[19]

By that evening she was free to go, knowing she had only to wait for a formal annulment. This was expected to take around six months. They could have claimed damages, 'but both Father and I have decided we take much higher ground by not asking',[20] and Mr Ruskin's ten thousand pounds was returned to him. This surely disposes of the claim that she had got married for money. She had no income of her own; Millais had only what he could earn. He had been very successful so far but he was not yet established. If he had been a more calculating young man he would never have got involved with the wife of England's leading art critic, a man who could, for all he knew, make or break him.

Ruskin immediately moved back to Denmark Hill; as Effie said, it only meant sleeping where he already lived. His parents closed the Herne Hill house and sacked the two young servants, who turned up at Lady

Eastlake's in distress. During the next fortnight he was seen around London, looking much as usual, and sent a long letter to the *Times* discussing Holman Hunt's *Light of the World*. Then on 10th May, as planned, the family crossed the Channel. He tried not to think about what had passed, leaving his father and lawyer to sort out the distasteful business. On the 16th he wrote to his old friend Acland saying he had been deceived by Effie and her parents, who had turned out to be 'mean and designing'. He believed that she had a 'literal nervous affection of the brain', and that 'the whole of her present wild proceeding' was 'in consequence of her having conceived a passion' for Millais, whom he did not name. But he assured him that he was not seriously upset. 'My real sorrows were of another kind. Turner's death – and the destruction of such & such buildings of the 13th century, were worse to me, a hundredfold, than any domestic calamity. I am afraid there is something wrong in this – but so it is; I felt, and feel – that I have work to do which cannot be much helped by any other hand, and which no domestic vexation ought to interrupt – & I have always had the power of turning my mind to its main work & throwing off the grievance of the hour'.[21]

His spirits rose as he got back among his beloved Alps. He planned another volume of *Modern Painters* and thought he might ask some young Pre-Raphaelites to help him set up art schools in the manufacturing towns. But in August he finally wrote to a young admirer, Frederick Furnivall, who had been urging him to clear his name. He hardly knew, he said, whether or not he should try:

> As to the accusation of having thrown my late wife in Mr Millais' way – with the view supposed by Lady Eastlake, I should as soon think of simply *denying* an accusation of murder. Let those who say I have committed murder – prove it – let those who believe I have committed it without proof, continue to believe it.

This was surely true. Rather than forcing Effie on Millais, he feared that she would be a bad influence on the gifted young man. Looking up the notes he had been jotting down over the last twelve months, he went on:

> One great difficulty is that no one will ever believe that Effie's general character in her domestic life was what it was – what it *must* have been in order to render my conduct explicable – For instance – would the kind of temper indicated in the following

dialogue – which I happened to put down one day as an example of our usual intercourse – be believed in a woman who to all strangers behaved with grace and pleasantness.

Effie is looking abstractedly out of the window.

John. 'What are you looking at, Effie'.

E.   'Nothing'.

J.   'What are you thinking of then?'

E.   'A great many things'.

J.   'Tell me some of them'.

E.   'I was thinking of operas – and excitement – and – (angrily) a great many things'.

J.   'And what conclusions did you come to'.

E.   'None – because *you* interrupted me'.

Dialogue closed.

This appears little – but imagine every question asked in a kind tone – every answer given with a snap – and that continuing the whole day – Imagine this behaviour in daily intercourse attended by the most obstinate opposition in serious things – and by an *utter* ingratitude for *all* that was done for her by myself – my father – and my mother – not merely ingratitude – but ingratitude coarsely and vulgarly manifested ... and you may understand – though I do not see how at present I could make the public understand – why I used no persuasion to induce my late wife to change the position which we held towards each other.[22]

That dialogue must have happened in the searing last months of the marriage when neither saw any way out of it. Likewise, Effie had said that John's 'extremely bland manners'[23] concealed his real violent nature. Each thought the other totally to blame, but did not complain except to the people closest to them. Each wished that the unfortunate union could be wiped out of memory.

Ruskin was glad to be free, naturally, but when he thought of Effie, which probably was not often, it was with resentment. She had been ungrateful and unworthy of him. He felt guilty for having married her against his parents' wishes. But he does not seem ever to have thought that he had done her wrong.

After her examination, Effie felt better. She asked her father not to hire a governess for Sophie, Alice and John; she found that she loved being with them and was glad to save him money by teaching them herself. They had a happy summer at St Andrews, where she went for long walks and gave them lessons on the sand.

Earlier than expected, the Grays heard that 'the Judge has signed a sentence declaring the pretended marriage a nullity and that Miss Gray is free from all bonds of matrimony'.[24] Ruskin in Lausanne confirmed that he did not wish to contest the case. On 15th July, the Commissary Court in Surrey granted a formal annulment:

> Therefore we John Haggard Doctor of Laws the Commissary aforesaid having heard counsel learned in the Law in this behalf on the part of the said Euphemia Chalmers Gray falsely called Ruskin do pronounce decree and declare that he the said John Ruskin being then a Bachelor did at the time libellate contract a pretended Marriage with the said Euphemia Chalmers Gray then and still a Spinster but since falsely called Ruskin and we do also pronounce decree and declare according to the lawful proofs made in the said Cause as aforesaid that the said Marriage howsoever in fact had between the said John Ruskin and the said Euphemia Chalmers Gray falsely called Ruskin was had and celebrated whilst the said John Ruskin was incapable of consummating the same by reason of incurable impotency wherefore and by reason of the premises we do pronounce decree and declare that such Marriage or rather show or effigy of Marriage so had and solemnized or rather profaned between the said John Ruskin and Euphemia Chalmers Gray falsely called Ruskin was and is null and void from the beginning to all intents and purposes in the Law whatsoever and by reason thereof that the said Euphemia Chalmers Gray falsely called Ruskin was and is free from all Bond of Marriage with him the said John Ruskin by this our definitive sentence of final decree which we give and promulge by these presents.[25]

This document, deeply embarrassing to Ruskin, was not published, but could be read in the archives of Doctors' Commons by anyone who wished. Effie's feelings were of awe, and gratitude to all who had helped her. She wrote soon afterwards to Rawdon Brown:

> How much have I to be thankful for! when I think what others may be enduring at this moment and *I* restored to health and freedom ... For what was I to be treated with such mercy and

goodness both in a spiritual and temporal point of view. Pray now with me that I may have a continuance of a quiet and simple life to be little known or heard of.[26]

The glad news reached Millais in the Peak District, where he was painting. He had not seen Effie for eight months, or corresponded since before Christmas, although he had written regularly to her mother and of course she had seen the letters. Now at last he felt he could approach her directly:

My dear Countess

I cannot see that there is anything to prevent my writing to you now, so I will wait no longer. I consider that I have a special right to be amongst the first of your congratulating friends, for no one has been so keenly interested in the trials you have gone through, or is so happy at this blessed termination – I had so thoroughly convinced myself of the improbability of ever speaking to you again that I find my brains unable to keep pace with the sudden alteration of affairs, and that I am writing this in a state of incredulity. I did not hope to hear of the decision until November and when I came down this morning I was surprised to find your Mother's letter upon the breakfast table, for I knew at once the news it contained. The best news I have ever received in my life. May God give you health and peace to enjoy the new life you have entered upon, and I think from your late pedestrian performances at St Andrews you are not wanting in the former – I will say nothing of the past. Recalling bygone events can only be distressing to you. You may always feel happy in having done your duty, for you have done John Ruskin even a greater service than yourself. You were nothing to him but an awful encumbrance, and I believe secretly the source of all his sullen irritability. Love was out of the question in such a nature so that by the separation you have caused him no more pain than a temporary exhibition of grief such as would naturally follow after your living so many years with him. Now dear Countess do not be distressed with any more backward thoughts but pray to God that the future may be as happy as the past has been otherwise ... This time last year there seemed no more chance of what has happened than that the moon should fall, and now you are Miss Gray again. If you could see me I am sure you would pity me for I am scarcely able to write commonsense I am so bewildered.

He told her he had only been pretending to paint, keeping away from his friends so that he could get used to 'this wonderful change'. It seemed years since they had been together. 'I must see you before returning to London, *if you will invite me*. Oh Countess how glad I shall be to see you again, this is all I can say now, and you must imagine the rest. I can never be sufficiently thankful for God's goodness to me – I really believe that I should have grown a selfish callous fellow if this alteration had not come about. Take all care of yourself *and write me a letter to assure me that you are the same Countess I knew at Glenfinlas*'.[27]

Effie's reply does not survive; she had asked him to burn her letters. But she must have reassured him that she had not changed, asked him a string of questions about what he had been doing recently, but explained that they could not meet just yet. Too many people were ready to believe the worst of them; they were surrounded, in Jane Austen's words, by a neighbourhood of voluntary spies. Perhaps she and her mother had already decided that they would be unable to get married for a year, the minimum time people were expected to wait after the death of a spouse.

Millais accepted her judgment. He would wait patiently; he had grown more cautious, and Lady Eastlake had warned him to keep away from Perth. 'Do not hurry so as to give people the chance of blaming you in any shape although beyond a few close friends it scarcely matters what the World says, the public will always be unkind if they can'.[28] He wrote to Mrs Gray at the same time about Ruskin:

He has behaved *most badly*, but he is half mad, and possibly embittered by discovering – when too late – that he ought never to have married – in that case according to his strange education and bringing up he is not to be judged so severely. You know what I thought of him at the time of his wretched treatment of the Countess, but now ... I cannot wish him but peaceful, and in health to go on writing as he likes. Now *she* is out of his possession I can forgive him, and I know she will also ... After his mistake he should have put up with everything. I believe that no living woman ever behaved as she did.[29]

As if to make the point that he and Effie were not together, he went in August to Winchelsea, at the other end of the island, and stayed there, with his friend Mike Halliday, until November. Here he started work on the backgrounds of two new pictures, *L'Enfant du Regiment* and *The Blind Girl*, one of his greatest works. The brilliant colours of the rainbow, landscape, butterfly and costumes reflect his new happiness and energy. His arrival did not go unnoticed by the local young women:

> What a difficult thing it is to behave properly. At this place there are lots of pretty girls who insist upon coming out bonnetless in the moonlight and invitingly passing and repassing us, and I have an almost insurmountable desire to stop them and speak, as most youths would, and when I get back to my bedroom I think what a fool I have been, and make up my mind to begin again.[30]

Meanwhile, Effie in Scotland was getting letters from her old teachers, the Misses Ainsworth, warning her that she was being watched. 'Millais, I do not hesitate to tell you, is the person to whom you are generally given, I deny it positively and I do not scruple to say I hope and trust no such thing will *ever* take place'.[31]

Hard as it was for her and him, she knew she must be very cautious. In October she wrote to Rawdon Brown, who had asked if she was thinking of getting married again:

> I am at present gaining health and strength and very happy teaching my sisters. I am not fit to marry anybody, believe me, and after what I have suffered could not do so without very much time for thought and deliberation, and you know it would never do to be wretched twice. If I marry it must be to somebody who wouldn't require me to live in London. I am very unfit for living in town although I should like to go occasionally. I could not be shut up in a street without pining, and I cannot have a man again be unkind to my dear Parents and other important items to leading a quiet life – which I think would be necessary – Then I would not marry unless I cared very much about somebody and who would let me be a good deal in Scotland ... Now all this will take a long time surely to get and leave me peace to teach music and lessons to my heart's content in the meantime.[32]

There was another reason for staying at home which could not be mentioned; Mrs Gray, at forty-six, was again pregnant. The baby, her fifteenth, was due in March 1855. Effie was very anxious to help her parents as they had helped her, and if her mother died she would certainly have to take some responsibility for the children.

She had not seen Millais since the night he left Edinburgh in November 1853. No modest woman could tell her friends that she was getting married (even if they could be trusted to keep quiet) before an engagement was announced. And it was also true that she did not want to make another mistake. They were hoping, rather than planning, to get together eventually. Neither could be quite sure that they would feel the same when they came face to face.

When Ruskin returned from Switzerland and Millais from Sussex there were some final sittings for the portrait, which had taken well over a year. Only his hands (which were smaller than most men's, and could not be done in his absence) remained to be painted, and Millais felt it was 'the most hateful task I ever had to perform'.[33] By the first week in December it was finished, and there could be no doubt that it was magnificent. Sir Charles Eastlake and his wife, who saw it before it was delivered, thought in spite of their deep dislike of the subject that it was 'one of the remarkable pictures of the world'.[34] Ruskin knew of no reason why he and the artist should not remain on good terms. He sent a chatty letter, asking Millais for his address, 'as I may often want to write to you'.[35] When there was no reply, he asked 'Why don't you answer my letter – it is tiresome of you – and makes me uneasy'.[36]

Millais was horrified and embarrassed. All his instincts were against being rude to anyone, but he eventually wrote back:

My dear Ruskin,
    My address is Langham Chambers, Langham Place, but I can scarcely see how you conceive it possible that I can desire to continue on terms of intimacy with you. Indeed I concluded that after finishing your portrait, you yourself would have seen the necessity of abstaining from further intercourse.
                            Yours truly
                            John Everett Millais
    The barrier which cannot but be between us *personally*, does not prevent me from sympathising with all your efforts to the advancement of good taste in Art, and heartily wishing them success.[37]

A deeply shocked Ruskin replied:

Sir
    From the tenour of your letter, received yesterday, I can only conclude that you either believe I had, as has been alleged by

various base or ignorant persons, some unfriendly purpose when I invited you to journey with me to the Highlands, or that you have been concerned in machinations which have for a long time been entered into against my character and fortune. In either case, I have to thank you for a last lesson, though I have had to learn many and bitter ones, of the possible extent of human folly and ingratitude. I trust that you may be spared the natural consequences of the one, or the dire punishment of the other.

I remain,
Your obedient servant
John Ruskin[38]

His father had read Millais' letter, and wrote angrily to him the same day. He told him that he would not allow the portrait to be exhibited, and it has not often been seen in public since. A week later Mr Ruskin gave his version of the marriage, as one-sided as Lady Eastlake's, to Charles Collins:

My Son caught by a pretty face married contrary to his parents *judgement* but not to their *commands* – Miss G concealed the embarrassed circumstances of her Father – courted my Son ... He found at once that the Woman had no Love for him and he lived with her accordingly – She soon filled his House with men of her own finding till he could not get a single hour for study without stealing away to his Father's House – In that house she professed the greatest pleasure in being with her Mother in law up to the marriage day, but no sooner she secured my Son than she used her utmost efforts to take him entirely from his parents and to make him a mere man of the Town. She wasted my property in the most reckless manner making away with £15000 in six years, but she would have been pardoned had she proved a Helpmate to my Son or a Daughter to Mrs R but she was neither – every kindness was lost upon her – she returned for care and fondness only neglect and even contumely, altho' herself both lowly born and lowly bred ... With the artfulness and falsehood inherent in her Character she told the World that those men whom she had forced on my Son destroying his domestic Quiet, were brought by him and left with her for improper ends, the latest and most preposterous falsehood ever invented by the most abandoned woman, and Millais whom my Son with the purest motive and single eye to his Improvement

105

in art, asked to join his Circle, among rocks and Waters which he wished him to study, was one of those whom she proclaimed to be among the persons brought improperly about her – In Scotland Mr Millais' Conduct was most improper when he left his work to follow my Son and Wife to Edinburgh – My Tone to Mr Millais may have seemed harsh for I did feel that he of all men should not have so readily ranked himself on the side of my Sons enemies and slanderers. I however speak for myself not for my Son. He has taken his part rightly or wrongly and scorns to propitiate those who give credit to any reports against him. He will neither say nor write a word in his own defence ... his praise of the artistic Labours of the preRaphaelites will bate no jot of their fervour or Intensity but it is clear to me that Mr Millais is not the man to understand or appreciate the Graduate and all personal Intercourse should at once terminate now and forever.[39]

So ended, in grief and rancour, the association between the greatest Victorian art critic and the most brilliant of the Pre-Raphaelites. But other members of the brotherhood, which hardly existed by this time, would still have a use for Ruskin.

The first months of 1855, known as the Crimean winter, were bitterly cold. London was covered in snow for weeks and the whole Gray family caught flu, except Effie, who nursed them. Her mother had erysipelas and there must have been great anxiety in a house which had lost so many children. At last, in mid-February, Millais arrived at Bowerswell in the snow. Perhaps it was then that he formally proposed, but after fifteen months apart each must have felt intensely shy. Effie wrote that 'this visit was only two days long, very anxious and distressing in many ways ... the cold hand of past sufferings opened by remembrance and Mama's illness not over'. They were both unwell and probably spent most of the two days coughing and sneezing. The children and her mother would have claimed a great deal of Effie's attention. It was not romantic.

Millais told her that he was preparing a new picture, *The Rescue*, for the summer exhibition. She advised him to go back and finish it, and to come back if he wished in May, 'when we could settle things for the future'.[40] No one but the Eastlakes knew about his flying visit, and it was still open to him to back out.

106

On 19th March, two days after her forty-seventh birthday, Mrs Gray gave birth to a boy and a week later became extremely ill. Effie was still nursing her in mid-April and told Millais it was not yet the right time to visit them. In May *The Rescue*, a huge painting inspired by a fire he had witnessed in London, was shown. It is night and a fireman is racing down a staircase to pass three small children to their mother. Millais had actually seen two firefighters fall to their deaths and wanted to show his respect for them. 'Soldiers and sailors have been praised on canvas a thousand times', he said. 'My next picture shall be of the fireman'.[41]

It was a striking picture and it won some unexpected praise. On 1st June Ruskin published a small pamphlet, *Notes on some of the principal pictures exhibited in the rooms of the Royal Academy 1855*. He would go on issuing these notes for several years, and made it clear that his judgements were not affected by personal feelings. 'It is the only *great* picture exhibited this year', he wrote of *The Rescue*, 'but this is *very* great'.[42]

By the time the *Notes* appeared, Millais was packing his bags. Perhaps, groping for words when he and Effie met in February, each wondered whether they had made a terrible mistake. He had written to Hunt in a great state of nerves:

Good gracious, fancy me married my old boy, I feel *desperately melancholy* about it which is rather different to most bridegrooms, but callous to all results as it is quite impossible to foresee the end of anything we undertake ... I take this fearful risk in desperation, I hate wasting my life, and fretting away in *Bachelorism*, and cannot myself change for worse (I may it is true make this girl wretched and so increase my state) but it is worth the risk and you must pray for me my dear old friend ... She dislikes naturally coming to London after her life in it, and I much fear it will never cease to live in her memory, and will always affect her spirits, but time will show. I have so little faith in my own ability to blot out this ruin in her life that I am often very desponding in the matter, but I cannot see how this marriage could have been otherwise, everything seems to have happened to work out this end.[43]

Lady Eastlake had advised them not to get married for two years; others thought they should not get married at all. Nevertheless, they decided that as soon as a decent interval had passed, they were going to do it. Early in June it became known that they were engaged and would live quietly in Scotland for the foreseeable future. Ruskin heard about this from the usual kind friends and wrote:

I am not able to calculate the probabilities on either side. I do not say that Millais does wrong *now* – whatever wrong he may *have* done. I am not sure but that this may indeed have been the only course open to him; that, feeling he had been the Temptation to the woman, and the cause of her giving up all her worldly prospects, he may from the moment of our separation – have felt something of a principle of honour enforcing his inclination to become her protector. What the result may be, to him I cannot conjecture; – I only know that if there is anything like visible retribution in the affairs of this life there are assuredly, dark hours in the distance, for her to whom he has chosen to bind his life.[44]

Millais went to a stag party, hosted by Wilkie Collins, and probably celebrated his birthday on 8th June with his family, arriving next day at Bowerswell. He spent the next three weeks there, falling in love with Effie and Scotland all over again. Unlike Ruskin, he fitted easily and happily into the household. His brother William joined them and he joked that he was 'getting resigned to my fate'.[45] They arranged that when they returned from honeymoon they would rent Annat Lodge, a fine Regency house a few minutes' walk away. It had a large garden with cedars and a splendid view of the hills.

Tuesday 3rd July was a beautiful day. The couple were not allowed to meet until the ceremony, so Effie spent the morning in her room. She recorded in her diary a year later, 'I saw from my window the young men playing at Bowls, whilst I sat reading and thinking of my past Life and my Life with Everett that was to come. Jeanie came in and told me that the Bridegroom looked so merry and pleasant it put one in good spirits to see him ... I said to myself this is no time for anything but happiness and comfort while I look back and see what wonderful things have happened ... how much cause I have to bless God for this day'.

At two o' clock the minister arrived and her father came to take her downstairs, saying, 'Come away, my dear lassie, this time I feel happy at putting you into good hands'. They went into the drawing room (not the room where she had married Ruskin), which was decorated with flowers. The children, cousins and servants crowded in. Neither she nor

Millais 'made any public demonstration on the occasion of meeting for the first time that day. On the contrary I think a looker on might have fancied we were very indifferent to each other'.

Effie was described on her marriage certificate as a spinster. Her baby brother was brought in and christened Everett; then the bride and groom drove to the station. Once they were alone in the carriage, Millais broke down. Three weeks on his best behaviour, while the gossips of Perth took a good look at him, had been a frightful strain. Effie wrote, 'instead of the usual comfort I suppose that the Brides require on those occasions of leaving, I had to give him all the sympathy. He cried dreadfully, said he did not know how he had got through it, felt wretched; it had added ten years to his Life, and instead of being happy and cheerful, he seemed in despair'.[46]

She herself was much calmer. She bathed his face with eau de cologne, held his head and opened a window, and as the train approached Glasgow he stopped crying. She was quietly confident that this marriage was going to be very different from the first – and it was.

PART FOUR
EFFIE MILLAIS

9

The Young Mother
1855–68

> Still, she never repented that she had given up position and fortune to marry
> Will Ladislaw, and he would have held it the greatest shame as well as sorrow
> to him if she had repented.
>
> *Middlemarch*, Finale

The young couple 'were very anxious not to be thought like new married people'.[1] Before leaving the train, Effie took off her white shawl and put on dark gloves, a grey plaid and a black veil. They travelled down the Clyde to Rothesay where they spent the night, and crossed next day to Brodick in the Isle of Arran.

Rigid propriety meant that they had hardly ever been alone since they walked over the hills near Brig o' Turk fully two years earlier. Now that they were legally married and allowed to be together as much as they wanted, everything was fine. They spent a happy fortnight in beautiful weather on Arran and then crossed the water to Argyll. Effie wrote home, 'I am so happy with him. You can imagine how much I appreciate his natural character. I really think if it was not rather wicked to say so that I would almost go through much misery – I was going to say all I had suffered – rather than miss being with him a day'.[2] A week later, 'I don't think I have laughed so much since I was Alice's age'.[3]

Millais was equally thrilled and happy. His letters are full of Effie's praises. He was amused to find that, as on her first wedding journey, she talked to everybody, interrogating a coachman about Scottish history (they discovered a ruined convent on an island in Loch Awe, which would inspire a painting in a few years' time). Writing to Mr Gray three weeks into the honeymoon he boasted, 'My dear Father, I look forward with some pride, I can tell you, to the day that I bring back to Perth your altered girl. She has such rosy cheeks and has become so jolly you will find her a different looking woman'.[4]

They went on to St Andrews, where they met the Grays and posed for a family photograph. At some point Millais sketched a coin, showing, instead of Victoria and Albert, his wife and himself in profile. They are both facing left and look extremely smug.

A few more weeks were spent entertaining friends at their new home, Annat Lodge; then he got down to work, determined to have several pictures ready for next spring. By September, Effie was pregnant.

In contrast to the bleak time eighteen months earlier, when Millais could hardly bring himself to work, the paint flowed freely. Effie was happy and eager to help him. She posed for days, almost making herself ill, for the central figure in *The Blind Girl*, although in the end Millais used a different face. She sat, too, for *Peace Concluded*, as the wife of an officer just back from the Crimean war. This shows her with golden hair wound in braids around her head, and gives a better idea of how she looked in the 1850s than *The Order of Release*. She played the piano while he worked and found him models, 'going into strange habitations', Millais joked, 'and seizing adults and children without explanation and dragging them here, and sending them back to their homes with a *sixpence* when I should have been doubtful between a sovereign and thirty shillings'.[5]

Around this time he created one of his very greatest works, *Autumn Leaves*. Set in the garden of Annat Lodge at twilight (the hills and the spire of St John's kirk are just visible), it shows four very young girls feeding a bonfire. The two in dark dresses were modelled by Alice and Sophie Gray; the other two are working-class children whom Effie recruited and who also posed for *The Blind Girl* and *L'Enfant du Regiment*. Some critics would complain that it had no meaning, but of course it is about transience. The darkening sky, serious faces, and the apple held by the youngest child remind us that all life fades. It was painted quite quickly; he would no longer spend hours on every leaf and straw.

He went to London in the spring to place his brilliant new pictures in the 1856 Exhibition; Effie, whose baby was due within weeks, stayed behind. He met Hunt, back from the Middle East, and Ford Madox Brown, who noted that he seemed passionately fond of his wife and very angry with Ruskin. His attitude had hardened since he wrote in 1854 that he wished him well. 'I can scarcely trust myself to speak of Ruskin, who certainly appears to me (now that I know *all* about his treatment of my wife) to be the most wicked man I have known in my life. This I say *without hesitation* and methodically'.[6] If he knew of the threats to beat her he would certainly have been furious. Gabriel Rossetti was now very close to the Graduate, 'always speaking of Ruskin as though he was a saint of the callender [sic] and not showing one word of simpathy [sic] for his wife',[7] and for some years it would be difficult for anyone to be on good terms with both men. Hunt of course chose Millais; Rossetti distanced himself from his old friends.

When Ruskin's *Academy Notes* came out he called *Autumn Leaves* 'by much the most poetical work the painter has yet conceived, and also, as far as I know, the first instance existing of a perfectly painted twilight'. He praised *Peace Concluded*, too, rather more than it deserved. 'This picture is as brilliant in invention as consummate in executive power; both this and *Autumn Leaves* will rank in the future among the world's best masterpieces, and I see no limit to what the painter may hope in the future to achieve'.[8] We don't know how he felt when he saw an unmistakable likeness of his former wife in this family group, but he had always thought she had a beautiful face.

As soon as he had arranged sales Millais rushed back to Scotland. On 30th May Effie gave birth to a boy, Everett; she was just twenty-eight. The celibate years had left her physically fit and she got through it quite easily, perhaps with the help of chloroform. Millais announced happily that 'another PRB has just come into the world. My wife was taken ill last night and is now the mother of a fine little boy':[9] To religious Victorians, there could be no clearer sign of the rightness of this marriage than the birth of a healthy son. Effie recovered, and in August they took the baby to Brig o' Turk and revisited the scenes where they had fallen in love. An etching, *The Young Mother*, shows her breast-feeding with hills and a lake in the background. Afterwards Millais started work on a huge, medievalist picture, *Sir Isumbras at the Ford (A Dream of the Past)*.

Much of it was painted out of doors at the Bridge of Earn in the autumn of 1856, with Effie keeping him supplied with soup and wine. The meaning is not obvious as, unlike his earlier Pre-Raphaelite works, it is based on no known legend. An aged knight, on a great black horse, is taking two small children across a river after sunset. Millais thought it was one of the best things he had done so far. The landscape and figures are superb; the knight's golden armour and peacock feathers contrast with the bare-footed and frightened-looking children. Perhaps he liked it because it includes the beloved Everett, whose distinctive features gaze sorrowfully out of the frame as he clings to the old man's waist. He would become famous as a painter of children but very few would be as memorable.

But the horse, which fills most of the foreground, was not quite right. Effie wrote that 'all the critics cried out about the huge horse, called it Roman-nosed, and said every kind of absurd thing about it, forgetful of the beauty of the rest of the picture'.[10] They were both shocked by the reviews when it was exhibited in May 1857. Several critics said it was monstrous, grotesque. A cartoon by Frederick Sandys called 'A Nightmare', which appeared in printsellers' windows all over London, depicted Millais himself on a braying donkey, overseeing the bearded, dwarfish figures of Rossetti and Hunt. The donkey was labelled, 'J.R., Oxon'.

The real J R wrote in his *Academy Notes* that Millais had gone disastrously downhill. 'The change in his manner, from the years of *Ophelia* and *Mariana* to 1857, is not merely Fall – it is Catastrophe'. Yet he could still see the picture's immense suggestiveness:

It might be a type of noble human life, tried in all war, and aged in all counsel and wisdom, finding its crowning work at last to be the bearing of the children of poverty in its arms ... Or it might be an image less of life than of the great Christian Angel of Death.[11]

Millais refused to read the *Notes*, but of course he knew roughly what had been said. Ruskin added that his second exhibition entry, *The Escape of a Heretic*, was 'at once coarse and ghastly, exaggerated and obscure',[12] which was true. The effort which could have gone into perfecting *Isumbras* had been put into a much inferior work. Millais was still painting superbly, but he was also turning out pot-boilers. Effie, their child and the scenery of Scotland had liberated his imagination, but he was living a long way from his old friends and would surely have benefited from the lively discussions they had had in his bachelor days. *Isabella* had been conceived just after the PRB discovered the early Italians; Hunt had made him revise his original plan for the *Huguenot*; Ruskin had got him to paint rocks and water rather than a straight portrait of himself. Now he was thinking more about what kind of work would sell. Over the next few years he would paint some accomplished but uninspiring pictures: *News from Home, The Love of James I of Scotland, Spring, The Ransom*.

If Ruskin was against him (he may have thought), was that surprising? In the mid-1850s the older man's reputation was huge. He seemed quite unembarrassed by the collapse of his marriage and would have been unaware of any dirty jokes that were going about. Painters greatly feared him, according to a bard in *Punch*:

I takes and paints,
Hears no complaints,
And sells before I'm dry;
Till savage Ruskin,
He sticks his tusk in,
Then nobody will buy.[13]

Licking his wounds, Millais exhibited nothing in 1858, instead working on smaller pictures and illustrations for a new edition of Tennyson. On 19th September 1857 Effie had a second son, George. These were probably some of the happiest years of her life. They had moved into Bowerswell; she was surrounded by her family and friends and had plenty of help with the children (though two babies called Everett in one nursery must have caused some confusion). They spent the winter of 1857–8 in a rented house in London, but she was still nervous about moving back there permanently. Her marriage was recognised by the church and state. But it could not be denied that she had repudiated her first husband, rather than enduring everything like a perfect Victorian wife. She knew that people were still talking about her, might snub her, and probably thought she was a lewd woman who could not live without sex.

But, this time, nothing unpleasant happened, and at least one man who met her was impressed. The painter George Price Boyce called in November, and, finding Millais out, 'had a long and very pleasant chat with his wife, who has a lovely and passionate face, and whose manner is particularly engaging and ladylike'.[14] Boyce was the creator of *Night Sketch of the Thames near Hungerford Bridge*. He had a sister, Joanna, who was also a good painter, but would die in 1860 after the birth of her third child.

Although heavily pregnant again in the following autumn, Effie was keen to help Millais with his new picture, *The Vale of Rest*. He had wanted to paint nuns ever since their wedding journey, and in this picture, which now hangs in Tate Britain, he depicted women who had renounced marriage and were looking forward only to death. For the background he used terraces and shrubs near 'the wall of our garden at Bowerswell, with the tall oaks and poplar trees behind it',[15] and the tombstones were done in the grounds of the disused church at Kinnoull. One nun is digging a grave while another looks gloomily at the spectator. There is a muted gold and purple sunset and a coffin-shaped cloud.

Effie was not a religious fanatic, but she did like to go to the

Presbyterian church on Sundays and felt that Millais should go too. She also thought it bad for him to work seven days a week, 'as he took no rest, and hardly proper time for his meals'.[16] So one day when he was struggling, unable to get the digging nun right, she and her mother quietly removed the picture and hid it in a wine-cellar. Millais was furious but 'gradually calmed down. When the picture was eventually returned to him, he saw at a glance where his mistake lay, and in a few hours put everything right'.[17]

Around this time, on 28th November 1858, she bore a daughter, Euphemia Gray Millais. They had been married for three years and four months, and the babies were coming rather fast. Soon afterwards, Effie became unwell. 'She had imprudently gone, one cold winter's day, to Murthly, to make a drawing of some tapestry in the old castle, for one of my father's pictures; and, sitting long at her task, she contracted a chill, which affected the optic nerves of both her eyes'.[18] The trouble cleared up, but it would come back.

In spring 1859 Millais went south for the Exhibition, bringing *The Vale of Rest* and *Spring* (sometimes called *Apple Blossom*), a picture of eight young women picnicking in an orchard. He saw Ruskin looking closely at the nuns, and probably moved away. Rumours reached him that the great critic thought 'I had gone to the dogs and am hopelessly fallen'[19] since Pre-Raphaelite days. So he expected Ruskin to attack both pictures, but did not expect the storm of abuse he got from other critics.

This year no one seemed to have a good word for him. Virtually all the reviews said that his new paintings, and particularly the women in them, were hideous. Ruskin was, in fact, not among the most abusive. He pointed out that there was no reason for nuns to look beautiful, and said that *The Vale of Rest* was 'a great work', but 'crude'. But he had no time for the second picture, and summed up, 'there is, I regret to say, no ground for any diminution of the doubt which I expressed two years since respecting the future career of a painter who can fall thus strangely beneath himself'.[20]

For weeks Millais feared that for the first time he would be unable to sell anything. He believed that 'ruin stared him in the face – ruin to himself, his wife, and family',[21] and even thought of emigrating to New York. 'I am dreadfully low-spirited', he wrote home, 'and the profession is more hideous than ever in my eyes. Nobody seems to understand really good work'.[22] Effie in Scotland would have heard a garbled version of what Ruskin had said, and thought he was wickedly trying to destroy her husband's career. She must have been very frightened, but did her

The Order of Release by Millais.

Clockwise from left:

1. Margaret Ruskin.

2. Effie Ruskin, painted by Thomas Richmond, 1851. Effie described it as, 'much prettier than I am … I look like a graceful doll'. © *National Portrait Gallery, London.*

3. Ruskin's self-portrait.

4. Rose La Touche, by Ruskin.

Clockwise from right:

1. Millais, painted by George Frederic Watts, 1871. © *National Portrait Gallery, London.*

2. Millais, c. 1854.

3. Effie, Millais and their daughters photographed by Lewis Carroll, 1865.

Clockwise from below:

1. Ruskin, 1894.

2. Bowerswell today.

3. Millais, 1896, the last photograph.

best to console him: 'I returned here last night and opened three letters from you – all so kind and nice that they quite set me up'.[23]

It was not all bad news. The novelists Thackeray and Reade were supportive, as was Hunt, and he eventually sold *The Vale of Rest* (*Spring* did not find a buyer for two years). But he had had a severe shock, and told Effie, 'Whatever I do, no matter how successful, it will always be the same story. "Why don't you give us the Huguenot again?"... I am so glad to hear you are getting well and strong again. That is better than all the sales of pictures'.[24]

In future he would be reluctant to paint large expensive pictures which nobody wanted. With three small children – and probably more to come – it was too risky. He arranged to do illustrations for a journal, *Once a Week*, which treated him and Effie to a precious six days in Paris. He also illustrated several novels – *Framley Parsonage, Orley Farm, The Small House at Allington* – as they appeared in serial form. Altogether he would do eighty-seven drawings for Trollope, who was impressed by his conscientiousness – 'in every figure that he drew it was his object to promote the views of the writer'.[25] He also worked on a series of woodcuts called *Parables of Our Lord*, using local, Perthshire backgrounds for Biblical scenes. Some of his designs were incorporated in a stained-glass window which can still be seen in Kinnoull parish church.

He and Effie talked again about moving to London, but continued shuttling between there and Scotland for some time. She was almost certainly the one who hung back, but he needed to be in the metropolis to make contacts. In November he met Catherine, the discarded wife of Charles Dickens, who 'hopes you will call and bring the children to see her'.[26] Meanwhile he approached Dickens himself and asked if he might paint his daughter Kate. She was to be a central figure in *The Black Brunswicker*, which tells a story very like the *Huguenot*.

It is the eve of the battle of Waterloo. Two lovers are embracing for the last time; the young woman is trying to restrain the man, an officer in a famous Prussian regiment, who is going to war and will be killed. Millais worked on this picture through the spring of 1860. Kate was soon to marry his old friend Charles Collins but at present she was still a young lady living at home. To protect her reputation, she attended his studio with a chaperone, was kept away from the other model and 'leant on the bosom of a man of wood'.[27]

It is a beautiful picture – the woman's silver dress is especially striking – but not as powerful as the *Huguenot*. It was, however, exactly the kind of 'human interest' painting which the public liked, and marked 'a watershed in Millais' reputation and his emergence as the nation's most popular painter'.[28] It sold for the record price of a thousand guineas, and was widely reproduced. This time Ruskin did not comment as he had ceased publishing *Academy Notes*.

Effie was not there to see the *Brunswicker's* triumph. In May 1860 she gave birth to a daughter, Mary, in Scotland, and by April 1861 was in London again. She was pregnant for the fifth time – we don't know by how many months. This was possibly the last time she set eyes on her former husband.

Ruskin was due to give a public lecture on 'Tree Twigs'. Mrs Gaskell, who always took an interest in Effie, was not there, but described what happened anyway:

> He was engaged to deliver a lecture at the Royal Institution on April 17, & great interest was made to obtain tickets & the place was crowded; and he entirely *broke down* in his lecture. Just within this last day or two I have heard from thoroughly good authority … that on looking up (after some arrivals had come in to the reserved seats, after he had begun his lecture), he saw *Lady Eastlake and Mrs Millais* sitting right opposite to him, and staring at him, which finished the breaking him down. All his friends are so indignant and sorry.[29]

According to Thomas Carlyle, Ruskin continued speaking after the first shock and the lecture was a success. Carlyle reported that Effie had gone 'with a termagant of a woman called Lady E. … on purpose to disconcert him'.[30] There is no doubt that Lady Eastlake hated Ruskin, but such behaviour was not characteristic of Effie, who avoided even speaking of him if at all possible. She may have found it hard to refuse the older woman, or may simply have been curious about the man she had not seen for seven years. She was angry, not only on her own behalf but also because of his attacks on Millais, and perhaps was not sorry to embarrass him. But it is likely that the sight of him deeply upset her, reviving old pains and humiliations, and she never attempted to see him again. A few days later her eye trouble flared up again, and at the end of the month she lost her baby. The doctor said that she would never have been well had it gone to term.

She spent the hot summer of 1861 in Scotland, recovering and also looking after her mother, who was unwell. Millais missed her acutely. As he wrote in some bemusement, various ladies had been saying 'immodest' things to him and asking how his wife dared to leave him alone. He was a strikingly good-looking man and they may have thought, given his history, that he had little respect for marriage. Effie was not afraid, then or in future, that he would stray. This young woman, who has been called a social butterfly, often fled from London to Bowerswell, sometimes at the height of the season. Apart from any responsibilities to her family in Perth, she needed to recover her health and knew no other way than to put some temporary distance between herself and her husband. She had said in a letter to Rawdon Brown, when pregnant with little Effie, that she hoped to have no more than three children. But in July they were reunited and she immediately got pregnant again.

They had spent a long time looking for a London home, not too far from Millais' parents in Kingston-on-Thames, not too near the artistic set in Little Holland House whom they found pretentious. The whole family moved at the end of the year to 7 Cromwell Place. On 6th April 1862 her sister-in-law Judith, William Millais' wife of two years, died after giving birth to a daughter. Four days later, Effie herself had a third daughter, Alice Sophia Caroline (known as Carrie). Her feelings, as she went into labour, can be imagined.

When she left her home eight years before she had been Mrs John Ruskin, an ornament of high society in London and Venice, the subject of a well-known painting and a target for idle young men. Now she was Mrs John Millais, the mother of several small children, with a scandal in her past and her looks beginning to fade. George Du Maurier, who met the couple three months after Carrie's birth expecting to see a *femme fatale*, was surprised: 'I was most disappointed in his wife (the late Mrs Ruskin, you know). She is quite passée – wasn't she fascinated by my singing though?'.[31] Her pink cheeks had faded, as Ruskin foresaw, and from now on she would have to rely on her brains and social skills. There was a cruel contrast with Millais, who looked happy and handsome.

Yet, to him at least, she was still a deeply romantic figure. In December that year they visited the empty mansion of Knole so that she could pose for *The Eve of St Agnes*. For three nights, by the light of a full moon, Effie stoically stood in a very cold room wearing only a greenish-blue shift. In the finished picture her dress has slipped to her knees and a pattern of moonlight and window bars falls on the floor. The room and its costly furniture are in shadow, the woman 'half-hidden, like a mermaid in sea-weed', in Keats' words. The surroundings were 'weird and comfortless'; both of them nearly froze and she said afterwards it had been 'the severest task she ever undertook'.[32] But they had their reward, because the picture is magnificent. Effie was not pregnant or nursing at the time and looks very slim for a woman who had now borne five children. As he could not show his wife partly clothed, Millais used a model's head.

This was by far his finest picture of the 1860s. The next year, their third son, Geoffroy, was born and Millais, still only thirty-four, was elected a full member of the Royal Academy. He continued to paint highly popular works. *My First Sermon* (1863), showed his four-year-old daughter Euphemia, dressed for church in her best hat and coat and looking solemn. The Archbishop of Canterbury, Charles Longley, thought it a touching image of 'the piety of childhood'.[33] Millais was never a pious man, and in *My Second Sermon*, done next year, the same little girl in the same pew is fast asleep. A few years later he painted his younger daughters, Carrie and Mary, in bed in companion pictures, *Sleeping* and *Waking*. Other people began asking him to paint their children. William Rossetti wrote, 'it is rather exasperating to find a man of such pictorial power and command of expression as Mr Millais knocking off picture after picture of little girls and boys'.[34]

We cannot know what Effie thought. She may have believed everything he did was perfect; she would certainly have appreciated his portraits of their children. On the other hand, if she suspected that he had declined since his brilliant youth, how could she say so? He was working six days a week, often drawing illustrations at night after painting all day, to support their family. She was doing everything she could to make it easy for him. A letter from a friend refers to 'your wife, who (as I have always told you) alone makes it possible for you to exist'.[35] And then there were the constant pregnancies.

In the autumn of 1864, expecting her seventh child, she consulted Dr Simpson about her persistent insomnia. For a long time she had been unable to sleep without drugs, and she was getting worn out by having a baby, on average, every eighteen months. She told her mother that she would like her to visit before instead of after the birth in case 'anything happened'. It was deeply ironic. Having turned her world upside down in order to have a family, she now found that marriage to a young man with a normal sex drive left her constantly pregnant and ill. There was no lack of love for the children and Millais, but it does explain why she often went to Scotland without him and why he went away on long fishing and shooting trips, perhaps to remove himself from temptation. Every time a Victorian woman went into labour she had a one in two hundred chance of dying, and death had already come very close to their family. Effie knew it might happen.

The baby, John Guille (pronounced Jewel), arrived safely in March. At the end of that year, 1865, Holman Hunt finally got married. It had taken him much longer than Millais and other members of their circle to settle down. After a long, tortured relationship with his model, Annie Miller, he had been looking for a congenial woman who was prepared to go with him to the Middle East. He and another PRB, Thomas Woolner, were friendly with the family of George Waugh, a chemist who had eight daughters. Woolner married the youngest, Alice; Hunt fell in love with the eldest, Fanny, who is the striking dark-haired woman in *Isabella and the Pot of Basil*. They had dinner with Millais and Effie, said goodbye to their families, and set sail in August 1866 for what was still called the Holy Land. But an outbreak of cholera stopped them in Florence, and there, in October, Fanny gave birth to a boy. She never recovered and died several weeks later, on 20th December 1866, after they had been married for less than a year.

'My wife has nearly died more than once in childbirth', Millais wrote in a letter of sympathy, 'and I know the terrible nature of the trial'.[36] It was nearly two years since Effie had last had a baby, and they may have thought she was unlikely to get pregnant again, but she did.

All this time they could not have avoided hearing Ruskin's name, which was constantly before the public. Millais may have run into him at the Academy; they were both polite, and would have acknowledged each other. They knew that he had not remarried, and would have heard about the death of his father in March 1864. It is unlikely that any of his books ever entered their house, but they took the *Cornhill Magazine,* which carried many illustrations by Millais, and which was the first to print Ruskin's great essay *Unto This Last.* It would be interesting to know whether Effie was aware of his lecture, 'Of Queens' Gardens', published as part of *Sesame and Lilies* in 1865.

Over the last few years he had been growing less interested in modern painters and much more in the condition of England. The first lecture in the volume, 'Of Kings' Treasuries', discussed the woeful state of public education; the second was about the education of women and their role in life. Ruskin was not, as some people think, a bigoted male chauvinist. He took an interest in a girls' school, Winnington Hall in Cheshire, and argued that girls should learn almost as much as boys, but for a different purpose:

A woman, in any rank of life, ought to know whatever her husband is likely to know, but to know it in a different way ... speaking broadly, a man ought to know any language or science he learns, thoroughly – while a woman ought to know the same language, or science, only so far as may enable her to sympathise in her husband's pleasures, and in those of his best friends.[37]

This was not intended to sound patronising. Ruskin did not expect women to be highly intellectual (although he did once say that Lizzie Siddal was a genius), but he had no doubt that women were, or ought to be, morally better than men. This man, whose marriage had collapsed, dreamed of a happy home ruled by a benign female figure:

The man, in his rough work in open world, must encounter all peril and trial ... often he must be wounded, or subdued; often misled; and *always* hardened. But he guards the woman from all this; within his house, as ruled by her, unless she herself has sought it, need enter no danger, no temptation, no cause of error or offence. This is the true nature of home – it is the place of Peace; the shelter, not only from all injury, but from all terror, doubt, and division.[38]

'Unless she herself has sought it'? Any reader who knew Ruskin's history must have seen this as a coded attack on the wife who had run away. He went on to say that, since a woman's role was to create a home:

... do not you see that ... she must – as far as one can use such terms of a human creature – be incapable of error? So far as she rules, all must be right, or nothing is. She must be enduringly, incorruptibly good; instinctively, infallibly wise – wise, not for self-development, but for self-renunciation: wise, not that she may set herself above her husband, but that she may never fail from his side.[39]

Effie had notoriously fallen from his side and he certainly blamed her. He was now free to dream about a different kind of woman, one who would create the ideal setting for him while he worked. Many people have pointed out that he was talking only about middle-class women – though he denied it – and that the ordinary person's home

124

was not quite the peaceful place he described. The poet Elma Mitchell commented in 'Thoughts after Ruskin' (1967):

> *Women reminded him of lilies and roses.*
> *Me they remind rather of blood and soap,*
> *Armed with a warm rag, assaulting noses,*
> *Ears, neck, mouth and all the secret places:*
>
> *Armed with a sharp knife, cutting up liver...*
> *And haul out sheets from under the incontinent*
> *And heavy old, stoop to importunate young,*
> *Tugging, folding, tucking, zipping, buttoning,*
> *Spooning in food, encouraging excretion,*
> *Mopping up vomit, stabbing cloth with needles...*

Effie was a middle-class woman who had been shielded from the heaviest housework but she certainly was familiar with looking after the young and sick. Ruskin, growing up in his mother's well-run house, knew nothing of these things. And, ironically, she had become exactly the kind of wife he admired, fiercely loyal to her husband and very interested in his work and that of his friends. She was also better educated than he was, speaking three foreign languages while Millais spoke none. If she heard about the arguments in this essay, she would probably have sighed and thought them quite impractical. She just wished that her six years with Ruskin could be wiped out of everyone's memory, including her own.

In May 1868, Effie had just turned forty and was heavily pregnant with her eighth child. As before, she knew that she might not survive. Her two aunts, dead twenty years ago, Joanna Boyce, Judith Millais, Fanny Hunt – all must have been in her mind. She was worried, too, about her sister Sophie. She and Alice were now in their twenties, still unmarried, and earlier that year Sophie had had a breakdown and been placed in a private asylum in Chiswick, where Effie visited her as often as possible. While she was thinking of these things, with the baby expected in four weeks, she received a letter. It was from a woman she did not know, Mrs Maria La Touche, and it was about Ruskin.

10

The Sick Rose
1858–75

It was wicked to let a young girl blindly decide her fate in that way, without any effort to save her.

Middlemarch, Chapter 29

We left Ruskin in the spring of 1855, hoping that there were 'dark hours in the distance' for Effie. Yet he must have known that he was extraordinarily lucky to have got out of the marriage, and his career had not been greatly harmed. The Victorians did not read celebrity gossip. Hundreds of people in literary London knew about the scandal, but the thousands who admired his books and attended his lectures knew him only as a thinker. He was also an eligible bachelor again. Somewhere among the surplus thousands there must have been a woman who would have taken Ruskin on his own terms, but he did not seek her out. Indeed he was shocked and annoyed when at least two women, in the early years after the annulment, tried to marry him.

He had several other interests. He arranged the Turner bequest, gave drawing lessons at the new Working Men's College, got involved in the building of the Oxford Natural History Museum. As his parents grew older, their influence weakened. He continued to be a dutiful son, but he went on long holidays without them and began to distance himself from their views.

The year 1858 was a turning-point. Up to this time he had been a fairly orthodox Christian, though worried that geology seemed to contradict parts of the Bible. But in that year he attended a service in a Protestant chapel in Turin and decided that the preacher was talking nonsense. Whether or not God existed, it could not be true that only a fraction of the human race would be saved. Of course, his mother could not be told that he no longer believed what she did. He was also beginning to disagree with the system that had made old Mr Ruskin so rich.

Was it possible to isolate art from the world around it? Plenty of talented painters could not make a living; the great majority of people had no chance even to look at paintings because they were struggling to stay alive. He was worried by the misery he had seen in Venice and England; did not people like himself, who had been born privileged, have a duty to others? As long ago as 1853 he had written in 'The Nature of Gothic' about the workman's right to a job that satisfies his creative instincts. This seemed to him as much a basic need as food and shelter; we have not yet caught up with him in that respect. In two lectures on 'The Political Economy of Art', given at Manchester in 1857, he argued that society was planned on the wrong lines, that all men should be brothers.

He was asking more and more searching questions about matters that were generally taken for granted, and concluding that mankind had gone profoundly wrong. Even the Alps could not console him by 1860: 'Once I could speak joyfully about beautiful things, thinking to be understood – now I cannot any more, for it seems to me that no one regards them. Wherever I look or travel in England or abroad, I see that men, wherever they can reach, destroy all beauty. They seem to have no other desire or hope but to have large houses and to be able to move fast'.[1] Twenty years later he would note that the pleasant green lane near his childhood home at Herne Hill was now choked with rubbish.

It was in 1858, but before his recoil against his parents' religion, that Ruskin first met the La Touche family of County Kildare. John and Maria La Touche were part of the Protestant Ascendancy. He was a banker and landowner, with a private park of eleven thousand acres; she was a pretty, cultivated woman, five years younger than Ruskin, who wrote novels and yearned for a more interesting life. They lived with their three children at Harristown Old House, near Naas, but often spent the winters in Mayfair. The wife was conventionally religious; the husband had been converted by the Baptist preacher Spurgeon and was fiercely Evangelical. In January, on one of her trips to London, Mrs La Touche got herself introduced to Ruskin and asked him to give drawing lessons to her daughters, Emily and Rose. Most eminent men would have excused themselves, but he found that he liked the idea.

Rose, the youngest child, had been born on 3rd January 1848, three months before the marriage of Ruskin and Effie. So she was just ten when they met and they bonded at once. Over the next few years they often met and exchanged letters. Ruskin took her to the British Museum, to lectures on Shakespeare, to Denmark Hill, where his parents made a great fuss of her and gave her a copy of *The King of the Golden River*. She was of course accompanied by her mother and sister. Mrs La Touche was thrilled to have made friends with such a distinguished man and may have thought that he nursed a chaste passion for herself. Mr La Touche never liked him much.

How could they guess that he was becoming dangerously obsessed with their daughter? Rose was a bright, friendly girl, fair-haired and blue-eyed, very fond of her dogs and cats. Living in Ireland as she did he could only see her occasionally, and there were long gaps when he did not see her at all, but she quickly became the centre of his consciousness. 'I had loved Rosie since she was ten years old', he wrote some time later. '... I have had no thought within me – ever since – but was in some part of it hers'.[2]

Ruskin's biographer Tim Hilton bluntly calls him a paedophile, which does not necessarily mean a child molester. He was not a criminal; of course he would never physically have interfered with a child. But that summer of 1858 in Turin, when he lost his faith in Protestant Christianity, he noticed among a group of neglected children – 'one girl of about ten, with her black hair over her eyes and half-naked, bare-limbed to above the knees, and beautifully limbed, lying on the sand like a snake'.[3] She obsessed him for years but he never saw her again, and soon afterwards he began fantasising about Rose, who was much the same age. He did not hesitate to share his thoughts with others. By February 1860 he was writing in his weekly letter to the pupils of Winnington Hall, who had never met her, in a way that does not seem appropriate. He had been 'reduced to a state of frantic despair', he said, 'by Rosie's going away'.[4]

One feels sorry for this little girl, growing up under intense pressure from her parents and the kindly uncle-figure who overlooked her education. Her best chance would have been to go to school and make friends of her own age, but this did not happen. Her father, unable to convert his wife or older children, taught her that nothing in the world really mattered except religion. 'I listened and took in all my father's doctrines', she would write. 'He taught me that there was but the one thing needful, one subject worthy of thought, one aim worth living for, one rule for conduct, namely God's Holy Word'.[5] Ruskin, on a visit to Ireland in the autumn of 1861, encouraged her to teach herself Greek. She tried, but a few weeks later became extremely ill. Two years later when she was fifteen she broke down again, and this time it could not have been Ruskin's fault. Her parents had an ugly row on the occasion of her first communion, and immediately afterwards she collapsed. For eighteen months she was unable to lead a normal life, as she recalled: 'Light hurt me. Food hurt me (not my head). Sometimes I was hungry but had such terrible pain after eating'.[6] Very possibly she had anorexia; the few surviving photographs show that she was unnaturally thin.

Ruskin did not see her between April 1862 and the end of 1865. During that time his father died and he inherited a large fortune, much of which he eventually gave away. He did correspond with the mother and daughter; Rose's letters urged him to be a serious Christian. He wrote *Sesame and Lilies* with her in mind, including a plea to women not to assume they knew the mind of God.

Eventually she seemed to get better. She showed no interest in an ordinary social life but wandered around the estate visiting cottages and fretting about the gulf between rich and poor, of which Ruskin had made her aware. In December 1865 her parents brought her to London for the winter. Her elder sister was already married and they thought it was time for her to come 'out'. Ruskin was enchanted. Just as he had done with Effie nearly twenty years earlier, he went about with her, wrote a poem for her birthday – her eighteenth – and a few weeks later proposed.

Rose was startled and told him that she could not yet say yes or no. If he agreed to wait for three years, by which time she would be of age, then she would answer. Her parents were appalled; Mrs La Touche's sentimental feelings changed to fury. By the standards of some societies, including her own, Rose was old enough to get married, but she had met very few young men and had been extremely ill. It was by no means certain that she was fit for childbirth. There was an age gap of twenty-nine years. Ruskin was not what Rose and her father considered a Christian. And then there was his mysterious past. Mrs La Touche must have known that he had been married but had probably believed whatever he told her; now she began to wonder what had really happened and whether he was even free to have another wife.

They took their daughter back to Ireland in April and made it clear that they wanted no further contact. And Rose? It seems that she did not want to make a commitment but neither did she want to lose him permanently. He was a kind and fascinating companion, and she was not very happy at home. They kept in touch through his young cousin Joan Agnew, who kept house for the aged Mrs Ruskin. So began a long period of communicating through other people.

Among them was Georgiana Cowper, or Cowper-Temple, one of the many soulful married ladies who admired Ruskin. Her husband had inherited Palmerston's stately home, Broadlands, where Ruskin was often a guest, and she also knew the La Touche family. He wrote to her describing his wretchedness as he counted the days to Rose's twenty-first birthday:

> I know the La Touches don't know what they are doing ... they think nothing of poisoning my life and thoughts day by day and killing me with an *infinite* pain. They took the child away from me – practically – four years ago – and since that day of April, 1862, I have never had one happy hour – all my work has been wrecked – all my usefulness taken from me. I am not given, indeed, to think much of that – and yet I know there are many who love me – whom I might have loved and helped – whom I cannot love because of this ... there are hundreds – literally hundreds, whom I know – among my workpeople alone – who are all more or less paralysed and broken because I am, I, who, weak as I might be – was once their leader – and now have no strength or heart to lead them. And there are others – (surely many others?) who *were* more or less helped by my work ... who are now discouraged by every word I say – and all through this.[7]

He did, however, find time in that summer of 1866 to get involved with the Eyre Defence and Aid Fund. For some years he had been close to Thomas Carlyle, who believed that the non-white races had no rights. The previous autumn Governor Edward Eyre of Jamaica had brutally suppressed a revolt by the black population. 'Till the expiration of martial law, on 13th November, 608 persons were killed or executed, 34 were wounded, 600, including some women, were flogged, and a thousand dwellings, mostly flimsy leaf-built huts, were destroyed. Afterwards other culprits were tried and punished under the ordinary law of the colony – in some cases even by death'.[8]

The governor became a hero to white supremacists. When news of his behaviour reached England the Jamaica Committee, led by John Stuart Mill and T H Huxley, was set up and tried to have him prosecuted for murder. Carlyle was the loudest voice on the other side, and unfortunately Ruskin was drawn in. Not that he ever expressed really vicious racist views, like Carlyle's, but this man who had written movingly about the rights of the worker was still the man who had written in 1848 that rioting mobs should be gunned down. He also disappointed his admirers in the years of the American Civil War by failing to condemn slavery.

Meanwhile he was by no means content to wait for Rose's decision. He talked wildly about going to Ireland and camping outside her gate. When the family visited London he hung around the streets hoping to glimpse her and ran after a carriage as it crossed the Thames, thinking she was in it. Rose sent a message through Mrs Cowper-Temple, reminding him that the three years were not up. 'It is not likely I shall stop caring for him', she wrote, but '... nothing will make me change and give him his answer sooner'.[9] The stream of half-deranged letters went on. He blamed Rose's mother for poisoning her daughter's mind and making him miserable. In March 1868, when he was preparing to lecture in Dublin and of course hoping to see her, he turned his fury against Rose herself:

> She ought to know – or to be told – and convinced that she has done (through false teaching and her own constant dwelling on her own sensations instead of other people's) – an ineffably false and cruel deed – and that she has to repent of it – and undo it – as soon as may be. What the effect on my mind actually has been – if she cares to know it – is this – that my ideal of womanhood is destroyed – and irrevocably – that my love and tenderness to all men is greatly deadened – my own personal happiness in *any* love, destroyed – my faculties greatly injured – so that I cannot now command my thoughts except in a broken way – and such bitterness mixed with my love for her, that though it is greater than ever – and possesses me even more fatally than ever – it is partly poisoned love, mixed with distrust and scorn – and even if she comes to me now ... I should and shall – always say 'she has cost me too dear'.[10]

It is possible that similar letters went to Maria La Touche, who was now seriously worried. Rose did not attend his lecture but sent him two rose petals, with a note: 'I am forbidden by my mother and father to write to you, or to receive a letter'.[11] In the same month, May 1868, her mother wrote to Mrs Millais to ask her advice.

* * *

Mrs La Touche's letter (which is lost) must have briefly distracted Effie from her many worries, but could not have been welcome. It seemed that she would never be allowed to get away from Ruskin, that there would always be three people in her marriage.

When she read it, it all sounded horribly familiar. Once again Ruskin had got to know a little girl as a friend of her parents, established a trusting relationship and then proposed marriage before she was of age. She may also have remembered his interest in her younger sisters, Sophie and Alice.

It probably never occurred to her to ignore this letter; after all, the La Touches had a right to basic information. She explained that Ruskin had refused to consummate their marriage and that it had been annulled by a church court back in 1854. She was not qualified to say whether he was free to remarry, but she did say that if the banns were called she would publish the court's decision. This would prove that she had not been divorced for adultery. She also mentioned, probably as a tactful way of closing the correspondence, that she was about to have a baby.

Mrs La Touche wrote back to thank her for her 'kind, and *most true* letter'. She added that 'my daughter earnestly begs me to express to you her deep gratitude ... for your generosity in granting the information that has saved her, and us all, from so much misery. She has especially requested me to say this to you, from her'.[12] She got a copy of the judgment in the case of Ruskin v Ruskin and took it to a solicitor, who told her that no clergyman could marry a man whom he knew to be impotent. Here are some of the passages which she copied out:

> ... if it be discovered, after a man has been divorced on the plea of impotency, that he is not really impotent, the divorce is *ipso facto* annulled, and the former marriage is held good.
>
> In the case submitted, the parties would either contract a marriage that would be a nullity – or else, if the lady *should* have children, they would necessarily be illegitimate. For, if they be her husband's, he would be liable to an action for bigamy, and the second marriage would be nullified by that.[13]

Divorces and annulments were still so unusual that ordinary people did not know what was or was not permitted; even the experts did not always agree. The church court which freed Effie had lost its powers under the Matrimonial Causes Act of 1857. It seems that Ruskin could indeed have got married again, certainly in a civil ceremony, and other lawyers whom he consulted over the next few years would reassure him.

We have no reason to doubt that Rose felt grateful. If she had been told that marriage was not possible, she would not have to make a decision and perhaps could hold on to Ruskin as a friend. What she knew about sex repelled her and she said more than once that she did not want to get married. 'I cannot be to him what he wishes', she wrote, 'or return the vehement love which he gave me, which petrified and frightened me'.[14] Plenty of well-brought-up young women (Elizabeth Barrett Browning, Charlotte Brontë, Hunt's second wife Edith) were quite capable of defying their parents if they really wanted to marry someone. Rose would be twenty-one within a year, and could have married Ruskin at any time in the six years after that. She did not want to.

On 15th June 1868, Effie gave birth to her last child, Sophia, who is the baby in her father's painting *The Flood*. She must have hoped that she would hear no more about her former husband and that the young woman was 'saved'.

In the same month the La Touches learned that their elder daughter Emily, the mother of two small children, had died far away, on a sea voyage from Mauritius. For the next few years the family was in deep grief, and when Rose describes her unhappiness, or when she or her mother sound unreasonable, this should be borne in mind.

Ruskin returned from Ireland without seeing her, and by the end of the year she was again very ill, with 'the slightest agitation' causing 'attacks of violent pain'. Her mother told Mrs Cowper-Temple that the family did not want 'to receive any letter that ever so remotely recalls the idea of Mr Ruskin and the outrage he has offered us':

> When he came to Dublin last spring he talked familiarly of Rose in many quarters; bringing, indeed, ignominy upon himself, but much injurious notice and curiosity upon her; and of course the disgusting history of his past has been raised here, and Rose spoken of in connection with it – to the intense indignation of her family and friends. Mr Ruskin had not even the humanity, knowing as he did Rose's tendency to cerebral disease, to spare her the perplexity and misery of having to hear, over and over again, his appeals and those of his friends, against the right judgment of her natural protectors.[15]

It was damaging for an unmarried girl to be talked about. However,

Rose was now so unwell that the doctors hinted that perhaps she should not get married at all.

In the summer of 1869 Ruskin revisited Venice, for the first time since he had lived there with Effie. Holman Hunt bumped into him and they toured the galleries:

> The valet waited at the door with a hitherto unnoticed volume of the original edition of *Modern Painters*. Ruskin beckoned him, and opening the book at the passage already marked, he began deliberately and without pause to read to the end of it ... When Ruskin had closed the book, he began: 'No, there is no exaggeration or bombast such as there might have been, the words are all justified, and they describe very faithfully the character of the picture, I am well content', and he gave the volume back to the man.[16]

Ruskin told Hunt that he now believed 'that there is no Eternal Father to whom we can look up, that man has no helper but himself'.[17] He could get very angry with Rose for thinking that she knew more than he did:

> If our faiths are to be reconciled, it seems to me quite as reasonable to expect that an Irish girl of 19, who cannot spell – reads nothing but hymn-books and novels – and enjoys nothing so much as playing with her dog, should be brought finally into the faith of a man whom Carlyle and Froude call their friend, and whom many very noble persons call their teacher, as that he should be brought into hers.[18]

Effie had never preached at him. She was religious, and had told him that he ought to take the Bible on trust, but it had not been a serious problem when they were together. Millais usually stayed at home and smoked his pipe on Sundays while she was in church. Both of them were fairly 'normal' and reasonable people for whom Christianity meant, primarily, decent behaviour; they could not have comprehended the agonies Rose caused herself and others in the name of her faith.

Yet Ruskin could not get the Irish girl out of his mind. In January 1870 he came face to face with her in the Royal Academy, which had moved from Trafalgar Square to its present home in Burlington House, and she cut him. She was now twenty-two, free to meet and marry whoever she liked. In February the unstable young woman was writing that she loved him, but 'it seems to be God's will that we should be separated'.[19] He consulted lawyers. He told Rose that 'I am in Law unmarried and in my conduct to my wife – I boldly say and believe – guiltless – though foolish'.[20] He said other self-justifying things to the Cowper-Temples and the novelist George MacDonald about his long-ago marriage. According to MacDonald's son:

> 'Was it true that you were incapable?' my father asked, pointblank.
> Ruskin laughed merrily and denied it unconditionally.
> 'Then why', pursued my father, 'did you not defend yourself?'
> 'Do you think, if she wanted to be rid of me, I would put any obstacle in her way? I never loved Euphie before I married her; but I hoped I might and ought to, if only for her beauty'. Then he proceeded to explain his deplorable foolishness; how, over-persuaded by his parents, he proposed to a girl whom he only admired. Curiously ignorant, he presumed that the necessary love would follow marriage, as he had been assured it would. But he was not the man to claim intimate relations, to him most sacred, without the only justification for them, namely that of loving the woman beyond anything in heaven or earth.[21]

Ruskin's parents were no longer in a position to say that, in fact, they had never wanted this marriage. Only his former wife knew whether he was telling the truth.

Effie and her husband were staying at Bowerswell in October 1870 when they were again dragged into Ruskin's affairs. Millais had sometimes cursed him when among close friends in the 1850s, but they had long since decided that it was more dignified to say nothing. He was near the top of his profession; they were happy together and had a family of healthy children aged between fourteen and two; Ruskin was no longer attacking his work. Yet it seemed to him that his wife could not forget the past, or would not be allowed to forget.

At the beginning of the month Mr La Touche wrote to him and he replied, 'I am distressed to hear from you that you are again troubled concerning your daughter. My wife was six years beside Mr Ruskin and he never so much as made an attempt to make her his wife'.[22] He told him that the legal information was at Doctors' Commons and that he would gladly answer any questions. Perhaps he did not mention it to Effie, because he knew how much it upset her, but a few days later Maria La Touche wrote to her direct.

The La Touches believed what their lawyer had told them. The great fear was that if Ruskin got their daughter pregnant (and who could say he would not?) it would become clear that he was not, after all, impotent. In that case the marriage could be struck down, his union with Effie re-established, Rose's reputation destroyed and any child she might have illegitimate. The Millais children would also become illegitimate because their mother would still be Ruskin's legal wife.

Mrs La Touche's letter read:

Dear Madam,

I trust you will excuse my writing to you once more on a subject which must be distressing to you; but you were so kind to me and mine two years ago, that I cannot help writing to you again on the recurrence of the danger from which I then believed your kindness had delivered us – Mr Millais kindly answered a letter from my husband on the subject; but what we now want, is a contradiction of the statements Mr Ruskin is now making to Mr Cowper Temple, who with his wife, has great influence over my daughter – and is using that influence eagerly, to justify Mr Ruskin in all things, and persuade my unhappy child that she is bound to reward his love and constancy, by at least hearing his defence and allowing him to renew his addresses – I think we owe it to you, to inform you of what is going on, that you may be at liberty to take whatever measures you think proper. I do this because on the 18th of May 1868 you wrote to me, 'If the Banns of Marriage are proclaimed, I shall feel obliged in justice to my own character to give it (the Decree) publicity'.

I need hardly say that this appears to me perfectly right –

I ought to tell you what Mr Ruskin's line of defence is – I trust you will not think me impertinent, but I am so anxious that you should know the truth, and *crush*, if it can be done, the falsehoods he is spreading –

He wholly denies the 'impotence' stated in the Decree; and he accounts for the word being there, by the fact which he fully admits, that he lived with you 'as with a sister' for six years – He states that you were never his wife; that no love on either side preceded or accompanied the 'marriage' which was arranged for quite other reasons between his family and yours – that your tastes and his were from the beginning quite incompatible; that he never loved you, and that *therefore* he respected you too much to be anything but a protector and companion to you – that he made every possible effort to make you happy, and that failing in doing so, and finding you desired your liberty, he resolved to retire altogether, make no reply to the citation, and no resistance to any measure which the law demanded in order to secure your freedom and happiness at the cost of his own reputation.

This story appears to Mr Cowper Temple not only creditable but extremely *credible* – it cannot of course be made *intelligible* to my daughter who is singularly innocent and pure-minded, but the Cowper Temples urge upon her that his past history is all *perfectly beautiful,* pure and heroic, and that his love is a glory to any woman – Any imaginative girl's head would be completely turned by the strain in which they speak and write to her.

We have secured the opinion of an eminent Lawyer, who says, that if Mr R. can prove that he is not 'impotent' it may be in his power to set aside the decree, and contract a legal marriage –

All that my daughter seems to wish is to be allowed friendship and correspondence with him; but we forbid this, on the ground that his seeking her in marriage was an outrage and an insult; and also on the ground, that such a friendship would be used by him with a view to marriage: to which we can *never* consent.

I think a wholesome reaction would be produced in my daughter's mind (for she would believe your evidence) if you could write me a few lines to contradict as strongly as you can, these statements of his –

That there was no profession or idea of Love when his marriage with you was arranged –

That he tried in all things to make you happy and 'behaved towards you in a pure, creditable and honourable manner'.

That he has every physical and moral quality for making a wife supremely happy, if only her disposition and tastes suited him – as he has persuaded my daughter is the case with her, and *her alone* of all women that ever lived –

I am convinced he made the same professions to you, and would treat her exactly as he treated you. From your knowledge of him, do you not also think so?

Forgive this long and very disagreeable letter; and with thanks for past kindness believe me dear Madam

Sincerely yours

Maria La Touche

Mr R. professes a desire that the 'fiercest light' may be thrown on his past history –.[23]

This letter seems to have had a terrible effect on Effie. It was not just that she was having to relive an agonising chapter in her life; it also seemed possible that her name might again be dragged through the courts, her marriage legally cancelled and her children pronounced illegitimate. For all she knew, Ruskin might have been impotent only with her. She was forty-two now and had lost her looks. She must often have compared herself with the lovely young women whom her husband and others painted, and felt most desperately insecure.

Millais was not worried about the legal position. He was fairly sure that Ruskin would never have any children. But it made him furiously protective of Effie and his next letter to Rose's father, so different from his usual affable tone, shows that both of them were seriously upset:

Dear Sir,

I have read a letter from Mrs La Touche to my wife and with every consideration for your domestic happiness I must beg that she is *not again* asked to answer the aspersions of Mr Ruskin. If your Daughter believes that others can be more interested in her welfare than her parents and that their advice is not sufficient in a matter so dear to her and to them, of what avail is it my wife reiterating a denial of Mr Ruskin's present statements – How do you suppose can I submit to my wife going at this hour through the indelicate inquiry necessary 'that the fiercest light may be thrown on his past History' –

The facts are known to the world, solemnly sworn to in God's House, and Mr R is open to assert what he pleases to the few credulous admirers as far as we are concerned, and according to the eminent lawyer you have consulted, he has the matter in his own hands as regards his ability to set aside the decree and contract marriage. Mr R's conduct was simply infamous and to this day my wife suffers from the suppressed misery she endured with him. She is now a happy woman with a lovely family, and every blessing and success has accompanied our marriage.

Yours etc
JEM

PS. Will Mr R now submit to a medical examination?[24]

Effie wanted to write directly to Rose, but Millais begged her not to. She did, however, answer Mrs La Touche and made a copy of the letter, which was discovered by her grandson in the 1940s and has been interpreted as an act of revenge against Ruskin. If you think it unkind (which I do not), recollect that it was written in a state of extreme distress and that Ruskin had been saying things about their marriage which she knew to be untrue:

Dear Mrs La Touche,

I have received your kind letter and I am truly distressed that you should again be in such trouble about your Daughter. Mr Millais is extremely averse to my being brought into contact even by correspondence with your Daughter who if she is still under the mischievous influence of Mr Ruskin and his friends will not think differently whatever I say. If your Daughter can for one moment believe such a statement as his that he should marry a young girl of 19 without professions of the most devoted kind, not only then but beginning years before and influencing my mind and overlooking my education for years from a much earlier period, how can any words of mine undeceive her? He pursued exactly the same course with me as with her, he always took the tone of his love and adoration being higher and above that of ordinary mortals, and immediately after the ceremony proceeded to inform me that I was not his wife and that he did not intend to marry me. He afterwards excused himself from doing so by saying that I had an internal disease. His Father tried to induce him to believe me insane and his whole conduct was simply as monstrous as his present statements are perfect falsehoods. Our marriage was *never arranged* by anybody. There was no inducement but the utmost determination on his part to marry me. Prior to his professions to me he had been devoted to a Spanish Lady and broke a blood vessel from disappointment that he didn't get her. I do not think she wished it but religion was given as the obstacle, but he had quite got over that – and on our visiting her years after he had no feeling about her then or before our marriage. Now that I am a married woman and happy with a family I think his conduct can only be excused on the score of madness as his wickedness in trying his dreadful influence over your Daughter is terrible to think of. I can easily understand the hold he has acquired as it was exactly the same over myself. His conduct to me was impure in the highest degree, discreditable and so dishonourable that I submitted to it for years not knowing what else to do, although I would often have been

140

thankful to have run away and envied the people sweeping the crossings. His mind is most inhuman; all that sympathy which he expects and gets from the female mind it is impossible for him to return excepting upon artistic subjects which have nothing to do with domestic Life. It is a perfect falsehood to say that I did not agree with his pursuits – No one more so. He not only gave me the opportunity but the means of education when abroad both with himself and others in acquiring knowledge in painting, sculpture, architecture, every branch of the fine arts, a slight knowledge of Latin, Greek and we read together the works of the ancients and as I am particularly fond of History everything he wanted for his writing of this kind. From his peculiar nature he is utterly incapable of making a woman happy. He is quite unnatural and in that one thing all the rest is embraced. He always pretended to me to the last that he was the purest and holiest of men and has peculiar influence over a young mind in making himself believed. But I do think your Daughter surely cannot put aside the evidence given by the laws of her country sanctioned by her own Church. I had no idea I could get away up to within a month of leaving him which I did under the care of my parents and *entirely* without his knowledge by the advice of lawyers. So far from his conniving at my leaving him, it was a great shock to them all and this statement of his is also entirely *false*. He once years before offered me £800 a year to allow him to retire into a Monastery and retain his name. That I declined. He was then under the influence of [Cardinal] Manning.

I think if your Daughter went through the ceremony with him that her health would give way after a time and she would be submitted to the same kind of treatment as I was. It is very painful for me to write all this and be again obliged to recall all these years of distress and suffering which I nearly died of and has hurt me even now dreadfully and my nervous system was so shaken that I never will recover that again. But I hope that your Daughter may be saved and come to see things in a different light and Believe me dear Mrs La Touche

Yours very sincerely
Effie C. Millais[25]

Mrs La Touche now realised that she had pushed too hard. She wrote back to Effie apologising for causing her pain, and saying 'I do believe that my child is now *quite* saved – She never would believe any evidence *but yours* … She has given a voluntary promise to her father, that she will have no more to say to Mr R – and we have a promise from her friends and his, never again to name him to her – by her own special wish'.[26]

But Rose was not saved. Over the next four and a half years many things undermined her physical and mental health – grief for her sister, eating difficulties, perhaps an organic disease, worries about how a Christian ought to live. In a heartbreaking letter to George MacDonald she wrote, 'It pained me and cost me more thoughts than my head could bear to find a poor family … living near here, father, mother and ten children really very *very* poor, so poor the newest baby whom the Mother was too ill to nurse could be fed on nothing better than bread and water, – and then to come down to dessert here and find forced strawberries and cream finishing up a "sumptuous repast".'[27] It should be said that John La Touche had done all he could to help victims of the Irish famine in the 1840s, but any sensitive person in the circumstances might have found it hard to eat.

She was under pressure from several directions. Her parents wanted her to forget Ruskin; her religion told her that he was quite possibly one of the damned. At the same time he was keeping up a relentless, though intermittent stream of appeals to meet her, and his friends surely made her feel that she was being unkind to a great man. The Cowper-Temples, who really should have kept out of it, again became involved, so did his cousin Joan and the MacDonald family. Many people, then and now, think that she treated Ruskin badly. Certainly her behaviour was inconsistent.

In 1871 (the year his mother died) Ruskin again told her that he had consulted lawyers and was free to marry. Her response was hostile, and for a while he tried to get over her. But in the summer of 1872 they met at the homes of friends. Except for the brief encounter at the Royal Academy, they had not been in the same room for over six years. The MacDonalds' teenage son Greville was amazed that she was still alive – 'her dinner once consisted of three green peas, and, the very next day, of one strawberry and half an Osborne biscuit'.[28] They were reconciled, then she turned violently against him. Ruskin thought she was mad, and his own behaviour became increasingly strange. He did not see her again until October 1874, by which time she was obviously dying. Her parents had stopped trying to keep them apart and they met several times in London, but she made him promise that he would never let her get between him and God. Rose died on 25th May 1875 in a Dublin nursing home, aged twenty-seven. According to Ruskin, who is not always trustworthy, she was out of her mind.

Her death certificate was lost when the Public Records Office of Ireland was destroyed by fire in 1922, so we cannot know exactly what killed her. According to some people at Harristown she had tuberculosis. Accounts of her bright colour and extreme thinness seem to confirm this, but tubercular patients do not usually become insane. There is no doubt that for years she had been refusing to eat normally and may well have been a victim of anorexia. She had also been having nervous breakdowns since the age of thirteen.

Was she, or was Effie, to blame for the unhappiness of Ruskin's middle years? He himself had no doubt that the 'poor girl' was 'the victim of her mother and that *accursed woman of Perth*.[29] Others had and have more sympathy for him than for her. But when he met Rose he was an adult; she was a girl of ten and then a fragile young woman. It seems unlikely that they could ever have had a happy marriage, if only because their religious views never could have been reconciled. Effie's letters did not poison her mind, as he alleged. It was Ruskin's own behaviour which made her angry – his obsessive pursuit, which 'petrified and frightened' her, his refusal to believe in her God. In September 1870 he wrote some letters to her aunt, a Miss Price of Tunbridge Wells, which were shown to Rose and upset her deeply. We do not know what was in them, but it has been conjectured that they were about sex.

They never spent very much time together, except when she was a child and when she was dying. If Ruskin had ever actually lived with her, his feelings might have cooled. Once she was dead, of course, she became a sacred figure and he would be obsessed by her for ever afterwards.

Perhaps there was no way to save Rose. Yet it is just possible that her life might have turned out differently if Ruskin had simply offered her steady affection. 'If it could have been so that I could have kept the *friend* who has brought such pain and suffering and torture and division among so many hearts – if there had never been anything but friendship between us – how much might have been spared'.[30]

And Effie? When she replied to Mrs La Touche the second time, was it an act of spite? Her letter 'is one for which Ruskin lovers find it hard to forgive her';[31] however, Ruskin lovers had not been married to him.

If she had wanted revenge, she could have spent the last fifteen years telling her story in detail to everyone she knew. Today, she would have been invited to tell the newspapers. In fact she and Millais were discreet; even his great friend Holman Hunt knew so little that he believed her first marriage had been arranged by the old Ruskins.[32] During that marriage she spoke to no one about its circumstances, and then after six years only to her family, close friends and lawyers. Afterwards she did not go around abusing Ruskin; on the contrary, she never mentioned him. She did not approach Mrs La Touche; Mrs La Touche approached her. Having been asked, she had either to tell the truth as she saw it or refuse to reply.

By that time she was a mother of daughters herself. She vividly remembered her misery as Ruskin's wife and could not have wanted another young woman to suffer it. Indeed, she identified with her, remembering that 'he pursued exactly the same course with me as with her'. Assuming such a marriage was legal, Rose would not have been able to 'get on with her life' if it did not 'work out'. Had he managed to make love to her even once, she would have been tied to an unstable man for as long as they both lived. Effie certainly could have remained silent, as Millais wanted. But it was her nature to be friendly and obliging, and it is hard to see how she could have given any other advice.

If she had seen the letters Ruskin was writing at around this time, she would have felt even more convinced that he was not quite sane. She might also have reflected that she and Millais had been just as unhappy in 1853 and 1854, but had got through it. However, as he had predicted, there were 'dark hours in the distance' for them both.

11

Modern Painters
1870–78

'Be just, Chettam,' said the easy, large-lipped Rector, who objected to all this
unnecessary discomfort. 'Mrs Casaubon may be acting imprudently ... But I
think you should not condemn it as a wrong action, in the strict sense of
the word.'

'Yes, I do,' answered Sir James. 'I think that Dorothea commits a wrong
action in marrying Ladislaw.'

'My dear fellow, we are rather apt to consider an act wrong because it is
unpleasant to us,' said the Rector, quietly.

Middlemarch, Chapter 84

1870 was the year of the Franco-Prussian war and the year that Millais'
father died (his remarkable mother had died six years earlier). 'A fine
old gentleman', his grandson called him, 'who had many friends and
never an enemy'.[1] Both parents were pleasant and easy-going people who
had never caused any problems for their daughter-in-law.

Around this time Millais was preparing two pictures for the Summer
Exhibition. *The Marchioness of Huntly* is a full-length portrait of an
ordinary young woman, Amy Cunliffe-Brooks, who was about to marry
into the aristocracy. Her father paid him the huge sum of two thousand
guineas, and the picture is beautifully done, but uninteresting. This
marked the beginning of his career as a fashionable portrait painter;
many people who could afford it wanted to be immortalised by the man
who, now Turner was dead, was the greatest living English artist.

The Boyhood of Raleigh is one of the most famous and brilliant Victorian
story-pictures. The background was painted at Budleigh Salterton on the
Devon coast and the two children were posed by his sons Everett and
George, now aged thirteen and twelve. Everett is Raleigh, the intense-
looking dark boy who will become a famous explorer; George is his

fair-haired companion. The boys had been sent to prep school, where Everett, the firstborn, got a disappointing report. He was said in 1868 to be lazy and disobedient and this frightened his father, who remembered how hard he had worked at the same age. George, however, was an excellent student.

On 9th June 1870 Dickens died and Millais, who had long since forgiven his attack on *The Carpenter's Shop*, made a striking black and white drawing of his bandaged head. It was greatly valued by his daughter Kate, who was still married, not very happily, to Charles Collins and had become a good friend.

In late summer the family went as usual to Bowerswell, where they had the distressing exchange of letters with Mr and Mrs La Touche. On the way back Millais conceived what would become his first major landscape, *Chill October*. It shows a backwater of the Tay, 'the haunt of duck and moorhen and other aquatic birds',[2] near the railway line between Perth and Dundee. There are no figures, just a grey sky, silvery-grey water, willows, reeds and a few birds in flight. He painted it on a narrow strip of land between the tide and trains, in wretched weather. Effie had been encouraging him to do this and over the next two decades he would paint some other superb Scottish landscapes when he could find time. He is not usually thought of as a landscape artist but the effect of these pictures, especially when seen in one room, is overwhelming.

Many of his friends 'were at a loss to understand what I saw to paint in such a scene',[3] but Vincent Van Gogh was impressed. He saw it a few years later while he was working in England and it haunted him for the rest of his short life. 'Once I met the painter Millais on the street in London', he wrote, 'just after I had been lucky enough to see several of his pictures. And that noble figure reminded me of John Halifax ... not the least beautiful of his pictures is an autumn landscape, "Chill October"'.[4] (John Halifax is the upright hero of Dinah Craik's novel *John Halifax, Gentleman*.) One imagines the uncouth young man accosting the famous R A, and Millais listening courteously. Victorian and Impressionist, both trying to push the boundaries of art, briefly came face to face.

In the summer of 1871 Effie took the fifteen-year-old Everett, who presumably was no longer in disgrace, to Paris. She left her husband and younger children behind. Millais was overwhelmed with work as usual, and was also deeply involved with a charity which helped the widows and orphaned children of artists. He had never forgotten Walter Deverell and another friend, John Leech, who had died young leaving helpless dependants. 'Millais is not only a leading man on the Artists' Benevolent Fund', wrote William Rossetti, 'but I have more than once been assured that he is himself extremely liberal in such matters'.[5] A dinner he organised that year raised £16,000.

By one account, Effie had been very unwell, but she loved travelling, which Millais did not. In 1865, several months after the birth of her seventh child, she had dragged him on a tour through Europe where they were introduced to Franz Liszt; Effie immediately got into conversation with him, probably in German, while Millais could only look on. Just as she had been eager to see Venice after the siege of 1849, she now wanted to see France in the aftermath of the war. She took the young boy around some battlefields, probably telling him stories from history. It turned out to be a dreadful mistake.

The war had released all kinds of germs. Once they were back in the Grand Hotel in Paris, Everett was diagnosed with smallpox. While Millais rushed round London trying to get a visa, Effie nursed her son around the clock. A letter to her brother George begins calmly but soon becomes almost a stream of consciousness:

> ... we are shut away from all the house and don't speak to a soul the servants are not allowed to come in and put Grocerys down in the passages weather fine and pure windows all open ... Poor Evie is a sad object at present he is not so delirious now so feels all his sores and does not know what it is his hands and face are one mass & eyes closed he has crises every now and then & it is dreadful as I am so afraid of his tearing his face the state he is in is better not to describe but I have lost all fear of the complaint and being obliged to do everything about him I don't mind it at all but the nights are dreadful especially last night I had to sing every conceivable thing and tell stories & he swearing frightfully every crisis & then suffering no sleep for us at all for him snatches 4 to 9, he is sleeping now after my singing him to sleep like an infant ... everyone dreads the disease so much.[6]

Everyone, it seems, except Effie, who refused to let the manager turn them out. Her friends in Paris (she seems to have had friends everywhere) threatened that if he did they would inform the papers and frighten English tourists away.

147

On the same day she wrote to Millais, 'Dearest Everett, Many thanks for your letters and saying you want to come but although of course I should like very much to see you I would dread you coming into contact with Evie'.[7] By the next day she may have snatched a few hours' sleep and told him 'it is far better for you not to expose yourself as we are getting on well'.[8] She wrote to her father that the teenager was recovering and would not be pockmarked. He was soon able to write letters himself, and she was soon making plans for the rest of the family and worrying that her mother was getting too old to look after the children at Bowerswell. She was seldom off duty, and, at forty-three, she found she was pregnant again.

In the same month, July 1871, Ruskin too was seriously ill at Matlock, vomiting repeatedly; for a while it was thought he might die. During his worst times he had dreamed he would get better if he could lie down in Coniston Water, and coincidentally soon afterwards he was offered a little estate called Brantwood, on the east bank of the lake. At the time it was a cottage with a few acres of rocky land, not the spacious family home it would become. He had several contacts in the north of England and wanted a base away from London. Without inspecting it, he paid £1500 for the house and grounds, which had wonderful views. On 5th December old Mrs Ruskin died, aged ninety. She had given him a hard time during the last few years, and he admitted that he had never loved her. The house at Denmark Hill was closed, and from then on he divided his time between Coniston, Oxford (where he had been appointed Slade Professor of Fine Art) and Herne Hill.

By the early 1870s Effie may have thought that the storms in her personal life were over. She had eight children, all good-looking and healthy. Her sisters had both married, Sophie in 1873 and Alice in 1874. A great many friends – writers, artists and interesting people of all sorts – flocked to their house in Cromwell Place.

Happy families are all alike. We know less about Effie's time with Millais than her much shorter time with Ruskin because there were no serious quarrels or crises, and because their children and friends would not anyway have thought it right to discuss her. There are several anecdotes about him, very few about her. The 'sacred doors of home ... closed upon her married life', to quote Mrs Gaskell.[9] A respectable woman did not get herself talked about, and in Effie's case there were particular reasons for being discreet. A pupil of Millais' called her 'his kind and hospitable wife'.[10] We know that they both loved concerts, inviting musicians to play at their home on Sundays, and that she translated when he met foreigners. We hear of her sending flowers to the elderly Landseer on his birthday, persuading Shelley's friend Edward Trelawny to pose as the sailor in *The North-West Passage*, waiting at table when Tennyson came to dinner because he objected to servants. Not many interesting letters survive.

Although there were no more live babies after 1868, Effie's health was still giving cause for concern. In February 1872 Millais told William Rossetti 'that his wife has been a great invalid for about a year and a half past, very seldom leaving the house; the illness, it seems, is in some way connected with her last confinement'.[11] It seems that she was struggling with a difficult pregnancy as in March her baby, a boy, was born dead. Millais would have been feeling wretched, and probably guilty.

In the next year he painted a portrait of his wife, which was hung in their morning-room. She is wearing crimson and holding the *Cornhill Magazine* and, according to one critic, 'the picture well communicates the independence, scepticism and insouciance evident in her letters'.[12] Comparing Millais' paintings of famous Victorians with their photographs we see that he was uncannily good at catching a likeness, so we may be fairly sure that this is how Effie looked at forty-five. By that time she had given birth to eight children, worked hard, worried desperately and often been ill. She suffered throughout her life from insomnia. It is an interesting face, but no longer that of a young woman. 'A strong, sad likeness',[13] says another critic. If you compare it with his portrait of the beautiful Lillie Langtry, which hung beside it in the Tate Britain Exhibition of 2007–8, the contrast is harsh.

Yet there was little doubt that they were a happy couple. Many Victorians, as they knew, had unorthodox private lives. Dickens and Irving were both separated from their wives and deeply involved elsewhere. Wilkie Collins divided his time between two women, neither of whom he married, and had a secret family. Gladstone did not commit adultery but was much mocked for his interest in prostitutes, and had an inappropriate relationship with a woman called Laura Thistlethwayte. Frith, the painter of *Derby Day*, had twelve children by his wife and seven by his mistress; the aged George Cruikshank also supported two households. Ford Madox Brown did not marry his second wife Emma until two years after their daughter was born. Rossetti was notoriously involved with William Morris's wife; Burne-Jones had a very public affair which dragged on for years and caused his wife great pain. William Bell Scott lived in a *ménage à trois*, Whistler had several liaisons before his late marriage and at least three illegitimate children. Compared to them all, Mr and Mrs Millais appeared stodgily respectable. Yet there was still a blot on Effie's name.

'Everyone' knew, of course, that she had been married to Ruskin and people sometimes referred to her as 'Mrs R, I mean Mrs M'. As the wife of a distinguished man, she could have expected to be presented to Queen Victoria, and indeed had been, back in 1850. Their eldest, and very pretty, daughter Euphemia was coming up to sixteen; in a few years she and her sisters would be thinking about marriage. It was the first duty of a Victorian matron to take them around, and in order to be admitted to the 'best' places, she needed the Queen's approval. In 1874, the Duchess of Sutherland tried to get her into a reception. She was unsuccessful. Victoria let it be known that she would not receive any lady who had been divorced.

The woman who gave her name to the Victorian age had a commonplace mind, strong opinions and was a natural stirrer-up of trouble. Early in her reign she had spread a rumour that an unmarried lady-in-waiting was pregnant when in fact the poor woman was dying of cancer. Everyone in her orbit, from Prime Ministers to her younger children, who were not allowed to leave her side, was expected to be constantly on call. She believed, apparently, that Millais had seduced Ruskin's wife (this is why he was not asked to paint her), and, having lost a beloved husband herself, was unlikely to feel much sympathy for a woman who had two husbands living. Various people tried to change her mind and failed.

When Effie was informed she wrote back:

I was distressed and shocked beyond measure on reading your kind letter last night. I am satisfied that Her Majesty would not do an act of injustice to any of her subjects, and would not if correctly informed of my case have denied me the privilege of presentation. I have never been divorced nor did I divorce Mr Ruskin. By the ecclesiastical law of England, the church of which Her Majesty is the head, and the civil law of the country I was given my freedom, the ceremony of marriage through which I had passed being declared null and void by the Bishop of Winchester ... His sentence can be seen any day in Doctors Commons which declared me stainless and blameless and free to contract marriage as a spinster, and I was married to Mr Millais more than a year later.[14]

Always polite, she added, 'I cannot tell you how it distresses me having put you in so unpleasant a position'. It was yet another reminder that, although the events were twenty years old, her first marriage had not been forgotten. Indeed, the fact that she and Millais had not met for a year after the annulment, and had then got married, suggested that they had known each other very well while she was still Mrs Ruskin. It was galling, when both of them had tried so hard to keep the rules.

Millais was furious, but asked the Duchess to take no more trouble:

Had Her Majesty permitted my wife to pass before she could not have done it, the indignity has completely upset her. One thing shall certainly be known and proved and that is she was pure, and entirely free from a shadow of misconduct in all that concerns her freedom ... *Injustice to my wife is not defensible on the score of her misfortune proving an awkward precedent.* Think what the Queen's prohibition carries with it – Every one, even to her own children, will conclude there must be something against her character, because she may not be presented there again. If she is not considered worthy of passing before Her Majesty, how is she to mix in the society in which we move – to go ... where the Queen may be? The present state of things is impossible.[15]

We do not know when the children found out about their mother's past. It could not be concealed; Ruskin was too famous, and there was a danger that they might hear about it first from school friends. How was it to be explained to teenage boys and girls in a famously prudish age? Perhaps something was said along the lines of, 'Your mother went through a form of marriage with Mr Ruskin, a long time ago. He is a very strange man who treated her cruelly and refused to have children. The Church courts decided that they had never really been married. She has done nothing wrong'. None of them recorded their feelings, and the family would not talk about it for two generations.

It ended in Millais taking his daughters to parties without Effie. She was not a social outcast, like George Eliot, and no one doubted that her marriage was legal. But it was painful to know that her husband could go to places where she could not, and that people were still sniggering behind her back.

*   *   *

151

After his wife Fanny died, Holman Hunt returned to England with their baby, Cyril, and left him with the Waugh family before going abroad again. Fanny's youngest sister, Edith, had fallen in love with him (he was a good-looking and distinguished man). But it seemed that nothing could be done, because in Britain a man was not allowed to marry his dead wife's sister. After an agonizing delay, Hunt and Edith went to Switzerland in 1875 and got married, an act which roused extraordinary hostility. Millais and Effie of course remained on good terms with them but their families broke off contact. Edith's sister, who was married to Thomas Woolner, never spoke to her again, and Woolner also turned against his wife's family and his old friends, telling people that Millais and Hunt had had an illegal homosexual relationship in their Pre-Raphaelite days. Hunt, no friend to gay rights, was furious; Millais could not believe it.

This marriage turned out well; the Hunts had a son and daughter and lived happily together until his death in 1910. He campaigned vigorously against the Deceased Wife's Sister Act, and saw it repealed in his eightieth year. Other friends managed to get around the conventions and find their own way to happiness. Kate Dickens had married Wilkie Collins' brother Charles when she was twenty, probably to get away from home. He was several years older and an invalid, and although they were fond of each other, it was hinted that he was another of the men who should not have got married. Kate seemed restless and got herself talked about. Five months after Collins died, in 1873, she quietly married the artist Carlo Perugini in a registry office; the church ceremony followed after her official year of mourning. But she had left it too late to have a family, and her only child died as a baby.

Again, Millais and Effie were supportive. The Peruginis were close friends, lived nearby and went on holiday with them in Scotland. Millais encouraged Kate, who was a member of the Society of Lady Artists, to develop her talent. He also did a striking picture of her, wearing black, as a late wedding present. 'His friendship was my constant pleasure, and at times my greatest comfort', she wrote.[16]

Another interesting woman whom he painted was the artist Louise Jopling. Born in 1843, she had married a compulsive gambler when she was only seventeen; after that marriage broke up she supported her children by book illustration. Her first husband died and soon afterwards she married Millais' friend Joseph Jopling, a less successful painter than herself. Millais was the godfather of their son and his superb portrait was a christening present in 1879. He tried in 1880 to get her into the Academy, but was unsuccessful; Effie sent her flowers when her son was gravely ill. Louise founded a professional art school for women and believed that they should have the vote, as did Kate. We know that Effie was also interested in 'the woman question'.

But although these and other portraits are remarkable, some people were still saying that Millais had not fulfilled his early promise. One of them was the novelist Margaret Oliphant, who wrote for *Blackwood's Magazine*. She was Effie's exact contemporary, having been born in Scotland a month before her, and they would eventually die in the same year. She too had been married to an artist, though an unsuccessful one, and knew what she was talking about. Twenty years ago, she wrote in 1875, she and her friends had thought of Millais as a 'glorious young revolutionary'.[17] Now 'the pre-Raphaelites have gone out like a sputtering taper', and he was painting nothing as good as the *Huguenot* or the *Order of Release*.

Look at Mr Millais now; he could once touch those higher strings which vibrate through the very soul ... Who does not remember the tenderness of love in that worn, blue-bearded Huguenot, grieved only to disappoint the poor girl's fond expedient of anguish, not to risk his life; and that hard self-repression of the weary wife, all worn with the labour of her mission, thrusting her order of release into the jailer's face, almost insolent in intense self-restraint of that love, and joy, and woe, which were ready to burst out in passionate floods if but the danger were over? Look at him now ... And this is all that his genius has come to.[18]

Nevertheless, the portraits were bringing in a steady income. In the first months of 1877 the family moved to 2 Palace Gate, a few minutes' walk away from Kensington Gardens. The house, designed by Philip Hardwick and now the home of the Zambian High Commission, is a very good one, although it has no garden and is not the Renaissance palace it has sometimes been called. Visitors can still see its fine curving staircase and the white marble columns in the hall. There was a spacious studio, white walls that made the most of the light, a marble fountain and dance floor. The Millais had troops of friends and a happy relationship with their children. All they had to worry about, it seemed, was Effie's intermittent poor health, and the Queen's coldness, and perhaps the reviews.

*   *   *

On 1st May 1877 the Grosvenor Gallery opened in New Bond Street. It was owned by Sir Coutts Lindsay, a rich amateur who wanted to make space for the artists he admired, including those who did not belong to the Academy. Millais had several pictures in the inaugural exhibition; so did Burne-Jones and so did the maverick forty-three-year-old American genius who had been based in London since 1859, James Abbott McNeill Whistler.

Among those who looked in was Ruskin, on a brief visit to London; he was now spending more and more time abroad or in the Lake District. He had not been very well or happy since Rose died. Indeed he thought it had destroyed half his public usefulness, but he kept himself busy, publishing a newsletter, *Fors Clavigera*, which was addressed to the working men of England and gave his views on whatever he happened to be interested in at the time. He did not write much art criticism these days, but he was annoyed by Whistler's new painting, *Nocturne in Black and Gold: the Falling Rocket*. This shows a night scene in London, with some vaguely defined trees, the river, and a shower of gold sparks exploding against a black sky. Whistler had lived in Paris and his work has much in common with the early Impressionists – and the late Turner. But Ruskin, Turner's champion, could not see it.

He decided to review the exhibition in the next *Fors Clavigera*. He praised Millais, praised Burne-Jones, but said that *The Falling Rocket* was disgraceful:

> For Mr Whistler's own sake, no less than for the protection of the purchaser, Sir Coutts Lindsay ought not to have admitted works into the gallery in which the ill-educated conceit of the artist so nearly approached the aspect of wilful imposture. I have seen, and heard, much of Cockney impudence before now; but never expected to hear a coxcomb ask two hundred guineas for flinging a pot of paint in the public's face.[19]

This of course is how many people react to modern art, and most artists were well used to the rudeness of critics. Turner had ignored it, Millais and the Pre-Raphaelites had endured it, but Whistler was not that sort of man. To use a twenty-first century idiom, sensible people did not mess with him. Though charming and sophisticated, Whistler was a tough character who had spent three years at West Point Military Academy and been expelled from his club for pushing his brother-in-law through a window. He sued Ruskin for libel.

The case did not come to court for a year and a half, and during that time Ruskin suffered a total collapse. He did not admit to worrying about Whistler. But in February 1878, writing before dawn in his study, he looked out at the grey mist over Coniston Fells and felt desolate, thinking of Turner, his father, and Rose. A week later he sent a crazy letter to George MacDonald saying that he and Rose had finally got married. After that he became temporarily insane.

Although he recovered quite quickly, his doctors would not let him attend the trial, which was fixed for November. It caused huge interest, and not only in the art world. The many painters whom he had attacked must have gloated; Ruskin had stuck his tusk in once too often. A comedy, *The Grasshopper*, whose hero is an 'artist of the future' resembling Whistler, was put on the London stage. Eminent artists and critics lined up to give their views on both sides.

Obviously, Millais could not get involved. He would not have wished to do so anyway, as he hated unpleasantness and indeed may well have agreed with Ruskin; he believed that Whistler was extraordinarily talented but had 'never learnt the grammar of his Art'.[20] He and Effie had certainly seen *The Falling Rocket* and must have looked forward to the case with some interest. By the time it came to court, though, they were hardly thinking about it.

When old Mr Gray died, in January 1877, his eldest son George, who had been farming in Australia, came back to live with his mother. It was understood that, although he was now the head of the family, Bowerswell was held in trust for all the brothers and sisters. For the last twenty years it had been a second home for Effie, Millais and their children.

Millais had painted portraits of several of his children as they became adolescents. George, the second-born, who had posed for *The Boyhood of Raleigh*, appears in one of them, a good-looking, fair-haired teenager. He had gone to Rugby, without Everett, and then to Trinity College Cambridge, the first member of his family to attend an English university. There was talk of his becoming a diplomat or a barrister. He loved the outdoor life and was not too careful of his health.

In 1877 he caught typhoid and Effie took him to France, with his sister Mary, to convalesce. According to his brother John Guille, 'a chill ensued, followed by consumption', but the family may not have realised that he had tuberculosis as doctors did not like to diagnose it until the last stages. Next summer, when Millais had finished *The Princes in the Tower* and *A Jersey Lily*, they went to Scotland earlier than usual, probably thinking that the fresh air and familiar surroundings would do him good. But once they were at Bowerswell he deteriorated very quickly. Effie and Millais had both been at the deathbeds of young people but they still could not believe it was happening. On 30th August 1878, three weeks before his twenty-first birthday, George died.

'It was a terrible blow to my parents', wrote John Guille, '... never dreaming that his end was so near'.[21] A week later, with the horror still fresh, Millais replied to a letter of sympathy:

> We have all had a very trying month for George went through great suffering and died *hard*. Wasting away to a skeleton he lived on, maintaining his senses to within a day of his death. He was such a fine character ... and the family feel they will never know anyone to supplant him. He was so wise, truthful, and straightforward. I have loved and honoured him from his earliest days.[22]

George was buried in Kinnoull churchyard near Effie's seven dead brothers and sisters. For several weeks, Millais was too depressed to work or do anything else. But at last he got himself to Loch Ness, where he had expected to spend the summer, and painted the ruined Castle Urquhart against a stormy sky and a background of hills. The water is grey and windswept; a single figure, possibly George, rows across it. The title is a quotation from Tennyson:

> *The tower of strength which stood*
> *Four-square to all the winds that blew.*

The actual words of this poem, 'Ode on the Death of the Duke of Wellington', are 'O fallen at length that tower of strength'. Millais had always looked for strength in his family and now he was struggling to get it from his painting. Three years later, when Louise Jopling also lost a son, he wrote to her, 'When George died, I felt grateful for my work. Get you as soon as possible to your easel, as the surest means, not to forget, but to occupy your mind wholesomely and even happily'.[23]

Effie did not have this resource. She had never been good at talking about her feelings, and we can only imagine what was in her mind as she got through September in Scotland, got past George's birthday on the 19th. Perhaps she remembered the Shakespeare lessons at school – 'grief fills the room up of my absent child'; perhaps she felt guilty for having resented her pregnancies. While Millais painted, she and her elderly mother must have spent hours together, talking about their lost children.

At this time Ruskin was not far away, staying at Crieff with William Graham, an art collector and member of parliament. His host owned *The Blind Girl*, which had been painted more than twenty years before, and Ruskin had every opportunity to study it and see how good it was. His mind was now back to normal, and he had almost certainly heard about the death of Millais' son. He left no recorded comment, but he was not heartless. He had wanted his former wife to suffer, but surely not like this. We know that Millais was much in his mind that autumn because he wrote an article, 'The Three Colours of Pre-Raphaelitism', which appeared in October and November. This praised the compassion of *The Blind Girl*, which, like Wordsworth's poetry, reminded the viewer that the 'meanest tramp' could evoke thoughts which 'lie too deep for tears'. He went on to say that Millais was

> our best *painter* ... no question has ever been of that. Since Van Eyck and Durer there has nothing been seen so well done in laying of clear oil colour within definite line. And what he might have painted for us, if *we* had only known what we would have of him! Heaven only knows. But we none of us knew – nor he either.[24]

Millais probably read or heard of this, and perhaps it was at around this time that he stopped hating Ruskin. Compared to the loss of George, nothing seemed very important. It was anyway a gesture, after all these years, across 'the barrier which cannot but be between us personally'.[25]

He and Effie continued stoically with their usual routine. In October they crossed to Paris, in deep mourning but doing their best to behave naturally, so he could accept a gold medal from the *Exposition Universelle*. He was also made an officer of the Legion of Honour. Effie acted as his interpreter and they visited the studios of French painters. But 'after the excitement of his Paris visit the loss of his son came back upon him with renewed force'.[26] They could only have been faintly aware of public events as the year ended – Ruskin's article, the death of the President of the Royal Academy and his replacement by Frederic Leighton, the case of Whistler v Ruskin.

* * *

157

The trial was held at the Old Bailey on the 25th and 26th of November 1878. Ruskin was not there, though his cousin's husband, Arthur Severn, was in court to look after his interests. Whistler was happy to go into the witness box and say that Ruskin had libelled him. The spectators were much entertained.

The arguments hinged on whether *The Falling Rocket* was, or was not worth two hundred guineas (£210). As in the *Lady Chatterley* trial eighty years later, a jury of ordinary people was asked to pass judgement on a work of art, with several experts called as witnesses. Ruskin had the more distinguished supporters – Frith, Burne-Jones and Tom Taylor, the art critic of *The Times*. All of them said that the picture was sloppily painted; Taylor thought it not much better than 'a delicately tinted wallpaper'. William Rossetti reluctantly appeared for Whistler.

Even Whistler's counsel acknowledged that the absent Ruskin was a great man. He 'held perhaps the highest position in Europe and America as an art critic, and some of his works were, he might say, destined to immortality'. For Ruskin, the Attorney General argued:

> If a man thought a picture was a daub he had a right to say so, without subjecting himself to a risk of an action … Of course, if they found a verdict against Mr Ruskin, he would have to cease writing, but it would be an evil day for Art, in this country, when Mr Ruskin would be prevented from indulging in legitimate and proper criticism, by pointing out what was beautiful and what was not.[27]

The high point of the trial was when Whistler was cross-examined about his methods. His conversation with the Attorney General went something like this:

Q How long do you take to knock off one of your pictures?
A Oh, I 'knock one off' possibly in a couple of days – (laughter) – one day to do the work and another to finish it.
Q The labour of two days is that for which you ask two hundred guineas?
A No, I ask it for the knowledge I have gained in the work of a lifetime (applause).[28]

The result was unsatisfactory for both men. The jury decided that Whistler had indeed been libelled, but gave him damages of just one farthing (a quarter of an old penny). Possibly they found him arrogant and did not much like *The Falling Rocket*; probably they thought Ruskin was technically guilty but had a right to say what he believed. Both had to pay their own costs. Whistler went bankrupt and was in financial difficulties for years. Ruskin was a much richer man, and anyway paid nothing because his admirers immediately launched an appeal. But he was outraged. For the last forty years he had been saying exactly what he liked in print, and now, it seemed, he was going to be muzzled. He brooded over it, and could not accept that it might have been much worse.

In the long term, Whistler was triumphant; his picture now hangs in the Detroit Institute of Art and is worth much more than two hundred guineas. In the short term, he dashed off a pamphlet saying there was no reason why art critics should exist:

A life passed among pictures makes not a painter – else the policeman in the National Gallery might assert himself ... Let not Mr Ruskin flatter himself that more education makes the difference between himself and the policeman ... We are told that Mr Ruskin has devoted his long life to art, and as a result – is Slade Professor at Oxford ... What greater sarcasm can Mr Ruskin pass upon himself than that he preaches to young men what he cannot perform? Why, unsatisfied with his own conscious power, should he choose to become the type of incompetence by talking for forty years of what he has never done?[29]

Probably, being Whistler, he was hinting that there were other things Ruskin had 'never done'. Meanwhile, his enemy had decided to give up being Slade Professor:

although my health has lately been much broken, I hesitated in giving in my resignation of my Art-Professorship in the hope that I might still in some imperfect way have been useful at Oxford. But the result of the Whistler trial leaves me no further option. I cannot hold a chair from which I have no power of expressing judgement without being taxed for it by British law.[30]

Whistler took it in style. He hung the farthing on his watch-chain, and a year later went to Venice to make some money, probably convinced that the English were philistines. Millais did not comment. He was about to paint the former Prime Minister, Gladstone, and was looking forward to it. Effie watched over his career, looked after her remaining children, got through the crowded days and sleepless nights.

12

The Old Man of Coniston
1879–1900

But he always regarded himself as a failure: he had not done what he once meant to do.

Middlemarch, Finale

John Guille Millais, the fourth son, was the highest achiever of Effie's children. He described himself in *Who's Who* as an 'artist, author, landscape architect and animal sculptor'; he was also an explorer, Fellow of the Zoological Society and expert on rhododendrons. From the age of thirteen he liked going off by himself to explore the coasts of Scotland: 'My father and mother were always opposed to these constant absences on my part, but being good-natured and broad-minded people ... they had got accustomed to my perpetual wanderings'.[1] Effie was distraught when the *Dundee Evening Telegraph* falsely reported that he had been drowned. When he grew up he travelled in Africa and the Arctic and published or illustrated more than twenty books, mostly about sport or natural history, but he is best remembered for his biography of his father, *The Life and Letters of Sir John Everett Millais.*

This book, though an invaluable source, says disappointingly little about Effie. She had been nearly thirty-seven when he was born, so he could not easily have imagined her as a young woman, and he could not discuss her marriage to Ruskin, of course. But he made it clear that his parents had been a united couple:

And here let me say at once how much of my father's happiness in after years was due to [Effie]. During the forty-one years of their married life my mother took the keenest interest in his work, and did all in her power to contribute to his success, taking upon herself not only the care of the household and the management of the family affairs, but the great bulk of his correspondence, and saving him an infinity of trouble by personally ascertaining the objects of his callers (an ever increasing multitude) before admitting them into his presence. A great relief this, for business affairs and letter-writing were equally hateful in his eyes; and in spite of himself, his correspondence increased day by day.

Possessed in a considerable degree of the artistic sense, she was happily free from the artistic temperament, whilst her knowledge of history proved also a valuable acquisition. When an historical picture was in contemplation, she delighted to study anew the circumstances and the characters to be depicted, and to gather for her husband's use all particulars as to the scene and the costumes of the period. Her musical accomplishments (for she was an excellent pianist) were also turned to good account in hours of leisure, and not infrequently as a soothing antidote to the worries that too often beset the artist in the exercise of his craft.[2]

'Free from the artistic temperament' means that she was calm and sensible. The letters written at times of crisis do not give a good idea of her normal demeanour. Millais depended on her judgement and admitted that when his work was going badly 'I sometimes go to my wife and have a good cry'.[3]

John was twelve when the family moved into 2 Palace Gate, thirteen when George died. By this time he was old enough to understand his father's importance. Millais was the highest-paid of all British painters; he was also generally liked. Whatever people thought of his recent work, no one doubted his charm and good nature. Louise Jopling relates:

He was dining out, and, of course, sitting next the hostess. On his right was a charming Society woman, who evidently had not caught his name when he was introduced to her, for she presently, during a pause, started the usual subject of conversation in May – the Academy. 'Isn't Millais too dreadful this year?' And then, seeing the agonised contortions on her hostess's countenance, she said, 'Oh, do tell me what I've done. Look at Mrs –'s face! I must have said or done something terrible.' 'Well', laughed Millais, 'you really have, you know'. 'Oh, please, tell me'. 'Better nerve yourself to hear. Drink this glass of sherry first'. 'Yes, yes, now what is it?' For answer Millais said nothing, but, looking at her, pointed solemnly to himself. When it dawned upon her who her neighbour was, she was spared any confusion by Millais' hearty laughter.[4]

Portraits from the 1870s show him still looking like a young god, but the years made a certain difference. He put on weight, he lost some of his hair, he used glasses for close work. But he was still bounding with vitality. He taught Life School at the Academy, where the students loved him, and spent many evenings at the Garrick Club. His friends included writers, scientists and musicians – George Du Maurier, William Makepeace Thackeray, Anthony Trollope, Charles Reade, George Meredith, Mark Twain, Henry James, Robert Browning, Matthew Arnold, Richard Owen, Arthur Sullivan. He was also close to Liberal politicians including John Bright, Sir William Vernon Harcourt, the Earl of Rosebery and William Gladstone. Having reeled off this dazzling list of names, his son adds that he cared nothing for a man's rank, which was probably true. 'As John Millais was to his friends in 1865, so he was in 1895',[5] one of them wrote.

After her babies were born and her health stabilised, Effie loved to entertain interesting people. Beatrix Potter, whose father Rupert sometimes photographed Millais' subjects, was the same age as their younger children and saw quite a lot of them. Her diary for 12th July 1884 records, 'Papa and mamma went to a ball at the Millais' a week or two since. There was an extraordinary mixture of actors, rich Jews, nobility, literary etc. ... Oscar Wilde was there'.[6] Both of them, however, tried to relax in Scotland, where they migrated for two or three months every autumn. Effie and the girls usually stayed at Bowerswell while Millais went shooting or fishing with friends. Middle-class Victorian men had an extraordinary passion for blood sports. Millais had originally thought that hunting was 'savage and uncivilised',[7] but had been persuaded to take it up by his friend John Leech in 1854. He found that long hours at his easel or desk gave him fearful headaches which were only cured by open-air exercise. Effie accepted that this, like an evening at the club, was his way of relaxing.

Although he had a high international reputation, he still disliked going abroad. Effie sometimes went without him, taking one or more of the children. She had plenty of friends of her own and had got used to managing by herself in the Ruskin years. But after decades of marriage, Millais was still writing that he did not like to be away from her for too long. Over the next few years her life would be dominated by births, marriages and another death.

* * *

In the first dreadful months after August 1878, Millais was thankful to throw his energies into the portrait of Gladstone. This had been his own idea, and while he was doing it they became friendly. It seems certain that he admired and voted for the Liberal leader, who was detested by the right wing. He had already painted Wilkie Collins, the philanthropist Shaftesbury and Thomas Carlyle. He had also done some memorable portraits of women, and not only young and pretty ones such as Lillie Langtry. The matron *Mrs Bischoffsheim* (1873) is an example.

Gladstone wrote long afterwards that he had never known anyone work with such 'extraordinary concentration'.[8] The portrait was done in a total of five hours and was described as 'unrivalled since the days of Rembrandt and Velasquez in its rendering of the mind and spirit of the man'.[9] Millais would paint him again a few years later, in red doctoral robes, and it is difficult to say which is the greater masterpiece.

The pictures of Louise Jopling and Kate Perugini were completed soon afterwards. He also painted an unpretentious self-portrait, by request, for the Uffizi Gallery. In 1881 he began work on Disraeli, who died before he had finished. Queen Victoria, indifferent to the fact that she had snubbed his wife, asked for a replica and made some helpful suggestions. She was graciously pleased with the result.

Throughout the 1880s Millais was very busy and in great demand as a portraitist. He painted two more Prime Ministers – Salisbury and Rosebery – John Bright, Cardinal Newman, Alfred Tennyson, Henry Irving and Arthur Sullivan, as well as many other people who were not particularly distinguished or interesting. They found him friendly, but not overawed. 'He calls Newman Mr Cardinal, and talks to him with his pipe in his mouth',[10] wrote one diarist. These portraits did not take him long. The rocks and plants in *John Ruskin* had cost months of labour but now he used plain, dark backgrounds. Sometimes he complained it was a waste of time, but his friends pointed out that he was painting history. In an age before colour photography, he gave us a whole gallery of famous Victorians.

After a year of misery, the family celebrated when their eldest daughter Euphemia got married on 29th November 1879. Her husband was a career officer, William Christopher James, the son of a judge. Effie organised a fashionable wedding followed by a ball, very different from her own modest wedding twenty-four years earlier. A son was born in October 1880 and named George Millais James. This boy (who would die in the Great War) was Effie's first grandchild. Another boy, William Milbourne James – the subject of *Bubbles* – was born in 1881 and was followed by two girls. All this must have been very healing. But at around the same time Effie and Millais were deeply worried about two other family members, Everett and Sophie.

As a ten-year-old, during the Ruskin crisis, Sophie had known something of what was going on. Two years later Millais painted her in *Autumn Leaves*, where she is the central figure. The children are so lifelike that it is hard to believe they moved and breathed a century and a half ago. He painted her again as a teenager with streaming hair and huge blue eyes, in 1857. Carlo Perugini painted her as an elegant young woman with dark red, piled-up hair and an intense, narrow face.

Sophie and her sister Alice, a pleasant and normal girl, often stayed with Effie as they were growing up and their parents saw that they met suitable young men. But neither of them married until they were pushing thirty; perhaps they were nervous, after what they had heard and seen. In March 1868 Sophie, who had been suffering from an eating disorder, broke down with 'hysteria'. Her parents, desperate to avoid another scandal, smuggled her away from Bowerswell, telling their neighbours that she was staying with her sister. In fact she was being treated in a doctor's house, near enough for Effie to visit her regularly, and she did not go home for a year.

In 1873 she married a long-time admirer, James Key Caird, a jute mill owner in Dundee, and had a daughter, Beatrix. They were not very happy together. According to Louise Jopling, she was a brilliant and fascinating woman. Millais painted her daughter in 1879; a fair-haired, worried-looking child. It appears that Sophie had further breakdowns and at last became hopelessly insane. Millais' final, 1880 portrait of her shows her looking haggard, with a sprinkling of grey hairs. She died far from her home, in London, on 15th March 1882, aged thirty-eight. Gabriel Rossetti died three weeks later.

Beatrix would also die, in 1888 at the age of fourteen. James Caird did not remarry and was a recluse in his last years. Long after Sophie was dead he became an eminent philanthropist, financing Shackleton's expedition to the South Pole and making many gifts to the city of Dundee.

There were rumours about Sophie – that she was in love with Millais, that she committed suicide – but we actually know very little, because it was one of those tragedies which respectable families did not discuss. We do know that several well-off Victorian women suffered from 'hysteria'. Her story is not unlike that of Rose La Touche, a bright and promising girl who had everything in her favour yet, somehow, for no clear reason, came to grief.

* * *

In the year that he painted Beatrix, Millais did a famous portrait of a luckier child called Edie Ramage. This little girl is dressed in pink and white with an eighteenth-century mob cap, and is about to eat a bowl of cherries. He called the picture *Cherry Ripe* and was paid a thousand guineas. It was commissioned by Edie's uncle, the editor of *The Graphic*, who printed it in a Christmas number, and 'quite amazing was the hold it took upon the public fancy'.[11] Copies went to 'the remotest parts of the English-speaking world',[12] fan mail poured in and Millais was besieged with requests to paint more of the same. He did paint several sweetly pretty pictures of upper-class children, including the Queen's granddaughter, Princess Marie of Edinburgh. They would do nothing for his long-term reputation.

Yet when he did a serious and ambitious picture, reminiscent of his Pre-Raphaelite days, the public was not interested. *The Ruling Passion* or *The Ornithologist* (1885) has an old man, probably with not long to live, showing his collection of stuffed birds of paradise to his daughter and her children. Millais could not resist putting his little grandsons in the picture and they could well have been left out. But it is memorable because it tugs at our imagination; juxtaposed, we see youth and age, brilliant plumage and death. Ruskin, who was still writing some art criticism, said that he had 'never seen any work of modern art with more delight and admiration'.[13] However, no one was prepared to buy it. Millais told Kate Perugini that he was 'not very hopeful ... I don't think, therefore, I will trouble the critics and public any more with what is called "an important picture"'.[14]

Yet only a month later he had proof that he was indeed greatly admired. Gladstone, on his way out as Prime Minister, recommended him for a baronetcy, the first time this had happened to a British-born artist. Others had been knighted, but this was a title he could pass on to his son and to future generations. He was thrilled. Of course he said that he did not care about being called Sir John, but he 'had long held that a distinction like this was not only an honour to the recipient, but to the whole body of artists, and an encouragement to the pursuit of Art in its highest and noblest form'.[15] One may wish that he had turned it down, just as one may wish that Effie had ignored Queen Victoria, but there are still plenty of people who think that titles are badges of merit. For her, in particular, it was important that they should be seen as an honourable and respectable couple.

The following year, 1886, Millais did the most celebrated of all his child-paintings, *Bubbles*. And this picture is now so well-known and so much abused that it is difficult to see it with clear eyes. He came across his grandson, Willie James, blowing bubbles, and thought it might be challenging to paint them and interesting to show the little boy's fascination with simple things. The child, who lived to be over ninety, did not remember posing. The bubbles were more difficult to paint, and a crystal sphere had to be used to get the lights and colours just right.

He did not expect it to be used as an advertisement for Pears soap. *Bubbles* was bought by the *Illustrated London News*, who sold it on to the manufacturers; Millais did not own the copyright. At first he was furious, but changed his mind when he saw that the reproduction was a good one. He believed that art ought to be widely circulated among those who could not afford to buy original work. But he would always be upset by the suggestion that he had painted it especially for Pears.

In the same year the Grosvenor Gallery held a major exhibition of his work. One hundred and fifty-nine pictures were brought from all over the country, including the *Huguenot*, which he had not seen for thirty years. He examined it closely and said to John Guille, 'Really, I did not paint so badly in those days, old man'.[16] But he seems to have felt, as did others, that he had lost some power since it was painted. According to Hunt:

> ... an ardent appreciator of his genius, Lady Constance Leslie, went early in the day to the exhibition. Ascending the stairs, she encountered the painter going out, with head bowed down. As she accosted him, and he looked up, she saw tears in his eyes. 'Ah, dear Lady Constance', he said, 'you see me unmanned. Well, I'm not ashamed of avowing that in looking at my earliest pictures I have been overcome with chagrin that I so far failed in my maturity to fulfil the full forecast of my youth'.[17]

He had told his old friend that he was discouraged by *The Ruling Passion*'s failure to sell. Buyers would pay only for portraits of themselves, or of winsome children. Millais and Hunt had several friendly arguments. Hunt, with a much smaller talent, had continued to paint exactly as he wished, stayed outside the Academy and considered himself the only true Pre-Raphaelite. Millais 'had been driven to believe that a man should adapt himself to the temper of his time':

> 'You argue', he said, 'that if I paint for the passing fashion of the day my reputation some centuries hence will not be what my powers would secure for me if I did more ambitious work. I don't agree. A painter must work for the taste of his own day. How does he know what people will like two or three hundred years hence? I maintain that a man should hold up the mirror to his own times. I want

proof that the people of my day enjoy my work, and how can I get this better than by finding people willing to give me money for my productions, and that I win honours from contemporaries? What good would recognition of my labours hundreds of years hence do me? I should be dead, buried and crumbled into dust. Don't let us bother ourselves about the destinies of our work in the world, but as it brings us fortune and recognition ... There is a fashion going now for little girls in mob caps. Well, I satisfy this while it continues; but immediately the demand shows signs of flagging, I am ready to take to some other fashion ... Why, if I were to go on like you do I should never be able to go away in the autumn to fish or to shoot, and I should be always out of health and spirits ... You take my advice, old boy, and just take the world as it is, and don't make it your business to rub up people the wrong way'.[18]

Millais' favourite among his own works was *The Vale of Rest*, followed by *The Order of Release* and *The Eve of St Agnes* (for both of which Effie posed). In an article, he wrote that 'no artist ever painted more than four or five masterpieces'. He could 'honestly say that I never consciously placed an idle touch upon canvas', but 'I confess I should not grieve were half my works to go to the bottom of the Atlantic – if I might choose the half to go'.[19]

The family was expanding. In 1886, their eldest son and third daughter both got married. Everett had been a real problem for several years. He and George had grown up together (there were only sixteen months between them), had posed together for *The Boyhood of Raleigh*, and were both devoted to their parents. But their characters were sharply different; George had been a completely satisfactory son whereas Everett refused to work and became a heavy drinker. It must have been difficult for him to be the son of a famous man and have an instantly identifiable name. When George died, Everett was the one to inform the Perth registrar. Struggling with his own grief, he may have wondered whether his parents would have preferred to lose him. Over the next few years his behaviour grew worse. In 1881, with yet another scandal looming, his family packed him off to his uncles, John and Melville Gray, in Australia.

When he got back, Everett had calmed down. He and his brothers never tried to compete with their father but liked the outdoor life as he did. He described himself as a traveller and naturalist, studied rabies and genetics at the Pasteur Institute and became a respected breeder of Basset hounds. He met a sensible woman, Mary Hope-Vere, was quietly married in France and soon started a family. It is likely, though, that the years of alcoholism had done permanent damage to his health.

The marriages of his sisters were entirely conventional. Three times Millais walked down the aisle with a lovely daughter on his arm and three times Effie gave a memorable party. Alice (Carrie) married Charles Stuart-Wortley, a Conservative member of parliament whose first wife, dead in childbirth, had been Trollope's niece. Sophia married an army officer. Mary, the second daughter, remained single.

By the end of the decade the Jameses had four children, Everett and his wife two and the Stuart-Wortleys one. Each wedding and birth would have been a great joy to Effie and she surely reflected that these things could not have happened if she had stayed with Ruskin.

A few months after the Whistler trial, Ruskin turned sixty.

Over the next ten years he was surrounded by a changing group of admirers and attendants. The most important was his cousin Joan, who lived with her family in his old home at Herne Hill. They all hoped that he would not get involved in any more controversies and that the breakdown of 1878 had been a one-off.

Joan's husband, Arthur Severn, did not find him an easy man. 'Although extremely kind and generous to a fault in some ways, he could be just the opposite', he wrote. 'No one dared contradict him on any subject without his flying into a passion. What he liked was absolute obedience and in return he would pet and flatter. His ideal was a "kind feudal system", everyone round him willing to help, to obey and to love him. To all such he would be kind and helpful, but woe betide the man or woman who ventured to differ or put him right'.[20]

For a while Ruskin lived quietly, writing, visiting the continent and sorting his vast collection of minerals, most of which he gave away. A house he had bought in the Walkley district of Sheffield became a library and museum for working men. He had, indeed, given away most of his father's money, and the Severns, who depended on him, were worried by his lavish spending. But he did own two houses, in London and the Lake District, and had a comfortable income from his books. He went fell-walking and rowed himself across Coniston Water. He kept up a vast correspondence with his readers, some of whom started Ruskin societies, where they discussed books and ethics, in northern and midland towns.

But in February 1881, soon after the death of Carlyle, he again went mad for weeks, recovered, and then broke down for a third time in the following year. During these attacks he was abusive and violent. In between them he could speak and write rationally, but they left him weakened, and his appearance changed. He had been a tall man, almost six feet, but now he lost several inches and grew a full beard. Probably, aware of his grandfather's end, those around him were afraid to let him use a razor.

In 1883 he resumed the Slade Professorship and gave more lectures, but by now his eccentricities were obvious to all. The undergraduates were thrilled, and his friends grieved, to see a great man making an exhibition of himself. He resigned for the second time, and permanently, in 1885, when Oxford University licensed experiments on animals.

These were the years of his friendship with Kate Greenaway, whom he hailed as a major artist. Of course most people thought that this was ridiculous. Kate may have been in love with him but, in her thirties, she was already too old for Ruskin. The real attraction, unfortunately, was her charming pictures of little girls.

He had been reconciled with Mrs La Touche and she sometimes visited him. This did not help him get over his obsession with Rose, who he believed was communicating with him from heaven. In 1885, when the La Touche family was in Coniston, he had a fourth attack of madness, his worst. Yet in the same year he had begun publishing his autobiography, *Praeterita*, which means 'things past'. This was written in beautiful lucid prose in the intervals between breakdowns and came out irregularly until 1889. Effie may have feared that he would say something about their marriage, but it is mainly a record of his childhood and youth, and does not mention her.

In the summer of 1887 he again became aggressive, and for a while Joan could bear no more. He left Brantwood and moved into lodgings in Folkestone, writing her several pathetic letters. From time to time he went to London, although he was afraid to approach his old home, and stayed in a hotel overlooking Trafalgar Square. There he witnessed the events of Bloody Sunday, 13th November 1887, when a great crowd of unemployed workers were attacked by the police. Ruskin went out to talk to them and said they were 'very nice fellows ... quite right, too, in demanding bread'.[21]

Wandering around the National Gallery, he introduced himself to Kathleen Olander, a Quaker art student of eighteen, who was naturally thrilled. He was now coming up to sixty-nine. After a while he proposed marriage and Kathleen, though startled, was prepared to consider a platonic union. But her horrified parents put a stop to it.

Private View of the Old Masters Exhibition, Royal Academy, 1888, by

Henry Jamyn Brooks, is a group portrait probably worked up from a photograph taken at the beginning of that year. It shows fifty-nine people, described by the National Portrait Gallery, where it now hangs, as 'the cream of late Victorian society'. Everyone at this party would have known that Ruskin was intermittently mad. Gladstone is there; as are many artists and aristocrats, some with their wives. Ruskin, shrunken and grey-bearded, is in one section of the crowd; Millais, tall and upright, in another. His daughter Mary is also in the group but not Effie; she would not have risked being in the same room. Mary (who is hemmed in by two middle-aged artists, and looks bored) would have taken a good look at this peculiar elderly man who had been married to her mother long ago. She could see him only as someone who had distressed and embarrassed her parents, and is said to have been very hostile to him in later life.

That summer Ruskin took a final tour through Europe, accompanied by friends, for he could not be trusted alone. He broke down in November. Joan took him back to Coniston which, apart from one trip to the coast, he never left again. His extraordinary mind had finally ceased to function. He went on writing for a few more months, but after 1889 his mental life came to an end.

Shortly before the Old Masters Exhibition, Millais had been in Scotland painting one of his finest wintry landscapes, *Christmas Eve*. This shows an ancient house reflecting the setting sun in its windows, bare trees and jackdaws pecking at the snow. The house is Old Murthly Castle, near Dunkeld, where he often went in autumn to fish and to be near the Gray family. After a break of several years, he was again painting landscapes. He sometimes sat in the open air for hours, pipe in mouth, ignoring freezing temperatures.

Dew-Drenched Furze was painted in the same part of the world two years later. This is an almost Impressionist picture, showing the sun struggling through November morning mist and 'firs, bracken and gorse bushes, festooned with silver webs'. It was 'a scene such as had probably never been painted before, and might possibly prove to be unpaintable'[22] but he succeeded, and it is a miraculous image of mist and dew – for him, unique.

Lingering Autumn is another Scottish picture from the same period. The third great late landscape is *Glen Birnam*, painted at the end of 1890. An old woman with a basket is walking by herself, her back to the viewer, through a winter wood. Each twig, head of bracken and animal pawprint in the snow is perfect.

He had overworked in the previous summer and wrote to Effie, 'I never looked forward to a holiday with greater pleasure as I am tired out. The anxiety of satisfying people in portraiture is almost intolerable'.[23] As he grew older, he looked forward more and more to escaping to Scotland and working, if at all, only on the subjects he chose. He was beginning to tire of casual socialising and only wanted to be with his wife and close friends. Yet they knew so many people, and there were so many demands on his time, that it was not easy. He was expected, and indeed willing, to be a public figure. He was a trustee of the National Portrait Gallery and supported the Sunday Society, which campaigned for museums to stay open seven days a week so that working people could visit them. He was also involved in negotiations to set up a new gallery of British art. Henry Tate, the sugar magnate, who owned a collection of modern pictures including *Ophelia*, proposed to give them to the nation and house them in a building on the site of the old Millbank prison. It met with some resistance.

The 1890s began well, with the marriages of their daughter Sophia and son John and the births of more grandchildren. But Effie's youngest brother Everett died, aged thirty-six. He had been the baby who was christened on their wedding day, and it was a chilling reminder of the passage of time. He was a stockbroker, interested in art, and left a legacy to Effie – one of the few sums she ever owned personally. Another concern was Millais' voice, which had grown strangely harsh and cracked.

In Scotland, on the night of 10th January 1892, their rented house caught fire and they got out in a hurry, just managing to save his newest picture. 'Your mother was wonderfully placid through all the turmoil',[24] Millais wrote to his son. They moved into Bowerswell, where they were always welcome, and he began work on another snow landscape. Climbing to an exposed road on Kinnoull Hill, he painted a woman and child, abandoned by the husband and father, and called it *Blow, Blow, Thou Winter Wind*. The boughs of the Scotch firs are forced upwards by a gale. It was a relief to paint something real, after too many London drawing-rooms, but sitting out of doors in a Scottish January did nothing for his health.

He returned to London in March quite unable to work, something which had not happened since the crisis almost forty years ago. A swelling in his throat was beginning to worry him. In the following year he was no better, and Effie's sight again began to give trouble. An operation did no good. This 'not only caused him great anxiety, but deprived him of her valuable and ever ready help'.[25] Effie could still get about but could no longer see to read. She was going to need her calm temperament.

That same year, 1893, W G Collingwood published a biography of Ruskin which referred very briefly to his marriage. Effie was not named, but her siblings felt that she was being attacked by innuendo. They were angry, but said nothing to her or to Millais, because of his poor health and her poor sight.

December 1893–94 was a year of horror. Neither of them was getting any better, and at Christmas their son Everett's three-year-old daughter, named Euphemia but known as Dorothy, died. In April Effie went to Germany for treatment by 'a famous oculist', and Millais, 'quite unable to work',[26] went to Bournemouth. From there he wrote to Effie, 'Have had a return of my head disturbance, so bad this morning that I thought of telegraphing for you, crying and having to leave the breakfast table, in short the old story over again',[27] which, by the way, surely answers the question of whether he still loved her.

On 28th May Effie's mother, Sophia Gray, died at Bowerswell. She was in her eighties and had survived nine of her fifteen children, two grandchildren and one great-granddaughter. Millais was not well enough to attend the funeral and wrote 'she has lived so straight, so good a life, that one ought to be thankful; but it will be a great sorrow to you'.[28]

There was more bad news from India, where their eldest daughter Euphemia had gone with her husband and little girls, leaving the two boys to be educated in Scotland. Major James, taking part in the barbarous sport of pig-sticking, had been thrown from his horse and suffered serious head injuries. He was invalided home in 1894 but did not get better. Later in the year he went back, and by Christmas was dead. A week later his daughter Phyllis, who is the child in *The Little Speedwell,* also died at the age of seven. That made four deaths in their immediate family between one December and the next.

Effie and Millais would have been distraught by their inability to help their daughter, far away in Lucknow, and the loss of another grandchild. Euphemia, the child in *My First Sermon,* who had been a beautiful girl and young woman, was now a widow at thirty-six. She eventually returned to England and died rather young.

They spent the winter with the always welcoming George Gray. Now in his sixties and unmarried, Effie's brother is said to have been a charming and humorous man who loved to entertain. 'The grey sky, the short winter days, the serious Scottish character, the quiet and repose of Bowerswell – antithesis to the unavoidable bustle and unrest of life in London'[29] were all very soothing. Millais could no longer stand the capital's winter fogs but he loved Perth, saying that the view north from the bridge was better than anything in the Riviera. He did the background to *St Stephen*, a representation of the first Christian martyr, in a disused stone quarry on Kinnoull Hill. The picture is very dark and shows a beautiful young man, as he had once been, lying dead.

Millais was suffering from cancer of the larynx, perhaps caused by heavy pipe smoking, and was facing up to the possibility that he would not get better. We don't know when Effie realised that she was going to lose her husband; it would not have been in character for her to tell anyone outside the family about the fear and grief which were eating her up. In public, they behaved as if his hoarse voice was a minor nuisance.

Frederic Leighton, the President of the Royal Academy, was ill too, and Millais was forced to take on some of his duties. He spoke at the annual banquet in May 1895: 'I have been intimately connected with this Academy for more than half a century. I have received here a free education as an artist ... and I owe the Academy a debt of gratitude I can never repay'.[30] In the summer he seemed to improve, but broke down again and spent one more quiet winter with Effie at Bowerswell. 'The green terraces and yew hedges ... the fir woods and the rushing Tay'[31] had been an inspiration ever since they got married.

Leighton died on 25th January 1896. It was obvious that Millais, though not keen, was his only possible successor. Younger men had their eye on the job but suspected that he would not be there for long. He was elected on 20th February as the tenth President of the Royal Academy, winning every vote except his own.

On the following day, he and Effie gave lunch to Constance Wilde, who was in England to visit her husband Oscar in Reading Jail. Many people had shunned her since the scandal, but the Millais, however successful, were never likely to forget old friends.

Some of the letters of congratulation which were now pouring in mentioned his wife, 'who will have to take so large a part in the new honour'.[32] Beatrix Potter noted:

Tuesday, February 25th – Met Lady Millais in Gloucester Road. She was being bullied by a lady in a velvet mantle, so I merely insinuated the remark that I was sure that she must be receiving more congratulations than she could attend to, whereupon she seized my arm to cross the street, expressing a wish to die together, there being a procession of female bicycles. I thought it a characteristic mixture of graciousness and astute utility, she walking with a black crutch-stick, but most amusingly elated.[33]

It was just after the election that Millais met the painter Philip Calderon in Kensington Gardens where he often strolled. 'It will kill me', he said in a hoarse whisper, pointing to his throat. 'But', he added, 'I am ready and not afraid; I've had a good time, my boy, a very good time!'[34]

There are several indications that Millais, in his last few months, was taking stock of his life. We don't know, though, exactly when he said, 'I have no enemies ... there's no man with whom I would not shake hands – except one, and, by Jove! I should like to shake him by the hand now'.[35] There was only one man, far away in the Lake District, who could have been meant.

Between February and May 1896 he threw himself into the usual preparations for the Summer Exhibition. His voice was all but gone. A journalist wrote afterwards:

There was something very pathetic in the way Millais lingered round the galleries of the Academy during the last days before it opened for the first time under his presidentship. He was in the rooms on the Saturday before the private view ... shaking hands with old friends, and saying, in a hoarse whisper, which told its tale tragically enough, that he was better.[36]

John Guille thought he would have tried to get monochrome artists admitted to the Academy; perhaps he would even have been able to admit women, but there was no time. By the end of April the cancer had been diagnosed, and on 11th May, late at night, he began gasping for breath. He would have died then and there if the famous surgeon Frederick Treves had not performed a tracheotomy by candlelight. They got some ozone into him, working at the cutting edge of surgery, and this kept him alive for the next three months, mostly without painkillers.

During this time a few old friends were allowed in to say goodbye. One of them, the Liberal politician William Harcourt, wrote on 16th June, 'Lady M. saw me first and was deeply moved. She begged me not to seem too shocked or depressed at the sight of him. I found the poor dear fellow (once so strong and gay) propped up in his chair with white beard and moustache, quite unable to utter'.[37] The beard had to be left because it was unsafe to shave, and he communicated by writing on a slate.

Millais had always behaved beautifully and this did not change when he was slowly dying. He showed an interest in all that was going on, asking to see photographs of the new Tate gallery and writing 'quite satisfied'. Whistler, whose wife had died that spring, sent his good wishes; so did the Queen's fourth daughter, Louise, who was one of the most intelligent of Victoria's children. She had studied art seriously and was a gifted sculptress and founder of the Ladies' Work Association. A few years later she would quietly agree with William Rossetti that the Boer War had been a mistake. Millais had painted her husband, a Scottish aristocrat, and she had never approved of her mother's treatment of Effie. Now she brought a message; the Queen had asked if there was anything she could do. Millais immediately wrote on his slate, 'receive my wife'.

So Effie took the train to Windsor on 3rd July and, in the words of the court circular, 'had the honour of being presented to the Queen'. No doubt the two women talked politely for a short time and Victoria expressed her sympathy. Although the older by nine years, the Queen was in better health, but then she had been carefully looked after all her life, and Effie was partially blind.

The inconvenience and embarrassment were worth it, because this proved to all who were interested that she was a respectable woman and that Millais, not the old man in Coniston, was her lawful husband. From then on she was with him day and night as his once robust frame slowly wasted away. Surrounded by his family – Effie, his eldest son and two of his daughters – John Everett Millais died at 5.30 in the afternoon on 13th August 1896. There were lavish official tributes and many sympathetic letters, because his courage during his long and very public ordeal had reduced some grown men to tears.

But it was the private letters and diaries which really showed how people were feeling. Burne-Jones wrote, 'I'm glad the torture is over for him, and the watching for his children and wife ... but I feel heavy enough and sad today, though I longed to see that it had come'.[38] William Rossetti called him 'my early and beloved intimate'.[39] Beatrix Potter noted:

Thursday, August 13th – Sir John Millais died Aug. 13th, interred into rest. He would have gone long ago if he had been an ordinary poor man ... I saw him last in November, walking in Knightsbridge, 'how is my little friend?', can't speak, can't speak!' He looked as handsome and well as ever, he was one of the handsomest men I ever saw ... I shall always have a most affectionate remembrance of Sir John Millais ...He gave me the kindest encouragement with my drawings (to be sure he did to everybody!) ... He was an honest fine man.[40]

The obituaries, which devoted much space to his distinguished career, said two things of special interest; that the best way of honouring him was to support the Sunday Society, and that he had married Euphemia, daughter of the late George Gray.

A few months later, Effie abandoned the Palace Gate house and headed for her favourite place on earth, Bowerswell. As her train sped through the Lake District she passed within a few miles of her former husband, who now knew little of what was going on around him. It seemed cruel that Millais, who was ten years younger and perfectly sane, had been the first to die.

There are not many records of her life over the next year. She helped her son John Guille with his projected biography and went on dictating letters, though she could not write them. She was near her brother George and her old friends, and Mary, the unmarried daughter, probably also lived with her. It is unlikely that she talked much about what she had lost; as she had written of her second wedding day, 'a looker on might have fancied we were very indifferent to each other'. But the first year after the death of a husband or wife is dangerous for the survivor. Her parents had lived to be seventy-eight and eighty-six; two of her brothers would go on well into their nineties, but she was not as tough. By 1897 it was known that Effie had cancer.

Willie James, the child in *Bubbles*, was now nearly sixteen, a naval cadet and about to join his first ship. Effie had been very kind to him and in later years he would be furious when she was attacked. Before going he spent some weeks at Bowerswell and remembered his grandmother clearly. 'Despite the ravages of time and illness that was soon to prove fatal, it was still plain to see why she had once been called the Fair Maid of Perth'.[41]

The gardens at Bowerswell had hardly changed since Millais painted them in the 1850s. The young boy recalled that Effie would wander off by herself to 'the top of the long walk where she so often sat during the last year of her life, and where I said goodbye to her before sailing for Australia'. Memories of the many good times in the past 'could still bring gleams of happiness to her tired eyes'.[42]

In the summer she seemed better and was probably very glad to have spent time with her grandson, but her pain was not yet over. Everett was not the second baronet for long. He died suddenly of pneumonia on 7th September, leaving his wife Mary, a new baby, a daughter aged four and an eight-year-old son who inherited the great name of Sir John Everett Millais. The boy would die young but the girl, Perrine Millais Moncrieff, became a distinguished ornithologist and an early champion of the environment in the New World.[43]

This tragedy 'came to her as a terrible blow, and robbed her of all power of resistance. Thenceforward she gradually sank'.[44] Everett was her firstborn, the baby who had been her reward for her struggle to free herself, the boy she had fought to save in Paris in 1871. She died – the certificate said 'tumour of intestine, perforation of bowel' – in the early hours of 23rd December 1897 at Bowerswell, aged sixty-nine. The newspapers, in their obituaries of 'Euphemia, Lady Millais', finally informed their readers that she had been married to Ruskin.

All this time, Ruskin lived on.

Younger people were dropping all around him, but his physical health remained good for a man in his seventies. He had retreated deep into himself after the last crisis and was cared for by Joan Severn, who kept outsiders at a distance. Interactions with others were minimal. He sent forget-me-nots to the funeral of Burne-Jones in 1898 – but that was probably organised by Joan – and began a letter, which he did not finish, to Gladstone's daughter after his death. His white beard had grown vast and spread over his entire chest.

Now that he was no longer writing or appearing in public, people were happy to acknowledge him as a grand old man. Books by or about him rolled off the press and his disciples multiplied, while the man himself sat passively in his study, looking out at Coniston Water and the distant fells. On his eightieth birthday, 8th February 1899, the *Times* announced that 'we are all Ruskinians now'. His admirers had prepared an illuminated address which they brought to the house and read aloud while he listened. He seemed deeply moved, but there was no conversation.

The new century did not officially start until 1901, but in the first days of 1900 there was a definite feeling that change was in the air. So many great Victorians had gone in the last decade – Tennyson, Newman, Gladstone, Huxley, Morris, Millais. The old queen had also turned eighty and was obviously on the way out. Now the Lakeland winter was closing in and there was influenza at Brantwood. Ruskin caught it, and drifted quietly away on 20th January. A funeral in Westminster Abbey was offered, but refused because he had made it clear that he wished to be buried either beside his parents or at Coniston.

His fame had spread worldwide. Tolstoy revered him; Gandhi would read *Unto This Last* in 1904 and it would change his life. Marcel Proust wrote, 'Only a few days ago we were fearing for the life of Tolstoy; that misfortune did not come to pass; but the world has been dealt a no lesser loss: Ruskin is dead. Nietzsche is insane, Tolstoy and Ibsen appear to be nearing the end of their life; one after another Europe is losing her "directors of conscience".'[45]

In an unnamed London club, there was a deplorable scene. 'There came a sudden clamour outside, the door burst open and another well-known artist rushed in dancing and frantically waving an evening paper. "Ruskin's dead! Ruskin's dead!" he cried; then sinking into a chair, 'Thank God, Ruskin's dead! Give me a cigarette!'.[46]

Aftermath: The Vale of Rest
1898 to the present day

Those who had not seen anything of Dorothea usually observed that she could not have been a 'nice woman', else she would not have married either the one or the other.

Middlemarch, Finale

'New generations with fresh struggles to engage in ever advance and sweep away many of the memories of individual lives',[1] Holman Hunt wrote after his oldest friend died. In the twentieth century, Ruskin and Millais would both become unfashionable and Effie's story would be much misunderstood.

John Guille's *Life and Letters*, dedicated 'to the memory of my dear father and mother', appeared in 1899. It is still a valuable source but, like most Victorian biographies, says nothing remotely embarrassing. Effie, as noted, is a shadowy figure, and her history is dismissed in a footnote:

> Miss Gray had been previously married, but that marriage had been annulled in 1854, on grounds sanctioned equally by Church and State. Both good taste and feeling seem to require that no detailed reference should be made to the circumstances attending that annulment. But, on behalf of those who loved their mother well, it may surely be said that during the course of the judicial proceedings instituted by her, and throughout the period of the void marriage and the whole of her after years, not one word could be, or ever was, uttered impugning the correctness and purity of her life.[2]

Ruskin was still alive at the time, or he might have said just a little more. Forty years after the marriage had ended, people were still talking

181

about it. Gladstone, who knew all of them, told his daughter Mary, 'Should you ever hear anyone blame Millais, or his wife, or Mr Ruskin, remember there was no fault: there was misfortune, even tragedy: all three were perfectly blameless'.[3] Others, including many who did not know them, were less charitable.

The attacks on Effie started within a year of her death, in Olivia Shakespear's novel *Rupert Armstrong*. The central character is a famous painter who, according to his daughter who tells the story, has not fulfilled his great promise:

'Your father is a very prosperous and successful man: he has perhaps the finest technique of anyone in England: he makes a good income and has been knighted. What more do you want, Agatha?'.[4]

This is the fault of his wife, Eve, who is not 'a merely vulgar woman, eager for display and social distinction',[5] but who dislikes being poor and has a great urge to experience life to the full. This does sound like the Effie who wanted 'to see and know everything'. The narrator says:

I believed that his gradual falling away from the finer ideals of his art had begun through the influence of my mother; her overmastering passion, her longing to live, to enjoy, to experience, had led to sordid issues: as means to an end, she must have money and position.[6]

Olivia Shakespear was young enough to have been Millais' daughter and clearly empathized with her own generation. Unhappily married, she had an affair with William Butler Yeats in the late 1890s and was close to him throughout their lives. He would have read the novel and known her feelings, which perhaps are echoed in his poem 'The Choice':

The intellect of man is forced to choose
Perfection of the life, or of the work,
And if it take the second must refuse
A heavenly mansion, raging in the dark.

Knowledgeable readers would easily have identified Rupert and Eve Armstrong. Edith Hunt, too, was spiteful about Effie, telling her granddaughter Diana that Millais would never have married her had it not been raining in Scotland in the summer of 1853. (She had been a child at the time and neither she nor Hunt had actually been there). Millais was always an attractive man and it is possible that several women were a little in love with him and resented his faded, and slightly older wife. Men, too, were less kind after she had lost her charming youthful looks.

And then there was the cancelled marriage to Ruskin. His earliest biographers were too embarrassed to say much about it. Hunt in 1905 tried to correct the false stories that were flying around, but did not get very far. He and others repeated in good faith what Ruskin had told them; that he had got married only to please his parents. To anyone who remembered the bossy old Ruskins, this might have seemed convincing.

Many people went on saying that Millais and Effie had eloped. A ridiculous film, *The Love of John Ruskin*, showed him nobly surrendering his wife to his friend and then acting as best man at their wedding. If she had rejected such a great man, there must have been something wrong with her, surely? The *Encyclopaedia Britannica* entry on Ruskin calls her 'essentially commonplace' and even today, when it is well known that Effie had a lot to put up with, critics are still harsh.

Meanwhile, the Gray and Millais families remained silent. They would have preferred the first marriage to be forgotten and the surviving daughters, Mary and Carrie, bought any personal letters which came up for sale. In 1924 Effie's brother, Albert Gray, was informed of the existence of Ruskin's 1854 statement, which had lain all this time in a solicitor's drawer. He wanted to buy and destroy it, but was not able to, and it was finally published in 1950 in J H Whitehouse's *Vindication of Ruskin*.

This statement had already been read by Willie James, who was now an admiral and a writer. His book *The Order of Release: the Story of John Ruskin, Effie Gray and John Everett Millais, told for the first time in their unpublished letters* (1947) gave an account of the marriage, a century after it took place, from Effie's point of view. It printed several of Ruskin's love letters and other letters he had dug out of a vast collection at Bowerswell, which was sold after the last brother died in 1946. James – or 'Bubbles' as he was sometimes known – called it 'a story of two men of genius and a beautiful woman'. He explained that the union 'was considered a subject to be avoided in conversation', and, given the family's silence, 'it was inevitable that Ruskin would find champions who would fix the blame for his disastrous marriage on his wife'.[7] He spoke as kindly as he could about Ruskin, stressing that Millais had wished him well and that Effie had not complained. But he could not quite bring

183

himself to admit that his grandparents had fallen in love while she was still married.

Among the letters here printed for the first time was Effie's to Maria La Touche in 1870. She was attacked for having written it by Whitehouse, Derrick Leon in *Ruskin: the Great Victorian* (1949) and later writers, most brutally G H Fleming, the author of two books on Millais and the Pre-Raphaelites who appears to dislike both his subject and his subject's wife.

Most of the criticism seems to me unfair. Effie did no harm. She was not wrong to leave a man who did not want her or to answer questions from a woman who was desperately worried about her daughter, and with good reason. She did not marry for money in either case and she did not ruin a beautiful relationship between Ruskin and Rose La Touche. Nor is it true, as has sometimes been alleged, that she and Millais became estranged. As if the eight children were not enough evidence, many loving letters of his survive, although most of hers to him have been lost. Everything we know strongly suggests that they remained faithful, wrote to each other when apart and were quietly devoted to one another throughout a marriage of forty-one years.

The serious accusation is that after he married her, Millais squandered his huge talents and became conventional. 'Everything was all right until Effie came along' wrote Roy Strong.[8] But Effie, her family and her Scottish home were closely involved with some of his greatest paintings: *The Order of Release, John Ruskin, The Blind Girl, Autumn Leaves, Sir Isumbras, The Vale of Rest, The Eve of St Agnes*. Many creative people do their best work when young – Tennyson is an example – so it would not be very surprising, and nobody's fault, if Millais' genius had faded away. Yet this is not so, because some of his late portraits and landscapes, like the wonderful *Dew-Drenched Furze* and *Glen Birnam*, are every bit as good as his early work. What he did do was turn out a very large number of pictures which are accomplished, but uninteresting.

'I hate married men', said J M W Turner. 'They never make any sacrifices to the Arts, but are always thinking of their duties to their wives and families, or some rubbish of that sort'.[9] Turner was reclusive, did not marry the mother of his children and allowed no one to interfere with his way of life. Millais had a deep sense of responsibility, had been the family breadwinner since his teens and had a chivalrous attitude to women. If he had not married Effie he would have married someone else and any children would have had to be supported; he had seen too much distress among widows and orphans of artists to let his own family go short. We know that he panicked in the late 1850s when critics, including Ruskin, damned his work. According to Hunt:

> In no other age would such an artist have been left without some national opportunity of exercising his genius ... While his works were still vehemently abused by the press, those of artists of mediocrity were lauded to the skies and certain of these painters were favoured by Parliamentary Commissioners of Fine Art. Now, persons of superficial reflection often say that Millais ought not under any temptation to have swerved from his higher inspirations, but great art cannot be produced even by men of the purest genius, if they are not supported by the country's demand for their work ... Surely a man of genius has a right to marry when he has established his commanding position, and being married he is called upon to support his family. Millais in this position found himself driven to despair and want of faith, in the possibility of teaching his countrymen the value of poetic art. 'I have striven hard', he said to me, 'in the hope that in time people would understand me and estimate my best productions at their true worth, but they (the public and private patrons) go like a flock of sheep after any silly bell-wether who clinks before them. I have, up to now, generally painted in the hope of converting them to something better, but I see they won't be taught, and as I *must* live, they shall have what they want, instead of what I know would be best for them. A physician sugars his pill, and I must do the same'.[10]

It was his decision. Effie, who was pregnant or unwell for most of the first fifteen years of their marriage, did not tell him what to do or paint, although she did do everything she could, like the women in 'Of Queens' Gardens', to help him. Perhaps he would have produced more masterpieces if they had continued living quietly in Scotland, but it is not clear that he wanted this. In the 1850s and 60s he and George Du Maurier wasted a good deal of time socialising: 'To both alike Society opened its arms, and for some years they mixed freely, if not frequently, with the gay and gilded throng'. Only when he was older did he avoid places where 'wealth is more favoured than talent, and vulgar display the chief feature of the entertainment'.[11] So perhaps we should not regret the pictures he did not paint and be thankful for the many great ones that he did.

Effie was an ordinary woman – a very intelligent woman, but one

185

who would probably not be remembered if she had not married two extraordinary men. But such men always have a very wide choice of wives, so we should not assume she was commonplace. Only a few Victorian women were celebrated for their own achievements; a much greater number 'lived faithfully a hidden life, and rest in unvisited tombs'. Instead she became a muse – first for Ruskin when he wrote *The King of the Golden River*, then for Millais when he painted *The Order of Release*. Her daughter Carrie, better known as Alice Stuart-Wortley, also became a muse, for Elgar; she was a good musician and is thought to have inspired his Violin Concerto. It was Effie's granddaughter, Perrine, who would be an achiever in her own right.

There was a feeling in mid-Victorian Britain that women could expect to suffer. After all, the Bible had said they would bring forth children in sorrow, which was why some religious thinkers opposed chloroform. Effie was one of the first women to get hold of it and give it to other people, believing that no one should have to endure unnecessary pain. In the same way, she came to believe she had the right to escape from a miserable childless marriage and form a happy one. She was one of the very few women of her time to do this and keep her place in society, showing that it might be possible for others. That is her contribution.

Bowerswell is now the City of Perth's war memorial site. There are several bungalows for elderly people in the grounds, but the house and terraces are not much changed. Brantwood, the house by Coniston Water where Ruskin died, is open to visitors, although his London homes at Herne Hill and Denmark Hill have disappeared. There are blue plaques on the house in Gower Street where the Pre-Raphaelite Brotherhood was founded and on Effie's married home at Palace Gate.

The three actors in this most Victorian of love stories are buried hundreds of miles apart. Millais is in the south aisle of St Paul's Cathedral next to Turner, with the motto *Ars Longa, Vita Brevis* ('art is long, life short') on his stone. His statue is near the modern entrance to Tate Britain and in 2007–8 thousands of visitors flowed past it to marvel at a new exhibition of his work.

Ruskin lies in Coniston churchyard under a Celtic cross of local green slate. His teaching on work, on art and on the natural world is as relevant now as it was when he wrote it, and his name lives on in the Ruskin School of Art and Ruskin College, Oxford, the first in the university to admit working-class men.

186

Effie is buried with her son George in Kinnoull churchyard, where Millais painted *The Vale of Rest*, on the east bank of the Tay. Her parents, brothers and sisters are nearby. Her stone is quite legible, but the church is disused; the graveyard is a wild flower sanctuary and the river splashes over a bank of pebbles a short way downhill. It is a peaceful place to browse on a fine day, to read the inscriptions and to remember the lives that are gone:

> *And soon all of us will sleep under the earth, we*
> *who never let each other sleep above it.*[12]

Appendix: Middlemarch and the Ruskin Marriage

George Eliot knew Millais slightly and they respected one another's work; he attended her funeral and in 1893 painted *The Girlhood of St Theresa*, based on the Prelude to *Middlemarch*. Her common law husband, G H Lewes, wrote to him on 3rd April 1877 asking if she might visit his studio privately, and other letters reveal that she met and called on him occasionally between then and 1880, the year of her death. We don't know whether she ever met Effie. It is on record that Millais liked *Romola* and that George Eliot was impressed by the *Huguenot*, writing that the woman's face in that picture is 'never to be forgotten'.

She was living in London, considering her own future, at the time of the Ruskin/Effie/Millais scandal, and we may assume that she and Lewes heard versions of the story, if not then, certainly in the next fifteen years before she began writing *Middlemarch*. We can also be certain that, although she admired Ruskin, she sympathised with all three.

Middlemarch studies two marriages which go wrong and is concerned with the question of how much one owes a husband or wife after love has died. In the main story an inexperienced young woman, Dorothea, marries an older man who is an eminent scholar. The marriage is short, childless, unhappy and probably unconsummated. They go to Italy where the young wife is left to amuse herself while he works on his great book. She meets someone of her own age, an artist with curly hair and an un-English name, to whom her husband has been kind. They fall in love but do not have an affair. Once free, Dorothea waits only a short time before she marries Will, giving up 'position and fortune'. They are happy and have children, but face a certain amount of unpleasantness, and some people say that 'she could not have been a "nice woman", else she would not have married either the one or the other'.

Of course there is no divorce or annulment in *Middlemarch* and Dorothea, as often happens in Victorian novels, is released from her bad marriage to Casaubon only by death. Equally, of course, George Eliot does not say that Casaubon is impotent and twentieth-century critics had to work out the likelihood of this for themselves. But there are clues; Dorothea gets pregnant in her second marriage, not her first, and Mrs Cadwallader, in Chapter 6, more or less spells out the situation:

'Between ourselves, little Celia is worth two of her, and likely after all to be the better match. For this marriage to Casaubon is as good as going into a nunnery'.

This means that if the elder sister has no children the younger sister's children will inherit the family fortune. Sophisticated Victorians could have read between the lines.

George Eliot knew less than we do about the Ruskin marriage (she never, of course, read the letters), and although she often put real people into her novels, her characters do not precisely correspond to the originals. Dorothea is not Effie; Casaubon is a much smaller figure than Ruskin and the dilettante Ladislaw is not the hard-working Millais, although George Eliot, who was ten years his senior, probably found him youthful and charming. Novelists are not always fully aware of what is going on in their imagination and she may have been unconscious of the parallels between the Casaubon story and a great Victorian scandal. But her conclusion is clear: Dorothea has the right to make a second happier marriage, whatever people say, and the author has some admiration for a woman who had managed to get the better of the marriage laws, as she never did.

Notes

Abbreviations

RG, The Ruskins and the Grays (Mary Lutyens, 1972).

EV, Effie in Venice (ed. Mary Lutyens, 1965).

MR, Millais and the Ruskins (Mary Lutyens, 1967).

JGM, John Guille Millais, *The Life and Letters of Sir John Everett Millais* (1899).

Mount Temple, The Letters of John Ruskin to Lord and Lady Mount Temple (ed. John Lewis Bradley, Ohio, 1964).

Millais-La Touche, 'The Millais-La Touche Correspondence', ed. Mary Lutyens, *Cornhill Magazine*, Spring 1967, pp. 1–18.

Ruskin, *The Works of John Ruskin* (eds. E.T. Cook and Alexander Wedderburn, 1903–1912).

Hunt, William Holman Hunt, *Pre-Raphaelitism and the Pre-Raphaelite Brotherhood* (1905).

Tate, Bowerswell Papers in Tate Britain.

Chapter 1

1 JGM, II, p. 257.
2 Margaret Ruskin to John Ruskin, 11th September 1847, in William James, *The Order of Release*, p. 44.
3 Effie to her mother, 2nd September 1840, Tate, vol. 1.
4 Winifred Gérin, *Elizabeth Gaskell* (Clarendon Press, 1976), p. 25.
5 Mary or Harriet Ainsworth *EV*, p. 5.
6 Effie to her father, 5th July 1841, Tate 1, 25.
7 Melville Jameson to George Gray, 15th July 1841, *RG*, p. 17.
8 William Rossetti, *Some Reminiscences*, 1, p. 178

9   Effie to her mother, 9th August 1841, Tate 1, 37.

10 *The Diaries of John Ruskin 1835–1847* (ed. Joan Evans and John Howard Whitehouse, 1956), p. 212.

11 Advertisement for the first edition of *The King of the Golden River* (1850).

12 John Ruskin, *The King of the Golden River*, Chapter 5.

13 *Diaries*, op. cit. 8th December 1843, p. 253.

14 Effie to Maria La Touche, 10th October 1870, in Mary Lutyens, 'The Millais-La Touche Correspondence', *Cornhill Magazine*, Spring 1967, p. 13.

15 *Diaries*, op. cit. 16th December 1843, pp. 254–5.

16 Ruskin to Frederick Furnivall, 18th August 1854, *MR*, p. 232.

17 Kate Perugini in Lucinda Hawksley, *Katey*, p. 359.

18 Effie to her parents, 28th April 1847, *RG*, p. 33.

19 Effie to George Gray junior, 29th April 1847, ibid, pp. 33–4.

20 John James Ruskin to George Gray, 28th April 1847, ibid, pp. 26–7.

21 George Gray to John James Ruskin, 1st May 1847, ibid, p. 29.

22 John James Ruskin to George Gray, 3rd May 1847, ibid, p. 30.

23 Effie to her mother, 7th May 1847, ibid, p. 37.

24 Ruskin, 'For a Birthday in May', II, pp. 243–4.

Chapter 2

1   John Ruskin, *Praeterita*, vol 1, paragraph 146.

2   Ibid, 1, paragraph 14.

3   Ibid, 1, paragraph 20.

4   Ibid, 1, paragraph 149.

5   John James Ruskin to James Hogg, Tim Hilton, *John Ruskin: The Early Years*, p. 30.

6   *Praeterita* 1, paragraph 50.

7   Ibid, 1, paragraph 243.

8   Hilton, *Early Years* op. cit., p. 48.

9   *Praeterita*, 1, paragraph 256.

10 Ruskin, *Modern Painters 1,* III, p. 617.

11 Ibid, III, p. 383.

12 Ibid, III, p. 449.

13 Effie to her mother, 18th June 1847, *RG*, pp. 41–2.

14 *Diaries*, op. cit. 25th August 1847, p. 364.

15 Margaret Ruskin to John Ruskin, 4th September 1847, *RG*, p. 52.

16 Ruskin to William Macdonald, 5th October 1847, ibid, pp. 61–2.
17 Mrs Gaskell to John Forster, 17th May 1854, *Collected Letters*, p. 287.
18 Ruskin to Effie, 11th November 1847, *RG*, p. 65.
19 Ruskin to Effie, 30th November 1847, James, p. 61.
20 Margaret Ruskin to John Ruskin, 27th November 1847, *RG*, p. 71.
21 Effie to Ruskin, 10th February 1848, ibid, p. 88.
22 John James Ruskin to George Gray, 22nd March 1848, ibid, p. 103.
23 Ruskin to George Gray, 17th March 1848, ibid, p. 101.
24 Ruskin to Effie, 16th December 1847, ibid, p. 78.
25 His real name was John Hobbs, but his employers had rechristened him. He was a skilled photographer and a strong republican, delighted to get out of the Austrian Empire. He left Ruskin soon after their return to England and was replaced by Frederick Crawley.

Chapter 3

1 Ruskin's statement of 27th April 1854, in *MR*, p. 191.
2 Effie to her father, 7th March 1854, ibid, p. 156.
3 Ruskin to his father, 13th April 1848, Leon, p. 117.
4 Effie to her mother, April and May 1848, *RG*, p. 112.
5 Effie to her parents, 3rd May 1848, Tate II, 20.
6 John James Ruskin to George Gray, 24th May 1848, *RG*, p. 117.
7 Effie to her mother, 23rd July 1848, ibid, pp. 127–8.
8 Effie to her mother, 28th June 1848, ibid, p. 121.
9 Ruskin to George Gray, 29th June 1848, ibid, pp. 122–3.
10 Effie to her parents, 17th August 1848, James, p. 123.
11 Ruskin to his father, 15th August 1848, Leon, p. 119.
12 John James Ruskin to George Gray, 24th August 1848, *RG*, pp. 135–6.
13 George Gray to Effie, 28th August 1848, ibid, p. 139.
14 Ruskin to his father, 29th August 1848, ibid, pp. 137–8.
15 Ruskin to his father, 4th September 1848, ibid, p. 140.
16 Effie to her mother, 17th October 1848, ibid, p. 164.
17 John James Ruskin to George Gray, 4th July 1849, ibid, p. 228.
18 Ruskin to George Gray, 5th July 1849, ibid, p. 233.
19 John James Ruskin to George Gray, 4th March 1849, ibid, p. 179.
20 Ibid, p. 180.
21 Ruskin to Effie, 25th April 1849, ibid, p. 185.
22 Ruskin to Effie, 27th April 1849, ibid, p. 185.
23 Ruskin to Effie, 24th June 1849, ibid, p. 220.

24 Ruskin to Effie, 29th April 1849, ibid, p. 187.
25 John James Ruskin to George Gray, 13th June 1849, ibid, p. 213.
26 George Gray to John James Ruskin, 22nd June 1849, ibid, p. 218.
27 John James Ruskin to George Gray, 4th July 1849, ibid, p. 226.
28 Ruskin to George Gray, 5th July 1849, ibid, pp. 231–4.
29 Ruskin to Effie, 2nd September 1849, ibid, pp. 249–50.

Chapter 4

1   Ruskin to W L Brown, 11th December 1849, *RG*, p. 254n.
2   Ruskin to Effie, 25th April 1849, ibid, p. 184.
3   Ruskin, *Modern Painters 1*, III, p. 257.
4   Effie to her mother, 30th September 1849, *RG*, pp. 257–8.
5   Effie to her father, 28th October 1849, *EV*, p. 54.
6   Ruskin, *The Italian Question*, 6th June 1859, XVIII, p. 539.
7   Effie to her mother, 13th November 1849, *EV*, p. 64.
8   Rawdon Lubbock Brown, *Oxford Dictionary of National Biography*, Volume 8, p. 102.
9   Effie to her mother, 22nd December 1849, *EV*, p. 90.
10 Effie to her mother, 24th February 1850, ibid, p. 146.
11 Effie to her mother, 24th November 1849, ibid, p. 75.
12 Effie to her mother, 11th March 1850, ibid, p. 156.
13 Effie to her father, 6th January 1850, ibid, p. 104.
14 Effie to her mother, 3rd February 1850, ibid, p. 132.
15 Effie to her mother, 27th November 1849, ibid, p. 77.
16 Effie to her mother, 24th February 1850, ibid, p. 149.
17 Effie to her mother, 24th December 1849, ibid, p. 99.
18 Effie to her parents, 21st June 1850, James, p. 160.
19 Effie to Rawdon Brown, autumn 1850, *EV*, pp. 170–1.
20 *The Times*, 7th May 1851.
21 Ruskin to *The Times*, 13th May 1851, XII, p. 322.
22 William Rossetti quoted in Rosenfeld and Smith, *Millais*, p. 54.
23 Ruskin to *The Times*, 30th May 1851, XII, p. 325.
24 Ruskin, XII, p. 319.
25 Ruskin, XII, p. 327.
26 Hunt, 1, p. 257

Chapter 5

1 William Rossetti, *Some Reminiscences*, 1, pp. 69–70.
2 Ibid.
3 Anthony Trollope, *An Autobiography*, Chapter 8.
4 Hunt, 1, p. 36.
5 Ibid, 1, p. 81.
6 Rosenfeld and Smith, p. 33.
7 Hunt, 1, p. 142.
8 JGM I, p. 52.
9 Rossetti, *Some Reminiscences*, 1, p. 71.
10 Ibid, p. 163.
11 Hunt, 1, p. 216.
12 Dickens, *Household Words* (1850), p. 266.
13 Hunt, 1, p. 305.
14 Edward Cheney to Lord Holland, August 1851, in *EV*, p. 225.
15 Ruskin to his father, 20th November 1851, Bradley, p. 65.
16 The same to the same, 27th December 1851, ibid, pp. 106–7.
17 Effie to her father, January 1852, *EV*, p. 249.
18 Ruskin to his father, 28th December 1850, Bradley, p. 110.
19 Effie to her mother, 27th June 1852, *EV*, p. 328.
20 Ruskin, 'The Nature of Gothic', X, p. 198.
21 Effie to her mother, *EV*, p. 264.
22 John James Ruskin to George Gray, 30th March 1852, *MR*, p. 4.
23 Effie to her mother, February 1853, ibid, pp. 29–30.

Chapter 6

1 Effie to her mother, 20th March 1853, in *MR*, pp. 37–8.
2 Effie to her mother, 27th March 1853, ibid, pp. 38–9
3 'The Fine Arts and Public Taste', *Blackwood's Magazine*, July 1853.
4 Effie to her father, 7th March 1854, in *MR*, p. 156.
5 Effie to Rawdon Brown, 20th June 1853, ibid, pp. 50–1.
6 Hunt, 1, p. 150.
7 William Bell Scott, quoted *MR*, pp. 276–7.
8 Millais to Holman Hunt, 28th June 1853, *MR*, p. 55.
9 Effie to Rawdon Brown, 1st July 1853, ibid, p. 56.
10 Millais to Hunt, 3rd July 1853, ibid, p. 59.
11 Ruskin to his father, 6th July 1853, ibid, pp. 60–1.

12 Effie to her mother, 10th July 1853, ibid, pp. 66–7.

13 Millais to Hunt, 17th July 1853, ibid, p. 69.

14 Statement of William Millais, 9th March 1898, Bodley MS Eng. Letts. c 228, fol. 62.

15 Alastair Grieve, 'Ruskin and Millais at Glenfinlas', *Burlington Magazine*, April 1996.

16 Ruskin to his father, 4th August 1853, in *MR*, p. 77.

17 Millais to Hunt, September or October 1853, ibid, p. 91.

18 Ruskin's statement, 27th April 1854, ibid, pp. 188–9.

19 Ruskin to his mother, 16th October 1853, ibid, p. 97.

20 Millais to Hunt, 20th October 1853, ibid, p. 98.

21 Ruskin to Hunt, 20th October 1853, ibid, p. 100.

22 Ruskin to his father, 6th November 1853, ibid, pp. 107–8.

23 Ruskin to his father, 11th November 1853, ibid, p. 109.

24 Millais to Mrs Gray, 19th December 1853, ibid, pp. 120–1.

25 Millais to Mrs Gray, 20th December 1853, ibid, pp. 122–4.

26 Ruskin to Mrs Gray, 27th December 1853, ibid, p. 126.

Chapter 7

1 Effie to her mother, 1st January 1854, in *MR*, pp. 128–9.

2 Effie's diary, dated 5th April 1856, quoted ibid, p. 138n.

3 Hunt, 1, p. 365.

4 John James Ruskin to Ruskin, 13th November 1853, in *MR*, p. 100n.

5 Millais to Mrs Gray, 17th January 1854, ibid, p. 131.

6 Millais to Mrs Gray, 3rd March 1854, ibid, p. 150.

7 Millais to Mrs Gray, 17th January 1854, p. 130.

8 Effie to her mother, 25th–27th February 1854, ibid, p. 140.

9 Ibid, p. 141.

10 Effie to her mother, 2nd–3rd March 1854, ibid, p. 146.

11 Effie to her mother, 25th–27th March 1854, ibid, p. 144.

12 Effie to her mother, 2nd–3rd March 1854, ibid, pp. 148–9.

13 Ibid, p. 148.

14 Millais to Mrs Gray, 3rd March 1854, ibid, pp. 150–1.

15 Effie to her father, 7th March 1854, ibid, pp. 154–7.

16 Millais to Mrs Gray, 15th March 1854, ibid, p. 157.

17 Effie to her mother, 23rd March 1854, ibid, p. 158.

18 Effie to her mother, 30th March 1854, ibid, p. 162.

19 Effie to her mother, 6th April 1854, ibid, p. 169.

20 Effie to her mother, 10th April 1854, ibid, p. 171.
21 Millais to Mrs Gray, 18th April 1854, ibid, p. 178.
22 *The Diaries of John Ruskin 1848–73* (eds. Evans and Whitehouse 1958), 17th March 1854, p. 491.
23 Mrs Gray to George Gray junior, 24th April 1854, *MR*, p. 180.
24 Effie to Mrs Ruskin, 25th April 1854, ibid, pp. 184–6.

Chapter 8

1 Ruskin's statement of 27th April 1854, first published in J H Whitehouse's *Vindication of Ruskin* (1950). *MR*, pp. 188–92.
2 Lady Eastlake to Mrs Gray, 28th April 1854, *MR*, pp. 198–9.
3 Lady Eastlake to Effie, 3rd May 1854, *MR*, p. 199.
4 The same to the same, 27th April 1854, *MR*, p. 195.
5 Millais to Mrs Gray, 6th May 1854, *MR*, p. 205.
6 Lady Eastlake to Effie, 25th June 1854, *MR*, p. 224.
7 Ford Madox Brown to Thomas Seddon, 13th July 1855 in *The Diary of Ford Madox Brown*, p. 144n.
8 Millais to Mrs Gray, 6th May 1854, *MR*, p. 206.
9 The same to the same, 10th May 1854, *MR*, p. 210.
10 Jane Welsh Carlyle to her brother-in-law, 9th May 1853, q. Batchelor, p. 133.
11 Hunt, II, p. 129.
12 William Bell Scott q. *MR*, p. 212.
13 Gabriel Rossetti to William Rossetti, 17th May 1854, *Letters of Dante Gabriel Rossetti 1835–60*, (ed. Oswald Doughty and John Robert Wall, 1965), p. 199.
14 Gabriel Rossetti to Ford Madox Brown, 23rd May 1854, ibid, p. 200.
15 Mrs Gaskell to John Forster, 17th May 1854, *Collected Letters*, pp. 287–8.
16 Millais to Mrs Gray, 27th April 1854, *MR*, p. 197.
17 Effie to Rawdon Brown, 27th April 1854, *MR*, p. 194.
18 Millais to Frederick Furnivall, 22nd May 1854, *MR*, p. 215.
19 Dated 30th May 1854, *MR*, pp. 218–19.
20 Effie to her mother, 30th May 1854, *MR*, p. 218.
21 Ruskin to Henry Acland, 16th May 1854, q. Batchelor, pp. 133–4.
22 Ruskin to Furnivall, 18th August 1854, *MR*, pp. 232–3.
23 Effie to her mother, 1st April 1854, *MR*, p. 165.
24 J I Glennie to Mr Gray, 15th July 1854, *MR*, p. 229.

25   The original document is lost. A copy is reproduced in Albert Gray, *The Marriage of John Ruskin.*
26   Effie to Rawdon Brown, 20th July 1854, Tate IV, 170.
27   Millais to Effie, 21st July 1854, *MR*, pp. 234–5.
28   The same to the same, 26th July 1854, *MR*, p. 239.
29   Millais to Mrs Gray, 27th July 1854, *MR*, p. 240.
30   Millais to Hunt, 25th August 1854, *MR*, p. 243.
31   Mary Ainsworth to Effie, 26th August 1854, Tate IV, 203.
32   Effie to Rawdon Brown, 9th October 1854, Tate IV, 211.
33   Millais to Mrs Gray, 3rd March 1854, *MR*, p. 150.
34   Lady Eastlake to Effie, 2nd January 1855, *MR*, p. 246.
35   Ruskin to Millais, 11th December 1854, *MR*, p. 247.
36   The same to the same, 16th December 1854, *MR*, p. 248.
37   Millais to Ruskin, 18th December 1854, *MR*, p. 248.
38   Ruskin to Millais, 20th December 1854, *MR*, pp. 248–9.
39   John James Ruskin to Charles Collins, 28th December 1854, *MR*, pp. 250–1.
40   Effie to Rawdon Brown, 21st March 1855, *MR*, p. 254.
41   JGM, 1, p. 248.
42   Ruskin, *Academy Notes* 1855, Vol. 14, p. 22.
43   Millais to Hunt, 22nd May 1855, *MR*, pp. 256–7.
44   Ruskin to Furnivall, 3rd June 1855, *MR*, pp. 257–8.
45   Millais to Charles Collins, 19th June 1855, *MR*, p. 260.
42   Effie's diary, 5th April 1856, *MR*, pp. 261–3.

Chapter 9

1   Effie's diary, *MR*, p. 263.
2   Effie to her mother, 20th July 1855, ibid.
3   Effie to George Gray junior, 27th July 1855, Daly 176.
4   Millais to George Gray, 2nd August 1855, *MR*, p. 263.
5   Millais to Hunt, *MR*, p. 266n.
6   The same to the same, *MR*, p. 265.
7   *The Diary of Ford Madox Brown*, 20th April 1856, p. 169.
8   Ruskin, *Academy Notes* 1856, XIV, pp. 56–7 and pp. 66–7.
9   Millais to Hunt, 30th May 1856, *MR*, p. 264.
10   Effie's diary, q. JGM, 1, p. 309.
11   Ruskin, *Academy Notes* 1857, XIV, pp. 107–9.
12   Ibid, p. 111.

13 Punch 1856, q. Lambourne, p. 38.

14 *The Diaries of George Price Boyce*, 19th November 1857, p. 19.

15 Effie's diary, q. JGM, 1, p. 329.

16 Ibid, 1, p. 328.

17 Ibid, 1, p. 332.

18 Ibid, 1, p. 334.

19 Millais to Effie, 18th April 1859, JGM I, p. 340.

20 Ruskin, *Academy Notes* 1859, XIV, p. 214.

21 JGM, 1, p. 336.

22 Millais to Effie, 10th April 1859, JGM I, p. 339.

23 The same to the same, 5th May 1859, JGM I, p. 343.

24 The same to the same, 17th May 1859, JGM I, p. 348.

25 Trollope, *An Autobiography*, Chapter 8.

26 Millais to Effie, 18th November 1859, JGM I, p. 350.

27 JGM, vol 1, p. 354.

28 Rosenfeld and Smith, p. 112.

29 Mrs Gaskell to Charles Eliot Norton, 24th June 1861, *Collected Letters*, p. 661.

30 Charles and Frances Brookfield, *Mrs Brookfield and her Circle* (Pitman, 1905), II, p. 500.

31 George du Maurier to his mother, 16th July 1862, *The Young George du Maurier*, p. 158.

32 JGM 1, p. 373.

33 Ibid, 1, p. 378.

34 William Rossetti, *Fine Art, Chiefly Contemporary*, p. 230. Ruskin was annoyed by *My First Sermon* and *My Second Sermon*, for reasons which are not hard to guess. He spoke contemptuously in a lecture of 21st January 1865 about people who take their children to church with 'lovely little Sunday feathers in their hats' (XVIII, 421).

35 W V Harcourt to Millais, 3rd October 1866, JGM I, p. 396.

36 Millais to Hunt, 6th January 1867, Daly, p. 220.

37 Ruskin, 'Of Queens' Gardens', in *Sesame and Lilies* (1865), para 74.

38 Ibid, para 68.

39 Ibid, para 69.

Chapter 10

1 Ruskin, *Modern Painters V*, VII, pp. 422–3.

2 Ruskin to Mrs Cowper-Temple, March 1868, *Mount Temple*, p. 133.

3 Ruskin to his father, 12th September 1858, *Letters from the Continent*, p. 171.

4 Ruskin to the Winnington children, 19th February 1860, *Winnington Letters*, p. 226.

5 Rose's autobiography, Burd, p. 158.

6 Ibid, p. 169.

7 Ruskin to Mrs Cowper-Temple, 29th September 1866, *Mount Temple* pp. 89–90.

8 'Edward John Eyre', *Dictionary of National Biography, Supplement 1901–1911*.

9 Rose to Mrs Cowper-Temple, 18th October 1866, Leon, p. 371.

10 Ruskin to Mrs Cowper-Temple, 21st March 1868 *Mount Temple*, p. 144.

11 Ruskin to Mrs Cowper-Temple, 13th May 1868, ibid, p. 155.

12 Maria La Touche to Effie, 21st May 1868, Millais-La Touche, p. 7.

13 Leon, pp. 402–3.

14 Rose to Louisa MacDonald, 1872, Macdonald, p. 121.

15 Maria La Touche to Mrs Cowper-Temple, 11th December 1868, Leon, p. 415.

16 Hunt, II, pp. 261–2.

17 Ibid, p. 265.

18 Ruskin to Mrs Cowper-Temple, 26th March 1867, *Mount Temple* pp. 114–15.

19 Ruskin to Mrs Cowper-Temple, 20th March 1870, ibid, p. 274.

20 Statement dated 20th September 1870, Burd, p. 122.

21 MacDonald, pp. 100–1.

22 Millais to John La Touche, 5th October 1870, Millais-La Touche, p. 8.

23 Maria La Touche to Effie, 8th October 1870, ibid, pp. 9–11.

24 Millais to John La Touche, 10th October 1870, ibid, pp. 11–12.

25 Effie to Maria La Touche, 10th October 1870, ibid, pp. 12–14.

26 Maria La Touche to Effie, 14th October 1870, ibid, p. 15.

27 Rose to George MacDonald, 14th–17th May 1872, MacDonald, pp. 111–13.

28 MacDonald, p. 120.

29 Ruskin to Robert Horn, 22nd November 1870, Leon, p. 482.

30 Rose to George MacDonald, 14th–17th May 1872, op. cit.

31 Mary Lutyens, Millais-La Touche, p. 1.

32 Hunt, II, pp. 90–94.

Chapter 11

1   JGM II, pp. 22
2   Ibid, II, p. 26.
3   Ibid, II, p. 29.
4   Vincent Van Gogh to Theo Van Gogh, 15th July 1877, p. 129.
5   *The Diary of William Rossetti*, 27th April 1873, p. 266.
6   Effie to George Gray junior, 29th July 1871, The Morgan Library and Museum, The Bowerswell Collection (MA 1338), Letter ZPQ 10.
7   Effie to Millais, 29th July 1871, ibid, Letter ZPQ 11.
8   Effie to Millais, 30th July 1871, ibid, Letter ZPQ 12.
9   Mrs Gaskell, *The Life of Charlotte Bronte*, Chapter 13.
10 JGM II, p. 61.
11 *The Diary of William Rossetti*, 8th February 1872, p. 160.
12 Rosenfeld and Smith, p. 198.
13 Daly, p. 204.
14 Effie to the Duchess of Sutherland, 2nd May 1874, Daly, p. 195.
15 Millais to the Duchess of Sutherland, 4th May 1874, Daly, pp. 195–6.
16 Kate Perugini to J G Millais, 1st July 1898, JGM II, p. 375.
17 Margaret Oliphant, 'Art in May', *Blackwood's Magazine*, June 1875.
18 Margaret Oliphant, 'The Royal Academy', *Blackwood's Magazine*, June 1876.
19 Ruskin, *Fors Clavigera*, July 1877, XXIX, 160.
20 JGM II, p. 354.
21 Ibid, II, p. 92.
22 Millais to Thomas Oldham Barlow, 6th September 1878, Rosenfeld and Smith, p. 200.
23 Millais to Louise Jopling, 5th June 1881, JGM I, p. 433.
24 Ruskin, 'Three Colours of Pre-Raphaelitism', XXXIV, p. 165.
25 Millais to Ruskin, 18th December 1854, *MR*, p. 248.
26 JGM II, p. 109.
27 Whistler's account of the trial is in *The Gentle Art of Making Enemies* (1890).
28 Lambourne, pp. 473–4.
29 Whistler, *Whistler v. Ruskin, Art and Art Critics* (1878).
30 Ruskin to Henry Liddell, 28th November 1878, XXIX, xxv.

Chapter 12

1 John Guille Millais, *Wanderings and Memories* (1919), 21.
2 JGM, 1, pp. 287–8.
3 Ibid, II, p. 380.
4 Ibid, 1, p. 443.
5 John Hare in JGM II, p. 300.
6 *Journal of Beatrix Potter*, p. 97.
7 JGM 1, p. 142.
8 Gladstone to John G. Millais, 4th November 1897, JGM II, p. 117.
9 Edward Poynter ibid, II, p. 114.
10 Diary of Anne Pollen in Brian Martin, *John Henry Newman* (1982), p. 135.
11 JGM, II, p. 118.
12 Ibid, II, p. 121.
13 Ruskin, *Notes on Millais* (1886), XIV, p. 496.
14 Millais to Kate Perugini, 7th May 1885, JGM, II, p. 174.
15 JGM, II, p. 174.
16 Ibid, II, p. 196.
17 Hunt, II, p. 392.
18 Ibid, II, pp. 372–5.
19 Spielmann, p. 18.
20 Severn, p. 94.
21 Hilton, *Later Years* p. 557
22 JGM II, p. 213.
23 Millais to Effie, 3rd August 1890, Rosenfeld and Smith p. 241.
24 Millais to Everett Millais, 11th January 1892, JGM II, p. 294.
25 JGM II, p. 299.
26 Ibid, II, p. 303.
27 Millais to Effie, 12th April 1894, Daly, p. 205.
28 The same to the same, May 1894, JGM II, p. 304.
29 Ibid, II, p. 312
30 Ibid, II, p. 362.
31 Ibid, II, p. 325.
32 Hunt to Millais, 24th February 1896, JGM II, p. 330.
33 Potter, p. 408.
34 JGM II, p. 381.
35 Ibid, II, p. 393.
36 Ibid, II, p. 331.
37 A G Gardiner, *The Life of William Harcourt* (1923), II, p. 411.

38 Burne-Jones to Helen Mary Gaskell, 14th August 1896, Lago, p. 112.
39 Thirlwell, p. 317.
40 Potter, pp. 418–19.
41 James, p. 10.
42 Ibid, p. 257.
43 Effie's grandson, the third baronet, known as 'Jack' in the family, died unmarried of septicaemia in 1920, aged thirty-one. He had been invalided out of the Royal Navy. In spite of very poor health he is said to have had a 'cheerful and sunny' nature. Two other grandsons, George James and Geoffroy Millais, and a nephew, Patrick Gray, were killed in the First World War.

Everett's daughter Perrine (1893–1979) married Malcolm Moncrieff and emigrated to New Zealand in 1921. She wrote the first pocket guide to New Zealand's native birds, helped found the Abel Tasman National Park and was the first woman president of the Royal Australasian Ornithologists' Union. Dr Robin Hodge has made a detailed study of her life and work.
44 *Daily News*, 24th December 1897.
45 *La Chronique des Arts*, 27th January 1900.
46 Lambourne, p. 488.

Aftermath

1   Hunt to Everett Millais, August 1896, JGM 1, p. 416.
2   Ibid, 1, p. 287n.
3   Mary Drew, *Acton, Gladstone and Others* (1924), p. 107.
4   Olivia Shakespear, *Rupert Armstrong*, p. 76.
5   Ibid, p. 142.
6   Ibid, p. 130.
7   James pp. 1–2.
8   'Down with Effie', *Spectator* 20th January 1967.
9   Bailey, p. 234.
10 Hunt, II, pp. 178–9.
11 JGM, II, p. 265.
12 Marina Tsvetayeva, 'I know the truth', translated by Elaine Feinstein.

Bibliography

There is no collected edition of Ruskin's letters. His published works, including lectures and articles, can be found in the thirty-nine-volume Library Edition edited by Cook and Wedderburn at the beginning of the twentieth century. The Ruskin Library at Lancaster University holds a large collection of his papers.

Effie's letters, and those to and from members of her family, were partially edited in the twentieth century by her grandson Admiral William James and later by Mary Lutyens. The Bowerswell Papers, as they are known, are now in the Pierpont Morgan Library, New York. Transcripts of selected letters written between 1840 and 1855 are available in the archives of Tate Britain through the kindness of Effie's great-grandson, Sir Geoffroy Millais.

There are several good biographies of Ruskin, but still none of Millais. Effie's story up to her second marriage was reconstructed in Mary Lutyens' three scholarly volumes, and there is a sympathetic account of her later life in Gay Daly's *Pre-Raphaelites in Love*.

Abse, Joan, *John Ruskin: The Passionate Moralist* (London, Quartet Books, 1980)

Amor, Anne Clark, *William Holman Hunt: The True Pre-Raphaelite* (London, Constable, 1989)

Bailey, Anthony, *Standing in the Sun: A Life of J M W Turner* (London, Sinclair-Stevenson, 1997)

Batchelor, John, *John Ruskin, No Wealth but Life* (London, Chatto & Windus, 2000)

Bell, Quentin, *Ruskin* (London, Hogarth Press, 1978)

Boyce, George Price, *The Diaries of George Price Boyce*, ed. Virginia Surtees (Norwich, Real World Publishers, 1980)

Brown, Ford Madox, *The Diary of Ford Madox Brown*, ed. Virginia Surtees (Yale University Press, 1981)

Burne-Jones, Edward Coley, *Burne-Jones Talking; His Conversation 1895–98*, ed. Mary Lago (London, John Murray, 1982)

Clarke, William M, *The Secret Life of Wilkie Collins* (London, Allison & Busby, 1988)

Cooper, Suzanne Fagence, *The Model Wife* (London, 2010)

Daly, Gay, *Pre-Raphaelites in Love* (London, Collins, 1989)

Du Maurier, George, *The Young George du Maurier, A Selection of his Letters, 1860–67*, ed. Daphne du Maurier (London, Peter Davies, 1951)

Funnell, Peter, et. al., *Millais: Portraits* (1999).

Gaskell, Mrs, *The Letters of Mrs Gaskell*, ed. J A V Chapple and A Pollard (Manchester University Press, 1966)

Gray, Albert, *The Marriage of John Ruskin* (unpublished manuscript in the Bodleian Library, 1938)

Hawksley, Lucinda, *Katey: The Life and Loves of Dickens's Artist Daughter* (London, Doubleday, 2006)

Hicks, Phyllis D, *A Quest of Ladies; The Story of a Warwickshire School* (Birmingham, Frank Juckes, 1949)

Hilton, Timothy, *The Pre-Raphaelites* (London, Thames & Hudson, 1970)

Hilton, Tim, *John Ruskin; The Early Years 1819–1859* (Yale University Press, 1985)

Hilton, Tim, *John Ruskin; The Later Years* (Yale University Press, 2000)

Holman Hunt, Diana, *My Grandfather, His Wives and Loves* (London, Hamilton, 1969)

Holman Hunt, William, *Pre-Raphaelitism and the Pre-Raphaelite Brotherhood* (2 vols, 1905)

James, William, *The Order of Release; The Story of John Ruskin, Effie Gray and John Everett Millais told for the first time in their unpublished letters* (John Murray, 1947)

James, William, *The Sky was Always Blue* (London, 1951)

Jopling, Louise, *Twenty Years of my Life* (London, John Lane, 1925)

Keates, Jonathan, *The Siege of Venice* (London, Chatto & Windus, 2005)

Lambourne, Lionel, *Victorian Painting* (London, Phaidon, 1999)

La Touche, Rose, *John Ruskin and Rose La Touche: her unpublished diaries of 1861 and 1867*, ed. Van Akin Burd (Oxford, Clarendon Press, 1979)

Leon, Derrick, *Ruskin: The Great Victorian* (London, Routledge & Kegan Paul, 1949)

Lutyens, Mary, *Millais and the Ruskins* (London, John Murray, 1967)

Lutyens, Mary, *The Ruskins and the Grays* (London, John Murray, 1972)

Maas, Jeremy, *Victorian Painters* (London, Barrie & Rockliff, 1969)

MacCarthy, Fiona, *William Morris* (London, Faber & Faber, 1994)

MacDonald, Greville, *Reminiscences of a Specialist* (London, Allen & Unwin, 1932)

McMillan, George K, *A History of Kinnoul Parish Church, Perth* (Perth, 2007).

Mancoff, Debra N, *John Everett Millais: Beyond the Pre-Raphaelite Brotherhood* (Yale University Press, 2001)

Marsh, Jan, *Pre-Raphaelite Sisterhood* (London, Quartet, 1985)

Marsh, Jan, *Dante Gabriel Rossetti, Painter and Poet* (London, Weidenfeld & Nicolson, 1999)

Millais, Euphemia Chalmers, *Effie in Venice. Unpublished letters of Mrs John Ruskin written from Venice between 1849 and 1852*, ed. Mary Lutyens (London, John Murray, 1965)

Millais, John Guille, *The Life and Letters of Sir John Everett Millais* (2 vols, London, Methuen & Co, 1899)

Millais, John Guille, *Wanderings and Memories* (Longmans, 1919)

Moyle, Franny, *Desperate Romantics; The Private Lives of the Pre-Raphaelites* (London, John Murray, 2009)

Potter, Beatrix, *The Journal of Beatrix Potter from 1881 to 1897*, transcribed by Leslie Linder (London, Frederick Warne, 1966)

Riding, Christine, *John Everett Millais* (2006)

Rose, Phyllis, *Parallel Lives; Five Victorian Marriages* (London, Chatto & Windus, 1984)

Rosenfeld, Jason and Smith, Alison, *Millais* (Tate Publishing, 2007)

Rossetti, William Michael, *Fine Art, Chiefly Contemporary* (London, Macmillan & Co, 1867)

Rossetti, William Michael, *Some Reminiscences* (2 vols, London, Brown, Langham & Co, 1906)

Rossetti, William Michael, *The Diary of W M Rossetti, 1870–1873*, ed. Odette Bornand (Oxford, Clarendon Press, 1977)

Ruskin, John, *Works* (The Library Edition, eds. E T Cook and Alexander Wedderburn, 39 volumes, London 1903–12)

Ruskin, John, *Ruskin's Letters from Venice, 1851–1852*, ed. John Lewis Bradley (Yale University Press, 1955)

Ruskin, John, *Letters from the Continent 1858* (ed. John Heyman, 1982)

Ruskin, John, *The Diaries of John Ruskin*, ed. Joan Evans and John Howard Whitehouse (3 vols, Oxford, Clarendon Press, 1956–59)

Ruskin, John, *The Letters of John Ruskin to Lord and Lady Mount-Temple*, ed. John Lewis Bradley (Ohio State University Press, 1964)

Ruskin, John, *The Winnington Letters; John Ruskin's correspondence with Margaret Alexis Bell and the children at Winnington Hall,* ed. Van Akin Burd (London, Allen & Unwin, 1969)

Severn, Arthur, *The Professor; Arthur Severn's Memoir of John Ruskin,* ed. James S Dearden (London, Allen & Unwin, 1967)

Snow, Stephanie J, *Blessed Days of Anaesthesia* (Oxford University Press, 2009)

Spielmann, M H, *Millais and his Works* (1898)

Strong, Roy, *And When Did You Last See Your Father? The Victorian Painter and British History* (London, Thames and Hudson, 1978)

Thirlwell, Angela, *William and Lucy: The Other Rossettis* (Yale University Press, 2003)

Trollope, Anthony, *An Autobiography* (1883)

Van Gogh, Vincent, *The Complete Letters* (London, Thames and Hudson, 1958)

Whistler, James McNeill, *The Gentle Art of Making Enemies* (London, William Heinemann, 1890)

Whiteley, Jon, *Oxford and the Pre-Raphaelites* (Oxford, 1989)

Acknowledgements

Some of my research was done in the beautiful city of Perth, and now I know why Effie kept going back there. I was warmly welcomed by those who now live and work at Bowerswell, and would like to thank, in alphabetical order, Maggie Burns, Maria Devaney (Perth Museum and Art Gallery), Kathleen Flood, Rhoda Fothergill, Ian Gray, Mansel and Heulwen James, George McMillan, the Reverend David Souter and Margaret Stewart. The house and gardens may be explored on request.

I am grateful to Dr Alison Smith of Tate Britain, who organised the great Millais exhibition of 2007–8 and kindly answered my questions, and to all those who look after the Tate archives. Thanks too to the helpful and friendly staff at the Ashmolean Museum; the Bodleian Library; the A.K. Bell Library, Perth; the Ruskin Library at Lancaster University and the Pierpont Morgan Library, New York.

Dr Robin Hodge of New Zealand gave me valuable information on Effie's granddaughter, the environmentalist Perrine Moncrieff. My oldest friend, Diana Forrest, read and commented on the manuscript as it was written, and my husband, John Hemp, was, as always, my rock.

Family Trees

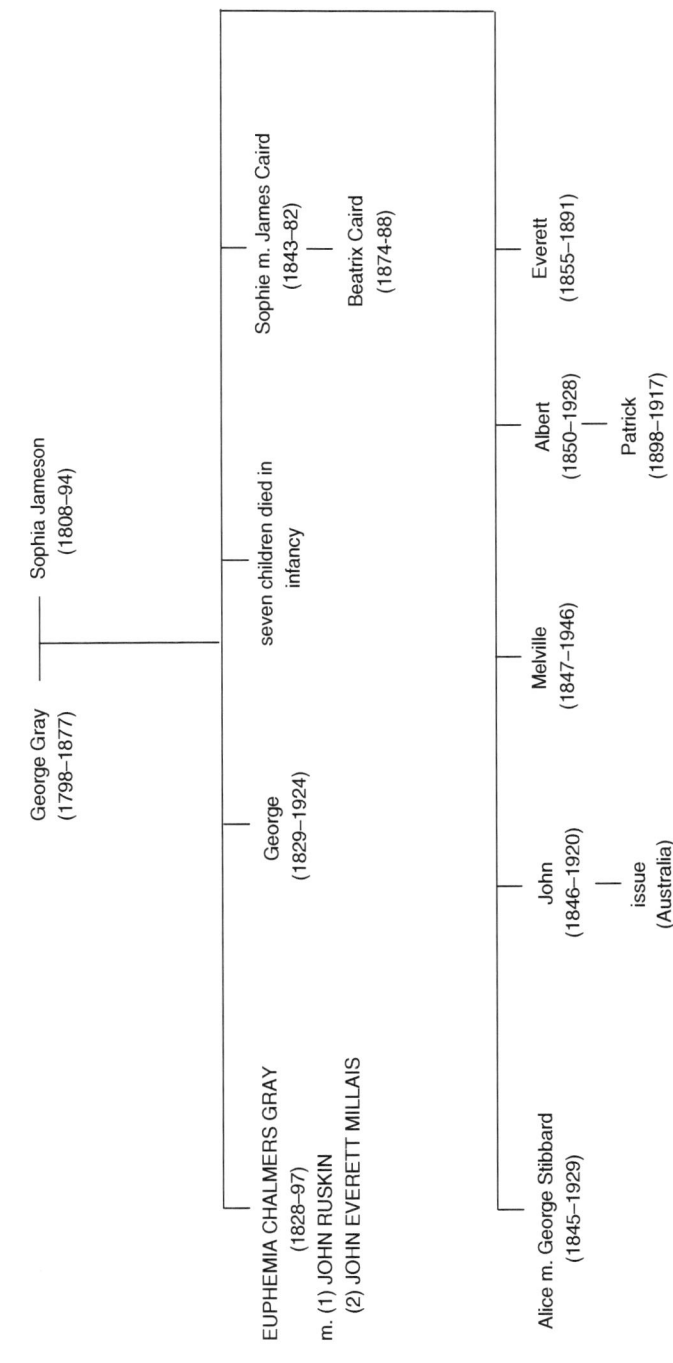

THE GRAYS

George Gray (1798–1877) — Sophia Jameson (1808–94)

EUPHEMIA CHALMERS GRAY
(1828–97)
m. (1) JOHN RUSKIN
(2) JOHN EVERETT MILLAIS

George
(1829–1924)

seven children died in infancy

Sophie m. James Caird
(1843–82)

Beatrix Caird
(1874–88)

John
(1846–1920)

issue
(Australia)

Melville
(1847–1946)

Albert
(1850–1928)

Patrick
(1898–1917)

Everett
(1855–1891)

Alice m. George Stibbard
(1845–1929)

211

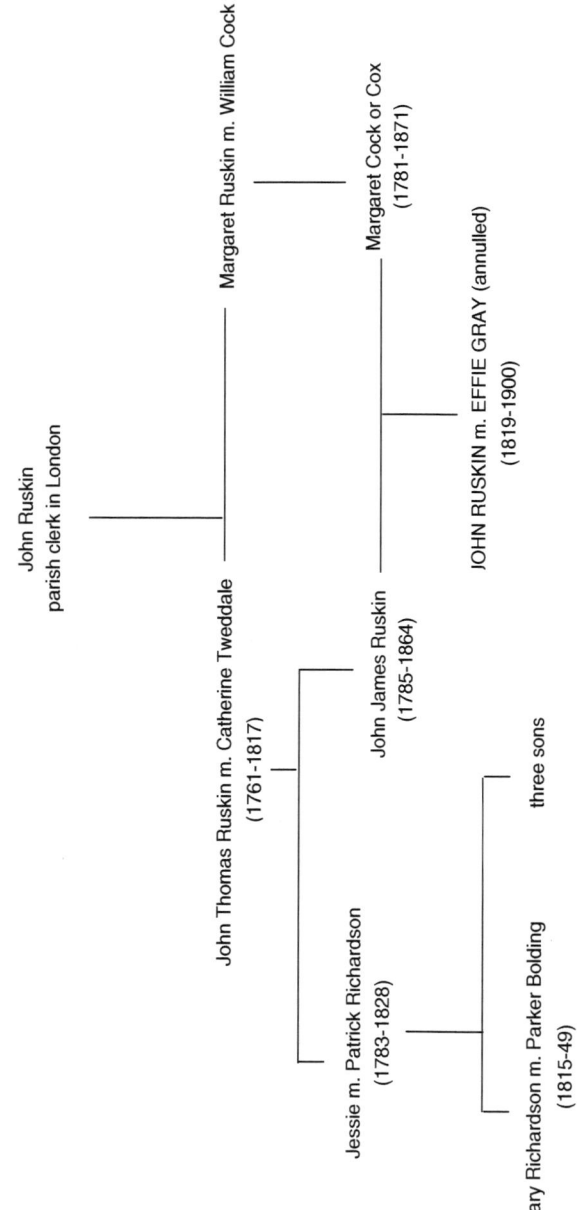

THE RUSKINS

John Ruskin
parish clerk in London

John Thomas Ruskin m. Catherine Tweddale
(1761-1817)

Margaret Ruskin m. William Cock

John James Ruskin
(1785-1864)

Margaret Cock or Cox
(1781-1871)

JOHN RUSKIN m. EFFIE GRAY (annulled)
(1819-1900)

Jessie m. Patrick Richardson
(1783-1828)

three sons

Mary Richardson m. Parker Bolding
(1815-49)

FAMILY TREES

THE MILLAIS

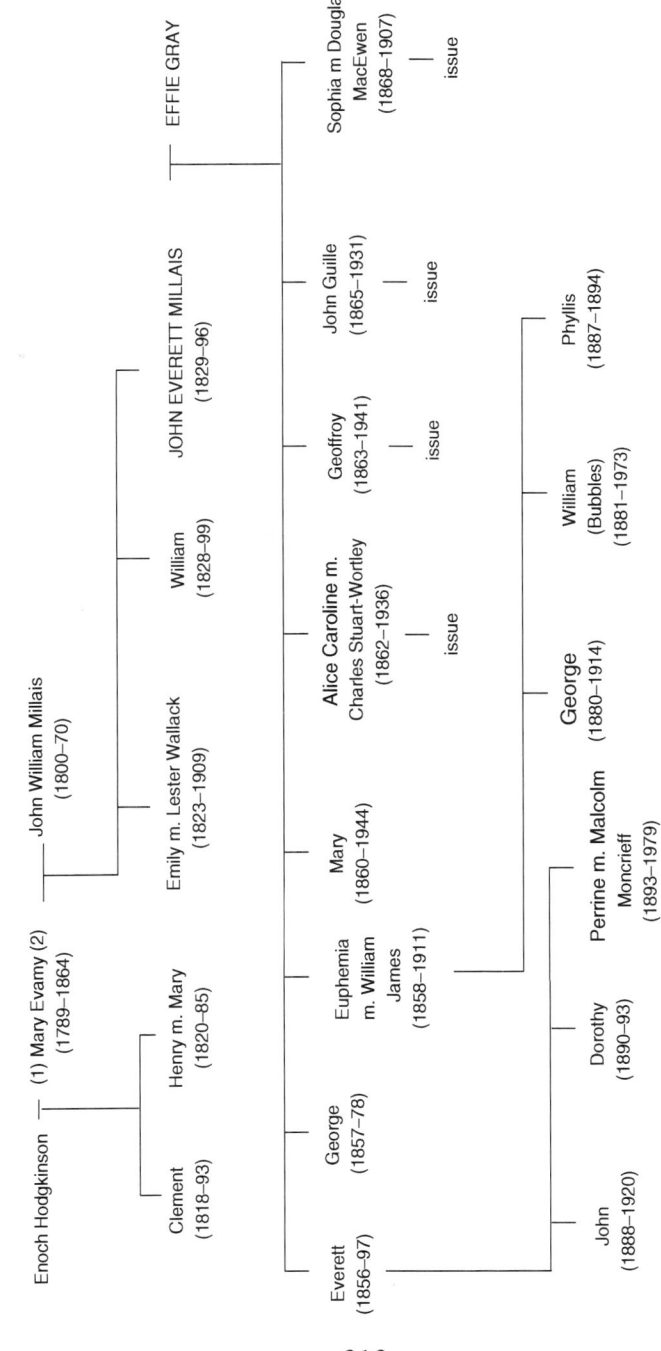

213

Index